HUN SEN
Strongman of Cambodia

HARISH C. MEHTA
AND
JULIE B. MEHTA

D0710199

GRAHAM BRASH
SINGAPORE

First published in 1999 by
Graham Brash Pte Ltd
144 Upper Bukit Timah Road
#08-02 Bukit View
Singapore 588177

ISBN 981-218-074-5

Printed by

Front cover photos:
*Right: A 19-year old Hun Sen with a pistol at his hip and an ammunition pouch clipped to his belt. This 1971
picture, taken one year after he joined the Khmer Rouger, survived miraculously. It was kept by a farmer in
Kompong Cham who presented it to Hun Sen in 1977. "This is the only picture where I had my two eyes," he
commented. He lost his left eye in combat in 1975.*
Bottom left: Hun Sen at Phnom Penh military ceremony.
Both photos courtesy of Hun Sen.
Top left: Silhouette of an Angkor Wat Spire, taken by Julie Mehta.

CONTENTS

To Kali,
Whom we discovered
In the golden spires piercing Khmer skies,
In the dried blood of Tuol Sleng,
In the sweetness of fruit
Among the lush new green
Of the old killing fields.

ACKNOWLEDGMENTS

There are many Cambodians to whom we owe a debt of gratitude—Prime Minister Hun Sen and his wife Bun Rany; his elder brother Hun Neng; King Norodom Sihanouk and his sons Norodom Ranariddh and Norodom Chakrapong; Sihanouk's half-brother Norodom Sirivudh; and, long-time supporter of the royal family Son Sann—for being generous with their time.

Among others who helped us, Indian army Colonel A.N. Bahuguna arranged a prized interview with Hun Neng. And Hun Sen's senior advisor, Prak Sokhonn, responded to our endless queries, and arranged for us to travel by military helicopter with the prime minister to the provinces. The final touches to the elaborate portrait of Hun Sen were given by his brother-in-law, Nim Chandara, who provided rare insights into the Hun family. At the last minute, when we still had a few unanswered questions, Ros Kosal, a prime ministerial aide requested Hun Sen to give us written answers. Stephen Troth, publisher and longtime resident of Southeast Asia, read the manuscript and suggested we write a short chapter on the history of Cambodia to put events in perspective. When the manuscript was finally coming together, Drs Anima and Tarun Banerjee helped us proofread. We thank them all.

CAMBODIA AND ITS NEIGHBOURS

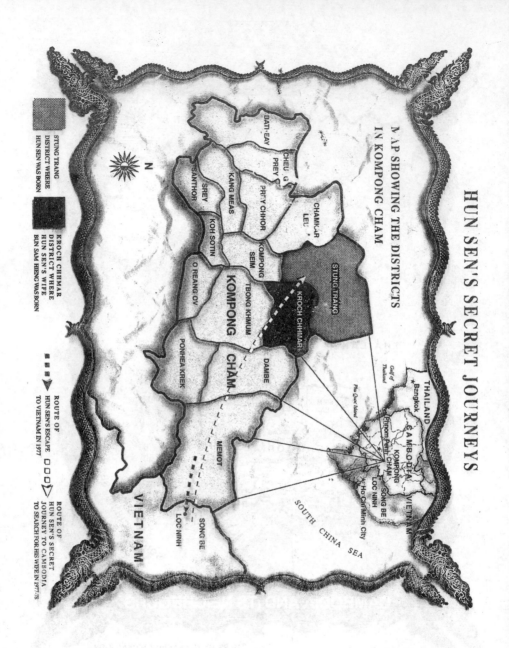

HUN SEN'S SECRET JOURNEYS

MAP SHOWING THE DISTRICTS
IN KOMPONG CHAM

STUNG TRANG
DISTRICT WHERE
HUN SEN WAS BORN

KROCH CHHMAR
DISTRICT WHERE
HUN SEN'S WIFE
BUN SAM HIENG WAS BORN

ROUTE OF
HUN SEN'S ESCAPE
TO VIETNAM IN 1977

ROUTE OF
HUN SEN'S SECRET
JOURNEY TO CAMBODIA
TO SEARCH FOR HIS WIFE IN 1977-78

N

BATI-EAY
CHEU G
PREY
SANTHOR
KANG MEAS
PRI-Y CHOR
CHAMKAR
LEU
SREY
KOH SOTIN
KOMPONG
SIEM
STUNG TRANG
O REANG OV
TBONG KHMUM
KROCH CHHMAR
KOMPONG
CHAM
DAMBE
PONHEA KREK
MEMOT
LOC NINH
SONG BE

VIETNAM

SOUTH CHINA SEA

THAILAND
Bangkok
Gulf of
Thailand
Phu Quoc Island
CAMBODIA
Phnom Penh KOMPONG
CHAM
LOC NINH
SONG BE
Ho Chi Minh City
VIETNAM

PREFACE

TEA WITH THE TIGER

Few forty-seven-year-old prime ministers have lived so many lives in a single lifetime—kompong child, pagoda boy, Khmer Rouge soldier, romantic hero, liberator, diplomat, strongman. This tiger holds the distinction of being a true cat, having survived more than nine brushes with death. It was this streak of luck, plus a canny sense of strategy and the will to survive that had made Hun Sen a seemingly invincible power, and kept him on top of the heap of Cambodian politics for two decades. Foreign minister at twenty-seven, prime minister at thirty-three, secure in his immense measure of confidence, he had always been the master manipulator, exuding charisma to reporters, ever since we first saw him in 1989. In his rapid ascent he had been dubbed a saviour, a democrat, and a dictator, all in the same breath.

Telling the strongman that we were writing his biography, and asking him for a series of intrusive interviews, was a highly sensitive matter. Harish casually broached the subject in the early 1990s with Prime Minister Hun Sen's assistant, Uch Kiman, who liked the concept. We knew the idea would fly, one day.

Some five years later, in mid-1997 Harish made a formal request, in writing, to a senior prime ministerial advisor, Prak Sokhonn. We were writing Hun Sen's biography, we said. Would he arrange ten hours of interviews with him? Within a week or so Prak Sokhonn got back to us. He had shown our letter of request to Hun Sen, who had just recently overthrown his first prime minister, Norodom Ranariddh, and Hun Sen had agreed.

We arrived at Hun Sen's sprawling villa on Boulevard Suramarit, facing the Independence Monument in Phnom Penh. We were to meet Prak Sokhonn there. After being screened by a reluctant young guard, we were admitted. The garden was ablaze with brilliant red hibiscus bushes and shrubs sculpted in the shapes of deer and dogs pranced around on a brutally cropped lawn. Prak Sokhonn was waiting for us. A tall, beaming man, he was an ex-editor of an army newspaper.

"When I started telling the prime minister about the both of you, he raised his hand to interrupt me," Prak Sokhonn said in early-December 1997 at Hun Sen's villa. "He said 'it's okay. I know them well. You can call them'.".

Prak Sokhonn said that we were to interview Hun Sen in the northwestern city of Siem Reap on December 3, 1997 ahead of the third Angkor Ramayana festival of dance which was to take place under the night skies at the ruins of the Angkor temples. But a Russian TV crew was not too happy that Hun Sen had given us an interview instead of them. Prak Sokhonn invited us to fly with him to Siem Reap.

"We will fly by Russian Antonov-24," he said, and, noticing our discomfiture, quickly added: "It's very safe."

We were not convinced. It was an Antonov, the same type of aircraft that had crashed earlier that year on the fringes of Phnom Penh's Pochentong airport. So we declined, and chose to fly by the European-built ATR-70, and arrived in Siem Reap, overflying the great Tonle Sap lake, ahead of Hun Sen's entourage.

From the air the Tonle Sap looked like a giant bowl of soup steaming in the sun, garnished by overhanging coconut trees, wild herbs, and endless ricefields and, up north, crested with hummocky mountains. It was in this rich cradle that many Cambodian empires had flourished, and then gone into terminal decline. It was there—right next to the soup bowl that was big enough and rich enough to feed a nation a diet of fish and rice—that we were returning to find the most elusive of answers.

Egrets, startled by the noise of the aircraft took to the air in flurries as our plane touched down at Siem Reap airport.

"It's winter. The temperature's a cool thirty degrees Celsius," said a taxidriver in fluid English, apparently relishing a bit of sarcasm. We looked forward to escaping from the heat into our airconditioned hotel room.

Pink lotuses bloomed on pools of stagnant rainwater, and a post-monsoon carpet of grass and waist-high paddy cloaked both the summer's dryness and the poverty of the land that sped past our taxi.

We checked into the Nokor Kok Thlok Hotel to await Hun Sen's arrival. The hotel manager said that the property had lain completely empty for two months after the military takeover in July.

"There were 150 tourists stranded here, and Hun Sen sent a special plane to evacuate them," he said. "But Siem Reap remained calm even at that time. They know how to control things around here."

In the morning army commandos began arriving, lugging assault rifles. They took up positions in a large vacant plot fronting the hotel. In the middle of the expanse was a helipad. As the sun rose the commandos waited under the sparse shade of a single palm tree. Beyond the helipad acres of palm fronds brushed the skyline, and, further on, the spire-like *gopuram* of Angkor Wat was visible in the clear air.

Hun Sen's arrival was delayed by two hours. Troops killed time, and a lot else. A plainclothes security guard tormented a grasshopper by flicking its eyes with his overgrown fingernail, blinding it, and ultimately squashing it to death. Seeing this a Cambodian official commented in French: *"Je suis malade."*

At 5 pm a pair of olivegreen helicopters drifted into view above the tree-line.

As they approached the beaming faces of Hun Sen and his wife Bun Rany were visible through the glass window of a new Franco-Italian helicopter. The powerful couple touched down, and entered the hotel, while their escort helicopter continued patrolling the evening skies. That night they were treated to Cambodian, Indian, Vietnamese, and Laotian classical dance at the Ramayana festival at the dark and brooding ruins of Angkor. Afterwards, Hun Sen led a dance around the swimming pool at the hotel.

The next morning Hun Sen was ready for our first interview soon after breakfast. Beside him sat interpreter Bun Sam Bo, advisor Prak Sokhonn, and a note-taker. Wearing a dark suit over an open-necked blue shirt, Hun Sen smoked steadily, his fingers deeply discoloured with nicotine. He spoke for two-and-a-half hours about his childhood, and his years in the Khmer Rouge, dragging hard on a cigarette in a huge effort to pull memories out of dark corners.

It was a promising beginning to the biography. He covered a lot of ground. Soon afterwards he flew out in his helicopter. We followed him to Phnom Penh. Two days later we interviewed him again at his *Roun Khlar*, or Tiger's Den residence, on the far edges of Takhmau city in Kandal province, twelve kilometres from Phnom Penh.

After leaving Takhmau city behind us a country road forked off the highway, and was abruptly punctuated by a roadblock. We were stopped by guards in military uniform. Beyond the roadblock a red-and-white radio antenna spiked the horizon. An artillery gun loomed out from under the flaps of a blue tent on the outer flanks of the camp. This was Hun Sen's home: an impregnable military fortress manned by a battalion of troops, ringed by watchtowers armed with machineguns, and dotted with artillery pieces. It was unapproachable, protected by marshes inhabited by local snakes. We drove along the dirt road, and halted under a bougainvillea-draped wrought iron gate. The residence was hidden behind high walls mounted with surveillance video cameras. The gate swung open onto a fashionably tiled pavement that climbed up to a wheatish villa with a red-tiled roof. Gabled windows, mock balconies, terrace washing lines swaying with white sheets, satellite dishes, and a profusion of antennae lent a lived-in look to the house. An elevated drive-in porch supported by Corinthian pillars overlooked a lake on which pelicans silently glided, and a mini-golf course where Hun Sen perfected his swing. The three-storeyed house built in November 1997 was surrounded by coconut trees, a swimming pool, a lake house, and waterfalls.

Inside, the house had a decidedly period-European touch with rich chandeliers, and 17th century *faux* French furniture. Pillars made of *beng* wood were rooted on marble floors.

Hun Sen's tastes were not always so extravagant. Originally he lived in a simple two-storeyed home, located right next door, that was built in 1989. The first home still existed. It was a large but plain structure. An ordinary reception area was furnished with a typically Vietnamese-style carpet, and heavily carved chairs. The plainness had been replaced by new opulence.

Hun Sen swept in wearing a dark blue suit and a blue shirt. He had just wound up a meeting with a group of Muslim students. Between small sips from a cup of Chinese tea he spoke into a microphone about his escape from Cambodia, the months spent in Vietnamese jails, the years consumed by his desire to liberate his country, his anger at its past rulers, and his rage against genocide.

The interview was proceeding smoothly until we asked him a question in which we referred to the Vietnamese military action to overthrow the Khmer Rouge as an "invasion". This brought forth a long, impassioned, and indignant response from Hun Sen, who was quick to correct our version of history, that it was never an invasion but an act of liberation from a genocidal régime.

"How could I, a Cambodian, invade my own country," he asked in carefully modulated English, a foreign language he found difficult, and had never felt the need to master.

By this time his equanimity had been disturbed, and we felt that it was time to end the interview. It had been a productive session with Hun Sen speaking on tape for more than two hours.

The next day we were to travel with him to Prey Veng province, east of Phnom Penh.

"You are coming with me, aren't you?" he said warmly. "Come tomorrow before 8 am. I am going to harvest rice."

He had forgiven us our "error" of history, and was soon seeing us off at the front porch.

The next morning we drove into his fortress at another point of entry further down the road, through another roadblock, past piglets tethered to a banana tree, barking dogs, and a watchtower manned by a smiling soldier. Four Russian-made helicopters stood on a concrete strip ringed by lotus ponds and water hyacinths. One by one the four helicopters lifted off, and flew low over the marsh towards our steaming rural destination.

After thirty minutes of cruising over lush terrain and pregnant waterways the four touched down in vast yellowing ricefields in the middle of a thousand villagers, their heads covered in colourful *kramas*. As soon as he hit the ground Hun Sen was hugging grandmothers and grandchildren. He then started cutting rice stalks with a *kandeav* (a kind of sickle) at a rapid pace and, within minutes, had harvested about twenty-five metres of the ricefield with the expertise of a ricefarmer. Afterwards, sitting under a makeshift tent he delivered a speech over a loudspeaker that was screwed onto the handlebars of a bicycle. All around him village folk squatted in fields covered with yellow dandelions and occasional patches of lavender water hyacinths.

Sweating profusely through his stonewashed shirt he told us: "I am a farmer. I am very poor. I am not like a prince."

His *krama* fell to the ground. A bodyguard picked it up and threw it over his own shoulder. A poignant act. Prime minister and bodyguard were one.

The biography would be incomplete without speaking to Hun Sen's wife. We explored the possibility of an extended session with Bun Sam Hieng, better known as Bun Rany, and Hun Sen agreed without hesitation.

The next day we met his wife, the farmer's daughter who had come, literally, through slaughter.

Dressed in a chocolate and ochre silk *ikkat sampot* Bun Rany's back was as straight as a ramrod. As the soft afternoon rays caught the gilded edges of the *faux* Louis XVI ornately carved sofas on the second floor of her swish new home in Takhmau her gentle drone almost sounded like a lullaby.

Our chat turned out to be a four-hour saga about her life and losses, her hopes and disappointments, her loves and lessons learnt, as she dredged up painful memories through a monsoon of tears.

At forty-four she boasted a slim enough waistline, and was generously endowed in the Cambodian way. She sat with her hands folded on her lap. With trendy black platforms and Dior bag, the wife of Cambodia's most powerful man exuded a quiet charm that was quite disarming.

Her porcelain skin was the perfect foil for the wiry jet black hair that had been cropped short on the orders of the Khmer Rouge during their rule. Now, decades later her long hair hung loose on her shoulders. A few typical Khmer sapphires adorned her long, burgundy-painted fingernails. The oft pushed back cuticles stood witness to some heavy-duty manicure sessions.

The interviews for the biography were half-done. Hun Sen agreed to answer dozens of questions in writing. Sure enough, his written answers were delivered right on schedule.

He said he would grant us one final interview a couple of months later. While we waited for the last interview to come through we put together all our other interviews with the other Cambodian leaders—Ranariddh and Son Sann being among the many we had spoken to. Some of the most insightful comments came from Hun Sen's childhood friends who lived with him in the pagoda during the mid-1960s, and from his teachers at high school.

One of our most prized interviews was with his elder brother, Hun Neng, whom we met in 1993. The brothers Hun were military allies. Their combined forces had helped overthrow the Khmer Rouge in 1979.

The final interview came through with the suddenness of the Cambodian rains. Prak Sokhonn said that the prime minister had only "one window" to meet us in early June 1998. Once again we drove to his home in Takhmau for a two-hour session. Hun Sen talked about his days as a pagoda boy, and the challenges he confronted when he became prime minister.

He gently inquired how his biography was progressing. Not once did he ask to see the manuscript. It appeared that he would rather not see the manuscript, and would have us write it the way we pleased.

It was clear that his staff adored, and admired, this man who had risen out of crushing poverty to become the most powerful leader Cambodia had ever known—more powerful even than Prince Sihanouk who was easily toppled, and more resilient than Pol Pot.

Prak Sokhonn who had, at that time, been with Hun Sen for more than four years, said that his boss was unlike most ministers.

"They sign documents without reading them," he said. "But Hun Sen reads every word. None of his aides dare make a mistake, which is met with a stern rebuke. But once he's had his say it's back to normal."

It was with the same care and concern that he built schools and irrigation canals across the country. He accepted donations, and pumped the money right back into the development projects. A strongman he was, but with a strong conscience and a sense of duty. And there was always a hint of another motive: to shower the people with largesse so as to win their support in the elections.

Harish C. Mehta
Julie B. Mehta

Phnom Penh, August 1999

THE PLAYERS AND THEIR RELATIONSHIP WITH HUN SEN

MAIN CHARACTERS

Norodom Sihanouk: Born in 1922 he dominated Cambodian politics on becoming king in 1941. He abdicated in 1955, and became the chief of state in 1960. His political career ended when he was ousted in a *coup* in 1970. He was reappointed king in 1993 after two decades in exile. Sihanouk was Hun Sen's chief adversary during the peace talks that began in France in the 1980s. Sihanouk gradually and tentatively grew fond of Hun Sen and even respected his authority, realising that the strongman provided the stability his country needed, and that it was impossible to remove him from the political scene.

Vietnamese Army Generals Van Tieng Dung, Tran Van Tra, and Le Duc Anh: The three generals who helped Hun Sen raise a rebel army. They planned and launched the Vietnamese attack on the Khmer Rouge in 1978-79. General Le Duc Anh later became the president of Vietnam, and remained close to Hun Sen who, in turn, owed the diplomatic support he enjoyed in Vietnam to his links with the generals.

Heng Samrin: Born in 1934 he joined the Khmer Rouge and served as a commander of the Khmer Rouge 4th Infantry Division from 1976-78. He led an abortive *coup* against Pol Pot, and defected to Vietnam in 1978. He became the President of the People's Revolutionary Council that governed the country after the Vietnamese overthrew the Pol Pot régime in 1979, and served for several years as head of state. Heng Samrin was one of the earliest mentors of Hun Sen, and nurtured the rising star.

Chea Sim: Born in 1932 into a peasant family in the Ponhea Krek district of Kompong Cham province, Chea Sim was recruited by the Vietnamese communists during the war against the French in the 1950s. He joined the Khmer Rouge, and became a committee secretary for Ponhea Krek. After the Pol Pot régime was toppled, he rose to become the minister of interior, and later the chairman of the national assembly of the State of Cambodia. He retained the post of chairman of the assembly that was formed after the elections of May 1993, and became the head of the senate in 1999. Like Heng Samrin, Chea Sim groomed Hun Sen in the 1980s to play a major role in government. But perceptions persisted that there existed a rivalry between Chea Sim and Hun Sen, and that the latter had not been sufficiently respectful to him. In the party hierarchy Chea Sim was Hun Sen's senior, and despite their differences the two men remained the best of friends.

Pen Sovann: Born in 1935 he entered the Issarak independence movement when he was just 13, and later joined the Communist Party of Indochina in 1951. Sovann served as bodyguard to Ta Mok who went on to become the dreaded Khmer Rouge general responsible for genocide. Sovann split with Ta Mok after independence in 1953, and attended communist training camps in Vietnam. He tried to mobilise Cambodians living along the Lao border to overthrow Pol Pot. After overthrowing the Khmer Rouge, the Vietnamese installed Sovann as secretary-general of the People's Revolutionary Party. He was elected prime minister in July 1981, but was sacked soon afterwards following policy differences with Heng Samrin. Sovann was seen as being disloyal to the Vietnamese. He was flown to Hanoi where he was jailed for seven years. Sovann blamed Hun Sen for his imprisonment. On his return to Cambodia in 1992, he was allowed to join the Cambodian People's Party but was sacked following rumours that he might join an opposition party headed by government critic Sam Rainsy.

Hun Neng: Born in 1949 in Kompong Cham, Hun Neng is an older brother of Hun Sen. His rise coincided with the meteoric ascent of Hun Sen. Jailed by the Khmer Rouge in the mid-1970s, Hun Neng was exiled to the hills of Kompong Thom for nine months. He played an important role in mobilising rebel military forces in Kompong Cham to overthrow Pol Pot. Later, Hun Neng studied economics in Phnom Penh, and served as an economic advisor to the local government of Kompong Cham. He rose to become the chief of a district, and was appointed the governor in 1985—the same year that Hun Sen became the prime minister. Hun Sen and Hun Neng were more than brothers; they were political allies.

Pol Pot: Mystery surrounds Pol Pot's date of birth. Some historians believe he was born in 1925, but French records date his birth to 1928. Given the name Saloth Sar, he grew up in a wealthy farming family in Kompong Thom province. He won a scholarship to study radio electronics in Paris in 1949, but was more interested in communism than science, and did not complete his studies. He returned home in 1953 to join the Cambodian Communist Party and became its secretary-general in 1962. He gave himself the name *bâng* Pol (*bâng* signifies elder), and later added Pot. A psychotic side to the intellectual was revealed when, as the supreme leader of the Khmer Rouge guerrillas, he presided over the killings of some 1.7 million innocent Cambodians. Hun Sen joined the Khmer Rouge in 1970, but he never met Pol Pot. Hun Sen defected from the Khmer Rouge in 1977, and soon turned into Pol Pot's biggest and most dangerous enemy. The Khmer Rouge repeatedly tried to hunt Hun Sen down and kill him, but without success. Eventually, Hun Sen was able to overthrow Pol Pot with the help of the Vietnamese army in 1979. Consigned to the margins of Cambodian politics, Pol Pot lived a fugitive's life in the jungles bordering Thailand. He died in April 1998 after being held in captivity by his own cadres who charged him with the murder of a colleague. Death cheated the Cambodian people of the opportunity to bring this notorious criminal to trial.

Khieu Samphan: Born in 1932 in Svay Rieng province, he was educated in Paris University. On returning to Phnom Penh, he founded the French-language journal, *L'Observateur.* He was a member of the national assembly as a member of Sihanouk's Sangkum Reastyr Niyum party, and served as secretary of state for commerce. He joined the Khmer Rouge in 1967, and at various times served as a Khmer Rouge head of state, and prime minister of the Khmer Rouge opposition, battling the Vietnamese forces from 1979-91. Samphan was one of Hun Sen's most vociferous critics, and locked horns with him during the peace talks through the early-1990s.

Son Sann: Born in 1911 in Phnom Penh, he was educated in Paris, and later served as the governor of the National Bank of Cambodia from 1954-68, and minister of state for finance and national economy from 1961-62. After the collapse of the Pol Pot régime, he created the Khmer People's National Liberation Front. He served as prime minister of the Coalition Government of Democratic Kampuchea, the régime in exile, from 1982-91. He remained a bitter critic of Hun Sen, blaming the Cambodian People's Party for the misfortunes that were visited on his country.

Norodom Ranariddh: Born in 1944 this son of Sihanouk was educated in Paris and Aix-en-Provence. He returned with a Ph.D. degree in law. He became the first prime minister of Cambodia following elections in May 1993. At the time, Hun Sen was the second prime minister, and the two men worked in close cooperation. But they fell apart, and Ranariddh was overthrown in a military takeover by Hun Sen in 1997. After the elections in 1998, the two men resumed their cooperation to form a coalition government, and were again on cordial terms.

Norodom Chakrapong: Born in 1945 this feisty son of Sihanouk rose and fell like a shooting star. A son of Sihanouk by another wife, he was a half-brother of Ranariddh. The half-brothers were bitter political rivals. Chakrapong defected from his father's party to join Hun Sen's government in the early-1990s. He quickly became close to Hun Sen who wanted to use his royal appeal to win votes in the general election. But they were irreconcilably divided after Chakrapong attempted to form a rebel autonomous zone following the 1993 election. Ranariddh and Hun Sen, seeing a common foe in Chakrapong, conspired to exile him. Chakrapong believed he was betrayed by the Cambodian People's Party.

Norodom Sirivudh: Born in 1952 this half-brother of Sihanouk also had a rapid rise and fall. A member of the Funcinpec party, he was appointed foreign minister in 1993. He resigned in October 1994, claiming he had serious differences with the Second Prime Minister Hun Sen. Sirivudh was exiled to France in December 1995 following allegations that he plotted to kill Hun Sen. Bitterly opposed to Hun Sen, Sirivudh turned into a relentless critic of Hun Sen and his style of government. He was allowed back to Cambodia in 1999, vowing not to return to politics.

Sam Rainsy: Born in 1949 this son of a former senior government official, Sam

Sary, went to study in France in 1965. There, Rainsy earned degrees in political science, economics, accounting and business management. While in France in the mid-1970s, Rainsy and his wife Tioulong Saumura produced a magazine, *The Voice of Free Cambodia*, highlighting the atrocities of the Khmer Rouge. Rainsy was employed in a French bank owned by the Michelin company. He returned to Cambodia in 1991 to make his debut in politics by joining Ranariddh's Funcinpec party. He was appointed finance minister, but was sacked from the government in 1994, and then removed from the party and the national assembly the following year. He became a bitter critic of Hun Sen and his government, and formed his own party, the Sam Rainsy Party.

Yasushi Akashi: A top Japanese diplomat, Akashi was appointed the chief of the United Nations Transitional Authority in Cambodia (Untac), the body mandated to organise and supervise the general election in 1993. Akashi's formal title was Special Representative of the Secretary General. After the completion of his Cambodian mission, he was appointed the head of the UN mission in Yugoslavia. He maintained a neutral position towards Hun Sen and the other political leaders.

Lt. Gen. John Sanderson: An Australian army general who served as force commander of Untac forces in Cambodia.

THE CAMBODIAN AND INTERNATIONAL PARTIES

Armée nationaliste sihanoukienne, or Sihanoukist National Army: It was set up in 1982 to fight the Vietnamese forces in Cambodia. Later it was known as the National Army of Independent Kampuchea, and served as the armed forces of Funcinpec.

Buddhist Liberal Democratic Party: Ahead of the election in 1993, Son Sann renamed the KPNLF as the BLDP in order to kindle latent Buddhism in the people, and show them the path to non-violence in national politics.

Cambodian People's Party: Better known as the CPP, it is the political party headed by Chea Sim, Heng Samrin and Hun Sen. The CPP evolved from the KPRP and the SOC. The leaders changed the name of the party in order to whitewash its tainted authoritarian image ahead of the elections in 1993, and also to cast off its communist ideology and adopt a more conciliatory democratic style.

Cambodian People's Armed Forces: Popularly known as CPAF, it is the armed forces of the CPP.

Democratic Kampuchea Party: The formal name of the political wing of the Khmer Rouge guerrillas, headed by Pol Pot.

Funcinpec: A French acronym for Front uni national pour un Cambodge indépendent, neutre, pacifique, et coopératif, or National United Front for an Independent, Neutral, Peaceful and Cooperative Cambodia. The royalist political party was created by Sihanouk in 1981 to fight the Phnom Penh régime of Heng Samrin and their patrons, the Vietnamese. After the peace accord was signed in 1991, Sihanouk handed over the party's leadership to Ranariddh.

Kampuchean People's Revolutionary Party: The KPRP was an offshoot of the Indochinese Communist Party (ICP) that played a vital role against French colonial rule and the Japanese occupation of Cambodia. The KPRP was formed in 1951 after the ICP was dissolved and reorganised into three communist parties for Vietnam, Laos, and Cambodia. The party in Cambodia split in 1962 into pro-China and pro-Soviet Union factions. Pol Pot led the pro-Chinese group that was vehemently anti-Soviet. In January 1979, the division became permanent when the pro-Soviet and pro-Vietnamese faction under Pen Sovann replaced Pol Pot as the leader in Phnom Penh.

Khmer People's National Liberation Front: Set up by Son Sann in 1979 to fight the Vietnamese forces based in Cambodia.

Khmer People's National Liberation Armed Forces: KPNLAF was the armed forces of the KPNLF.

National Army of Democratic Kampuchea: NADK was the guerrilla armed forces better known as the Khmer Rouge.

Paris Peace Accord: The peace agreement, formally known as the "agreements on a comprehensive political settlement of the Cambodia conflict," was signed in Paris on October 23, 1991, and ended the fighting between the four Cambodian factions that agreed to work towards elections under the supervision of the United Nations.

State of Cambodia: Better known as the SOC, it was the government that ran the country under various names from 1979 till the elections of May 1993. The

SOC had its origins in the KPRP as most of its member

Supreme National Council of Cambodia: The SNC was cre
accord to represent the sovereignty of Cambodia through the tran
until the elections. It represented the country externally and occupied
the United Nations.

United Nations Transitional Authority in Cambodia: Untac was created under
the Paris accord to organise and supervise elections, and demobilise and disarm
the Cambodian factions. Its mandate ran from late-1991 through late-1993.
Elements of the UN remained in Cambodia in 1994-95.

ABBREVIATIONS

ANKI	National Army of Independent Kampuchea
ASEAN	Association of Southeast Asian Nations
BBC	British Broadcasting Corporation
BLDP	Buddhist Liberal Democratic Party
CPP	Cambodian People's Party
FUNCINPEC	National United Front for an Independent, Peaceful, Neutral, and Cooperative Cambodia
FUNK	National United Front for Kampuchea
ICP	Indochinese Communist Party
KPNLF	Khmer People's National Liberation Front
KPNLAF	Khmer People's National Liberation Armed Forces
KPRP	Kampuchean People's Revolutionary Party
NEC	National Election Commission
NGC	National Government of Cambodia
PNGC	Provisional National Government of Cambodia
RCAF	Royal Cambodian Armed Forces
SNC	Supreme National Council
SRN	Sangkum Reastr Niyum
SEAZ	Samdech Euv Autonomous Zone
UN	United Nations
UNTAC	United Nations Transitional Authority in Cambodia

...1 Sna village, Stung Trang district, Kompong

...ıdra Dhevi in Phnom Penh, and lived in the Naga

197... ...blican government underground movement known
as the *maqu...,* ...ımer Rouge under the patronage of Sihanouk. Wounded
five times in heavy ... ...ng.

1975: Appointed Chief of Special Regimental Staff of the Khmer Rouge in the Eastern Region. Lost left eye in the final assault on Phnom Penh. Married Bun Sam Hieng, better known as Bun Rany. (The couple have three sons and three daughters, one of whom was adopted. The first child, a boy, Hun Manet was born on October 10, 1977. Other children: Hun Mana, female, born on September 20, 1980. Hun Manit, male, born on October 17, 1981. Hun Many, male, born on November 27, 1982. Hun Maly, female, born on December 30, 1983. The couple adopted a sixth child, a girl, whom they named Hun Maline).

1977: Appointed Deputy Regimental Commander of a Special Regiment of the Khmer Rouge in the Eastern Region. Escaped to Song Be province in South Vietnam to avoid being purged by Pol Pot. Formed a 20,000-strong force of Cambodian nationalists, and prepared to overthrow the Khmer Rouge.

1979: Flew back to Phnom Penh after the Khmer Rouge régime was toppled. Appointed foreign minister in the People's Republic of Kampuchea government.

1981: Appointed deputy prime minister.

1985: Appointed prime minister—possibly the youngest premier in the world. Won one hundred per cent of the votes in a secret national assembly ballot.

1986: Relinquished the post of foreign minister to concentrate on his job as premier.

1987: Took back the foreign minister's post in order to build his stature ahead of the peace talks. Met Prince Sihanouk for first peace talks in France.

1989: Planned and executed the final withdrawal of the Vietnamese forces from Cambodia.

1991: Signed a peace accord in Paris in October with Sihanouk and two other Cambodian factions, bringing the civil war to an end.

1993: Lost the election. Formed a coalition government with Norodo'n Ranariddh as first prime minister, and Hun Sen as second prime minister.

1996: Relationship with Ranariddh soured.

1997: Armed clashes erupted in Phnom Penh between the forces of Ranariddh and Hun Sen. Overthrown by Hun Sen, Ranariddh went into self-imposed exile while facing criminal charges for illegally importing weapons. The world's press acknowledged the emergence of Hun Sen as a strongman.

1998: Ranariddh, granted amnesty by Sihanouk, returned to contest elections in July. Hun Sen won the election and was appointed prime minister.

1999: Under Hun Sen's leadership, Cambodia became the 10th member of the Association of Southeast Asian Nations. He had eventually secured international acceptance after struggling for decades to gain legitimacy.

PROLOGUE

A SHORT HISTORY OF CAMBODIA

Of all the Cambodian leaders to have headed governments in Phnom Penh since independence from France on November 9, 1953, Hun Sen is destined to be the longest-serving, and the most resilient with a record fourteen years in power till 1999. In good health, and in firm control of government, he appears set for an even longer innings as prime minister. With his remarkable staying power he has carved for himself an equal political stature with former chief of state, Norodom Sihanouk, by at least one yardstick — their tenure in active politics. Sihanouk's political career as the head of government lasted fifteen years — he abdicated the throne in favour of his father in 1955 paving the way for his election as chief of state in June 1960, and ran the country till he was toppled in a *coup* in March 1970. Sihanouk's previous role as king lasted fourteen years till his abdication. Other Cambodian leaders had much shorter stints — Lon Nol's government survived just five years, while Pol Pot and Norodom Ranariddh were in power less than four years each.

During those fourteen years in power (1985 to 1999) Hun Sen tenaciously deepened his control on the government in four distinct phases starting with his appointment as prime minister in early-1985. In the second phase from the general election in May 1993 to 1997 he served as the second prime minister, but wielded more power than First Prime Minister Ranariddh, a son of Sihanouk. In the third phase (1997-1998) Hun Sen consolidated power after overthrowing Ranariddh. The fourth phase began with the victory of Hun Sen's Cambodian People's Party in the general election of 1998, and his reappointment as prime minister.

The story of Hun Sen and his country is inextricably woven into the fabric of a 2,000-year saga. In order to understand the controversial man who has ruled Cambodia with an adamantine grip, and his troubled nation, it is necessary to travel down that patterned past of two millennia and see him in the cross-currents of Khmer history. It is a history riddled with fiery civil strife within the shifting boundaries of a Khmer kingdom ruled by chieftains in the first eight centuries of the last millennium followed by 1,000-odd years of bloody wars with the Cham kingdoms in the east (present-day Vietnam), and the Siamese (Thais) in the West. While wars were waged the unparalleled edifices of Angkor (a corruption of he Sanskrit word *nagara*, meaning city), and a whole civilisation of temples was being built by thousands of men toiling incessantly. As a wave of Hinduism spread through Southeast Asia the Khmer kings built magnificent temples to celebrate the gods of the Hindu pantheon and the Buddhist faith.

The spirit of adventure among Indian seafarers to discover *Suvarnabhumi*, or land of gold, brought in its wake a continuous flow of Indian emigrants through the many trading posts in Southeast Asia. They arrived at the lower Mekong Delta at the southeastern corner of Cambodia and the southern-most point of Vietnam, known as Funan, derived possibly from the Khmer word *phnom*, meaning mountain in modern Khmer, and *bnam* in ancient Khmer from a Chinese root word.

Sometimes the Indian traders' stops at the new ports of call were unscheduled due to bad weather or the onslaught of the monsoons, a not very well understood phenomenon that forced their ships to anchor for months before sailing back home. The temptation then, as it is now among long distance business travellers, was to sink roots in a new land.

The beginnings of Indian colonies in Cambodia, like those in other parts of Indochina, are in oblivion, but are echoed in local legends and traditions. Though these legends cannot be regarded as true chronicles of events they possess historical importance in as much as they have preserved the popular beliefs about the foundation of Indian influences in these lands.

In the process of settlement beside fertile riverine deltas which yielded enough fish and rice to live comfortable existences, many of the merchants married local women and imperceptibly passed on their social, religious, and cultural genes over hundreds of years. The new religions—Hinduism and Buddhism—were thus transmitted in the new languages of Pali and Sanskrit. There is evidence of Indian influences such as Sanskrit literature, temple rituals, a legal system, astronomy, and a whole new written script being willingly adopted by the Khmers who imprinted it onto the weave of the complex nation we now know as Cambodia. The earliest inscribed evidence of the Indianisation of Cambodia comes from a heavily Sanskritised Khmer inscription from the Angkor Borei region, dated 612 AD.

It was the roving British ambassador, Sir Malcolm MacDonald, who popularised the charming legend about the beginnings of the Khmers as recorded by Chinese visitor K'ang T'ai in the 3rd century AD. In his book *Angkor and the Khmers*, he writes of an Indian prince, Kaundinya, a staunch devotee of a Hindu god who was pleased with his piety. It was sometime in the 1st century AD that the prince dreamed the god gave him a divine bow and asked him to set sail on a trading vessel. At dawn he went to the temple and found the bow he had seen in the dream. Then he embarked on his voyage. The god changed the course of the winds so that he arrived at Funan.

Lieu-Ye, or Willowleaf, the princess of Funan, came to pillage the wayfaring seaman. Kaundinya shot an arrow from the divine bow, piercing the queen's vessel, and forcing her to surrender. As was the custom among her simple people, Her Majesty was completely naked. Willowleaf did not even wear a figleaf. Deploring this display of savagery, Kaundinya at once presented his prisoner with a roll of cloth with which to wrap herself. By her captivation of him they were later married. The *History of the Liang Dynasty* has preserved a similar story about Kaundinya. It is interesting to note that the brahmins, or priestly class, of the Kaundinya clan are mentioned in an inscription of Mysore in southern India belonging to the 2nd century AD.

From Chinese records it appears that the wealth and pomp of Funan lasted until the 6th century AD. The territorial ambitions of the adjoining state of Chenla, and other principalities jostling for power in the region, changed the fortunes of Funan. There was civil strife and Chenla became the dominant base from which different dynasties wielded power between the 7th and 8th centuries, though interestingly, strong and consistent diplomatic ties were maintained with China, with wealthy tributes sent to the Chinese court. There is some evidence, for instance, that a successor of Kaundinya, possibly Jayavarman I, referred to by the Chinese chroniclers as Cho-ye-pa-mo, sent merchants to Canton to promote trade between 420-478 AD during the Song period.

Theories abound on the origins of the ancestry of the Khmer nation. Few inscriptions are available about Funan. Other than the 5th century records of a benevolent monarch, Maharajadhiraja (the king of kings) Devanika, the consensus among scholars regarding post-Funan Khmer reign is that Chenla was possibly a loose confederation of states. The names of King Bhavavarman, Chitrasena-Mahendravarman, Isanavarman, and Jayavarman I feature prominently in inscriptions and records of the 7th and ? h centuries.

A glowing account of Funan is written in the history of the Tsin dynasty (265-419 AD). It says: "The kingdom of Funan is more than 3,000 li to the west of Lin-yi (Champa), in a great bay of the ocean...There are walled towns, palaces, and houses. The people mostly take their food on silver utensils. The taxes are paid in gold, silver, pearls, and perfumes. They have many books. In writing they use an alphabet derived from India. Their funeral and marriage ceremonies are like those of Champa."

The sometimes tempestuous and mostly towering destiny of Angkor came in the form of a visitor—Jayavarman II—whose lineage is perhaps the most debated issue in the ancestry of Khmer kingship. Little is known about this man. There is a staggering lack of inscriptions from his reign. Though generally believed to have been installed as monarch in 802 AD on Mount Mahendra, there is a strong possibility of him being present in the region of Prey Veng as early as 790 AD.

However, it was only an 11th century inscription from Sdok Kak Thom that linked Jayavarman II definitely with the Sailendra dynasty of Indonesia, before he returned to Cambodia. Most of the evidence points to him being made prisoner and taken to Java when the monarch preceding him was killed by the Sailendras. His return to Cambodia was historic in that he established an empire that would stretch from the Gulf of Tonkin (present-day Vietnam) in the east to Kanchanaburi (present-day Thailand) in the west.

Ian Mabbett and David Chandler in *The Khmers*, pay measured tribute to the reign of Jayavarman II, the architect of the Angkor empire: "The very fact that it was later looked back upon as the beginning of a pan-Khmer régime indicates that there was, however gradually it was consolidated, a real discontinuity between the jostling principalities of 'Chenlala' and the empire that came into being during the 9th and 10th centuries."

During the reign of Jayavarman II the *devaraja,* or god-king, cult flourished as a highly ritualistic form of belief and worship where *lingas,* or the phallic icon of the Lord Shiva, once installed and consecrated in temples by Brahmin priests who performed Brahmanical rites and chanted specific Sanskrit mantras, were believed to hold the power of the king, seen to be god on earth. The power bestowed on the families of royal priests by Jayavarman II became a permanent feature of court life for later monarchs to emulate.

Towering temples built in the shape of a mountain functioned as the locus of the cult of the *devaraja*, through which the king's sacred personality was enshrined in a *linga* and worshipped. Upon his death the temple became the god-king's mausoleum, not unlike the Ramses Pharoahs of Egypt. The *linga,* uniting both political and spiritual power, became the property of the ruler (*devaraja*), and a symbol of his divinity.

The Khmers' passion for the construction of fabulous temples was driven, in part, by a deeper motive to survive by paying obeisance to their many gods. In their daily lives there were natural elements to be conquered—the blessings of water and harvests were to be sought. So, the Khmers reasoned the gods had to be appeased. In Khmer society, which was basically an agricultural one, fertility was an important factor.

Later, of course, as French scholar George Coedès emphasises, in the 12th century the cult of the god-king was honed to perfection when Khmer emperor Suryavarman II, a staunch follower of Lord Vishnu, built a sanctum in Angkor Wat and installed an image of Vishnu that was believed to hold the very essence of Vishnu's power, transferred to the monarch as the god who was king on earth.

The kings of Angkor believed with unquestioning faith that to perpetuate their power they needed to build more temples. So desperate had Jayavarman VII become in his bid to propagate his image through the cult of the god king, that in just under forty years he built no less than twelve mammoth structures— the best known being the Angkor Thom and Ta Prohm.

So, between 802 and 1431, when the Thais finally beseiged Angkor after relentless raids, a line of great Khmer kings dominated the vast political stage of ancient Cambodia—beginning wi h Jayavarman II, and including such stalwarts as Rajendravarman II (944-968), uryavarman I (1020-1050), Udayityavarman II (1050-1066), Suryavarman II (1 13-1150), Jayavarman VII (1181-1219), and ending with the weaker ones such as Thommo Soccorach and Ponha Yat in the 15th century. It was Jayavarman VII who extended the Khmer empire right up to present-day Kanchanaburi in Thailand.

These kings ruled over a lush and fertile land, sometimes blessed with up to four rice crops a year, and the fish from the huge Tonle Sap lake in the heart of the country that fed the thousands whose blood and sweat built the magnificent temples, and still others who fought the constant wars with the Cham and the Siamese armies. Vivid scenes of battles the Khmers fought with the Chams on one front, and the Siamese on the other, are chiselled on the walls of the Bayon and Angkor Wat, bearing witness to the valiant and brave who died to protect the Khmer motherland.

The history of these conquest-filled centuries has been pieced together from the stupendous monuments, sculptures, and excavated antiquities—but most importantly with the help of nearly 900 inscriptions in Pali, Sanskrit, and Khmer from the Angkor region.

From the time the Siamese armies ransacked Angkor, and the Cambodians shifted the capital from Angkor to the region of Phnom Penh in the 1440s, little is available by way of historical records until the 1940s. Thus the 500 years between Angkor's fall and this century are obscured. What is known for certain is that between the middle of the 15th and 16th centuries, Cambodia was a state ruled by the Thais. Then came the tussle to take over Cambodia—a constant struggle between Thailand and Vietnam lasting nearly 150 years until the 1860s.

The accession to the Cambodian throne of King Ang Duong in 1848 brought a twelve-year period of unprecedented peace sometimes described as the golden years. Duong, who suffered several years of captivity in Thailand, continued paying obeisance to the Thai king even after his release, while his country remained under Thai protection. At the same time Duong was frightened of Vietnam's motives.

Trapped between two powerful neighbours, Thailand and Vietnam, Duong perhaps had no choice but to seek the protection of the French. An insecure Duong sent gifts to the French Emperor, Napoleon III, via the French consulate in Singapore. But the Thais resented his overtures to the French. Duong sought French assistance both to defend his country from Vietnam, and to avoid the humiliation of remaining under the protection of the Thais.

The French grasped the opportunity, demanding teak and trading privileges from Duong in return for protection. In 1863, Cambodia willingly became a French protectorate. Duong breathed easy, and France gradually tightened its control over both Vietnam and Cambodia.

In the early stages of colonial rule the Cambodians were grateful to France for pressuring Thailand to return to Cambodia in 1907 its provinces of Battambang and Siem Reap after a century of occupation. But discontent was simmering in the villages. While the Khmer court appreciated the French presence, the over-taxed villagers suffered under the colonialists.

A flashpoint was the murder of a top French official and his Cambodian staff. In the early-1920s the acting French resident in Prey Veng, Felix Louis Bardez, dramatically increased the tax collections, and was promoted as the resident in Kompong Chhnang. In April 1925 Bardez visited a village in Kompong Chhnang that chronically reported low tax yields. He summoned tax evaders, handcuffed them, and threatened to imprison them. He then ate lunch while refusing to let the prisoners eat. A crowd of bystanders was incited by Bardez's arrogance, and attacked Bardez, killing him, his interpreter, and a militiaman.

These injustices gnawed at the hearts of the Cambodian intelligentsia in whom anti-colonial feelings readily took root. Nationalists such as Pach Chhoeun, Sim Var, and Son Ngoc Than succeeded in starting the first newspaper in Cambodia, *Nagara Vatta*, in 1936. It was no mean achievement for them to have convinced the French to grant them a licence—a process which normally took several years and usually ended in rejection. Rather than run the risk of opposing the French, the editors patiently bided their time. A perfect opportunity to challenge French authority presented itself when Japanese troops landed in Cambodia in May 1941. The paper took an increasingly pro-Japanese and anti-colonial line, leading to a dozen editorials being censored. The paper cleverly exploited two developments: it took full advantage of French military weakness, and Japanese sympathy for anti-colonial movements.

The French preference for Norodom Sihanouk as a future king was a gamble that would ultimately cost them their Cambodian colony. On April 25, 1941 Sihanouk was crowned king. The French colonialists saw in the debonair young Sihanouk an urbane, Westernised playboy who could be counted on to preserve French interests, which he did till the early-1950s.

The surrender of Japanese forces on August 16, 1945 saw a resurgence of French influence in Cambodia. The prince, previously labelled "comical" and "exotic", suddenly turned independence-minded. On a visit to France in February 1953, Sihanouk told the French President, Vincent Auriol, that many Cambodians did not feel any loyalty towards the French flag, adding that he himself had been faithful to France. From there, Sihanouk travelled to Canada, the United States and Japan, raising the question of his country's future, and complaining about French reluctance to loosen their grip.

On returning home, Sihanouk openly demanded independence. In a show of petulance, he went into exile in Thailand, and refused to communicate with French officials. In June 1953 he announced a royal crusade for independence. The French, fighting a bitter war in Vietnam, did not wish to risk another war in Cambodia, and ultimately relented, granting independence to Cambodia in November 1953. Sihanouk's non-violent campaign had triumphed. From then on he saw himself as another Mohandas Gandhi who had only a few years earlier won India its independence from the British in a non-violent manner. Later, a park was built in the centre of Phnom Penh prominently featuring a bust of Mahatma Gandhi.

Sihanouk then plunged headlong into politics. He abdicated in favour of his father, Norodom Suramarit, in March 1955 to pursue a nakedly ambitious political agenda. The very next month Sihanouk created his political party, the Sangkum Reastr Niyum, marking the beginning of the Sangkum era, a period of plenty, with farmers reporting bumper harvests, and Sihanouk personally laying the foundations of industry.

But Sihanouk took his nationalism too far and made a series of monumental blunders, putting himself and his country on a collision course with the United States. Sihanouk's biggest mistake was to openly provide support to Ho Chi Minh's Viet Minh forces that were battling American troops in South Vietnam. Sihanouk allowed the Viet Minh to travel across Cambodia over what came to be known as the 'Ho Chi Minh Trail'. The Americans frowned upon this strategy that sabotaged their own war efforts in Vietnam, and also alienated an influential group of Cambodian politicians that was growing increasingly close to Washington. Sihanouk's anti-Western proclivity became evident when he cut off diplomatic relations with America's two strongest Asian allies—Thailand and South Vietnam—in 1961 and 1963 respectively. Three months after breaking with Saigon, Sihanouk made yet another error by rejecting American aid in November, and went on to write scathing anti-American editorials in his captive journals such as *Kambuja Monthly Illustrated Review,* arguing eloquently in favour of his country's neutrality. By 1964 the US and South Vietnamese forces launched attacks on Cambodian villages, with the result that Cambodia's diplomatic relations with the USA were ruptured in May 1965, and its neutrality lay in tatters. By 1969 the USA had begun secret bombings of suspected Vietnamese sanctuaries inside Cambodia.

Against the backdrop of thousands of Cambodians dying in American bombing raids, Sihanouk left for France for his annual holiday in January 1970. By this time, his political adversaries within Cambodia such as Sisowath Sirik Matak, had begun plotting against him. In Sihanouk's absence, Matak and a few army officers visited the house of Prime Minister Lon Nol and, at pistol point, ordered him to support a vote in parliament to overthrow Sihanouk the next day. The *coup* was launched like clockwork on March 18. The national assembly voted 86-3 to remove Sihanouk, agreeing unanimously that they lacked confidence in his governance. Lon Nol stayed on as prime minister, with Matak as deputy. The new Republican government instantly won recognition and financial aid from Washington. Sihanouk, in exile, took up residence in Beijing.

At this time, a communist movement was gathering steam in the countryside. It was led by Saloth Sar, a French-educated intellectual who later adopted the name Pol Pot. He won a scholarship to study radio electricity in Paris, but he neglected his course work, and is believed to have joined the Communist Party of France. Soon, he and other young Khmer communists in Paris began to perceive Sihanouk's absolute monarchy as authoritarian. Saloth Sar wrote a polemical article calling for the elimination of the monarchy. Sihanouk was furious, and he cut off scholarship funds. Saloth Sar returned to Phnom Penh in 1953 to join the Indochina Communist Party, and take charge of the newly emerging Khmer People's Revolutionary Party. The epicentre of his anger was the French presence, American domination, and Sihanouk's authoritarianism. Sihanouk's police launched a campaign of terror against the communists, whom Sihanouk derisively labelled, in French, the "Khmers rouges", or Red Khmers. Pol Pot then found inspiration in Mao Zedong's brand of communism, and sought to recreate the Maoist model in Cambodia through class struggle, and agrarian reforms. By the time Sihanouk was toppled, the influence of the Khmer Rouge had spread over vast swathes of the countryside.

The new Khmer Republic resumed diplomatic relations with Thailand and Saigon in May 1970. Sihanouk exhorted Khmer Rouge leaders Pol Pot and Khieu Samphan to overthrow the Lon Nol régime and reinstate him as the rightful ruler. In April 1973 Sihanouk visited zones controlled by the Khmer Rouge, who were fighting the forces of Lon Nol on many fronts. In anticipation of the advance of the Khmer Rouge into Phnom Penh, the US Embassy was hastily shut down on April 12, 1975.

The Khmer Rouge entered Phnom Penh on April 17. Massacres began on the first day, and continued for almost four years. At the end, the death toll was estimated at 1.7 million innocent Cambodians who were tortured and starved to death. The Khmer Rouge permitted Sihanouk to return to Phnom Penh in December 1975 where he remained virtually under palace arrest, and unaware that his Khmer Rouge friends had evacuated cities, banned money, and turned the country into a concentration camp.

It was in this vitiated atmosphere, with Cambodians killing one another, that Hun Sen grew up. Unable to pay for his education, his parents sent him to school in Phnom Penh. The child was an ardent admirer of Sihanouk, and was deeply pained when he was removed in a *coup*. When Sihanouk called upon his countrymen in 1970 to rise and join the movement to overthrow Lon Nol, Hun Sen responded. He gave up his studies, and went into the jungles to join the Khmer Rouge, unaware of their murderous intent. Hun Sen eventually broke ranks with the Khmer Rouge in 1977, and defected to Vietnam where he was initially kept prisoner. Later he sought Vietnamese help to fight Pol Pot, whose inhuman régime was toppled in 1979.

This book contains the untold story of Hun Sen. It is also the story of a country that fell victim to Sihanouk's ill-conceived diplomacy and Cold War politics that together conspired to create the conditions, first, for the Khmer Rouge to come to power and, then, for a strongman like Hun Sen to rise from obscurity, overthrow the genocidal régime, and take control of his war-wracked country.

With Hun Sen tightening his grip, the country became stable by degrees, with investors reporting that never before had business confidence been so high. When the old cancers of corruption and crime proved difficult to remove, Hun Sen warned his own partymen to change their ways, or risk being sacked. Clearly, Hun Sen was bent upon building a transparent and economically prosperous Cambodia. Ironically, the most formidable stumbling blocks to his vision were the influential politicians and powerful civil servants within his own government.

ONE

KOMPONG DAYS

CHILD OF THE FULL MOON

Tuol Krosang village would never be quite the same again.

The little-known hamlet near Takhmau city, home to rice farmers and swarms of egrets, was aflutter with the arrival of birds of a different kind. When Hun Sen moved into his country home right next door in 1989, the tiny settlement was buzzed by howling helicopter engines, rasping rotor blades, and the sounds of an army camp. Through gaps in rows of flowering krosang trees, and groves of mango, banana, and palm, the villagers could see the ungainly metallic birds lift off and touch down at helipads far beyond the marshes. They knew that neighbour Hun Sen had come to stay.

They were bewildered at the rapid rise of this poor kompong boy. Regarding him with a curious mixture of fear and reverence, they knew he was now stronger than ever, and were grateful to him for liberating them from the genocidal Khmer Rouge who starved, tortured, and killed about 1.7 million Cambodians in the mid-1970s.

"Among strong students I was strong," Hun Sen told us in mid-1998, one year after he overthrew first prime minister Norodom Ranariddh, a son of King Norodom Sihanouk. "Among strong soldiers I was strong. Now, among strongmen I am strong."

Picking up a copy of *Time* with a cover picture of president Suharto of Indonesia, another strongman with whom he was often compared, he said with a grin: "He's gone. I am still here."

Long before Suharto was toppled Hun Sen had voiced his innermost desire: "I want to develop my country like the other Southeast Asian strongmen did."

The Cambodian strongman who turned forty-six in 1998 was born neither into great wealth, nor into power. After his family lost its modest wealth he was no different from a poor village child. His parents did not plan for his future, and would have been happy to see him become a rice farmer.

It was at midnight under a full moon on Tuesday, August 5, 1952 that Hun Sen was born.

"According to Cambodian belief children born in the year of the dragon, especially on Tuesday, are very stubborn," Hun Sen said during an interview with the authors. "We should correct my birthdate. It has been wrongly mentioned in the media as April 4, 1951."

In later life his stubbornness and, equally, his resilience confirmed the accuracy of ancient Khmer beliefs.

He was born in Peam Koh Snar village in the district of Stung Trang in Kompong Cham province, on the eastering bend of the Mekong river. His mother gave birth at home, not at a hospital. His maternal grandmother was a midwife who delivered all the children in the family.

Blessed with the mighty river the province was the rice bowl of a very poor and very wet country. He sloshed through country roads during the rainy season when the village was flooded. People there made their living off the river, or by farming. His family lived in a typical open-plan Khmer-style home: a wooden structure built on stilts, and divided into three areas—two living spaces, and an area for cooking.

His parents named him Hun Bunall. Four decades later people in the village would still call him by his childhood name.

"They tried to find a name for me that bore a close rhythm to the name of my father," he said. "My father's name was Hun Neang so they named me Hun Nal. Also, when I was born I was rather fat, and according to rural custom when a boy is fat he is called Nal."

When the teenager left home to study in Phnom Penh his name was changed a second time. He was variously called Sen and Ritthi Sen. In an ancient Khmer story Ritthi Sen was the name of a boy who suffered at the hands of his eleven stepmothers.

He changed his name a third time when he became a guerrilla in 1970.

"When I took to the jungle I did not use the name Sen or Bunall," he said. "Instead, I used the name Hun Samrach. Samrach means one who completes all his life's work. But for me this name was inauspicious. I was wounded many times while bearing this name."

After completing an intelligence mission in Kompong Cham in 1972 he abandoned his old names, and decided to adopt the name Hun Sen.

"But my relatives call me Bunall even now," he said.

The habit of changing names ran in the family. His two older brothers Hun Long San and Hun Long Neng had both dropped their middle names. Besides them, Hun Sen had three younger sisters—Hun Sengny, Hun Sinath, and Hun Thoeun—who all lived through terrible times.

"One older brother died even before I was born," he said.

In 1945 when the Japanese took over all command positions in Cambodia following their invasion of Indochina in 1941, Hun Sen's father, Hun Neang, was a Buddhist monk in the pagoda of Unalong in Kompong Cham, and his mother, Dee Yon, was a housewife. Hun Neang was a disciple of a holy man named Samdech Chunnat. After Hun Neang was disrobed he joined the Issarak movement that strove to liberate the country from the French colonial rulers. But the family suffered a blow when a group of Issarak members kidnapped Hun Sen's mother for ransom. The kidnappers were aware that Hun Sen's grandfather was rich.

The affluent family was forced to sell its property to pay off the kidnappers. Fortunately his mother was released without being harmed. But life became more difficult as the family, having lost most of its land, became poorer. Desperately in need of money to support the family Hun Neang joined the government as a militiaman. He was trained by the French, and led his troops to attack the Issarak. After Cambodia became independent in 1953 he became the chief of a self-defence force in his commune.

"He had the blood of a soldier," Hun Sen said of his father.

Hun Sen's maternal grandmother exerted tremendous influence over the family. Although she was a midwife she acquired a working knowledge of the local laws, and advised people on their legal problems.

Hun Sen's mother could not read or write, but she had a good head for mathematics. All she could write was her own name, the name of her husband, and their six children. After Hun Sen moved into his country home in Takhmau in 1989 his parents continued living in his well-guarded villa at Boulevard Suramarit near the Independence Monument in the capital. As a result of the armed clashes on the streets of Phnom Penh on July 5-6, 1997 between the forces of Hun Sen and Ranariddh, his mother's health was affected, and she was moved to the Calmette hospital in Phnom Penh. She turned seventy-seven that year, and his father seventy-five.

Hun Sen's voice broke when he said: "According to the doctor my mother cannot live more than six months. She was given a lot of treatment, but the doctor gave her no more than six months."

She died in early-1998. A childhood friend of Hun Sen's, Chhim You Teck, who worked as a medical assistant at the Calmette Hospital, said that his mother was suffering from a serious liver ailment. The grieving son went into a month of mourning. He cancelled all appointments, and postponed an interview with us.

Living amid poverty and sickness Hun Sen learnt the art of survival. He spent six years studying at the Peam Koh Snar Primary School in the village. The lack of a high school in the village left his parents with no choice but to send him to Phnom Penh to study at the Lycée Indra Dhevi from 1965 to 1969.

"I did not finish my high school studies, but later I did complete my study programmes by learning while continuing to work part-time," he said. "I enjoyed studies very much."

He excelled in mathematics after being coached by his mother, and developed a fondness for Khmer literature. A keen sportsman, he liked athletics and volleyball, and continued playing when he became the prime minister.

At school, he immersed himself in Cambodian poetry, dipping into verse by Preah Bat Ang Duong, the teachings of Krom Ngoy, and books on education written by Tiv Ol.

He was moved by the sheer power of sentimental stories such as *Kolap Pailin* (Pailin Rose), *Phkar Srapoan* (A Faded Flower), Tum Teav's Romeo and Juliet, and ancient works such as the Hindu epic, Ramayana. He read with pleasure the works of Preah Chinavong, Preah Thinnavong, Luong Preah Sdech Kan, and the Cambodian *sastras*, which were ancient stories written on palm leaves. He did not have a taste for popular movies with the exception of film adaptations of ancient Khmer stories which he enjoyed.

Even as a teenager he had a sharp political mind. This instinct developed prematurely, even precociously, owing to the widening social and economic inequalities in Cambodian society. As a child he respected and admired the chief of state Prince Norodom Sihanouk, but he hated the corrupt officials and members of parliament.

"These people never went to the villages to get in touch with the people, nor did they keep the promises they made during the election campaigns," he said. As a boy he deeply mistrusted the rich and the powerful. "I hated the impudent children who came from families that had authority and wealth, and who despised the poor. They did not read their textbooks, and were not good at studies, yet they always passed the examinations," he said.

Early on, he developed a dislike for the Khmer Rouge, as well as for the Khmer Serei, an anti-monarchy movement backed by the United States. "I was shocked by the acts of aggression and the bombing of Cambodia carried out by the USA and South Vietnam," he said.

When he was at school he wanted to be a teacher when he grew up. But after he joined the national liberation front led by Sihanouk in 1970 he wanted to become a pilot.

"My aspirations and dreams had to be abandoned due to the war and the genocidal régime," he said. "Political events altered my desires, compelling me to enter politics, which I did not want to do. I led a rough life, full of suffering and the pain of separation caused by living far from my parents since childhood."

The scars would still be visible though the wound had healed.

"After I was married I seldom met my wife and children," he said. "Not until 1979 did I have a family reunion. But a good deed always brings a return, and although I was separated from my parents and family, I enjoyed the love and sympathy of the people and friends who looked after me. It was because of them that I could survive."

NOT too far away, yet worlds apart from Hun Sen's village, a little girl was growing up in Rokarkhnau village in the Kroch Chhmar district of Kompong Cham.

As the sunbeams caught the treetops covering the little hillock bordering picturesque Rokarkhnau, making the frail tributary of the Rokarkhnau river gleam like a narrow sheet of silver, a seven-year-old girl could be spotted skipping over the stones on the riverbed. Like most children, whenever she got the opportunity, the fair-skinned Khmer girl kicked up her heels in the ankle-deep waters of the little stream.

It was the summer of 1961. And as she neared the door of her father's farmhouse, little Bun Rany could smell the *pra hok* frying in the family pot. She could almost see the reassuring smile on her grandmama's face as she ladled out the rice and fried fish.

The rainy season was far more troublesome. It meant waiting to be ferried to school in a flimsy little dinghy across the turbulent waters of the now benign sliver of water.

At any rate she was glad she was nearly home. It had been a long day at school, and an opponent had dug her elbow deep into little Bun Rany's ribs at basketball practice. The anticipation of drinking the cool water from the family well made Bun Rany walk a little faster.

The district of Kroch Chhmar was a fairly prosperous one, with most farmers like Lin Kry, her father, living comfortably off the yields of the somewhat parched but fertile land. The Chinese-Khmer family traced its ancestry to Canton in China, and had integrated smoothly into Cambodian society.

Hun Sen would not meet Bun Rany for several years, but his world would change the day he saw her.

PAGODA BOY

Standing on the windblown jetty, Hun Sen, now thirteen, hugged his mother desperately, and said goodbye with a sinking feeling. The boat slowly pulled away from Kompong Cham, and headed upriver.

Tears flowed on both sides. She had hurriedly put twelve riels into his pocket. It was worth thirty-four American cents. She had given him a small packet of rice that was knotted into his *krama*. The only clothes he took with him were what he was wearing. Her heart cried out for the boy. There was little she could do for him. The family had lost its wealth, and its land. They could barely afford to pay his school entrance fees in Phnom Penh. They could not rent a small room for him, or pay for his meals. They were forced to entrust their bright little boy to the care of Buddhist monks at the Naga Vann Pagoda in Phnom Penh. The boat moved upstream, and out of sight of his waving mother, taking the young man to his new life in Phnom Penh, then, as always, a city of wealth and poverty, of silk and open drains.

On his journey back to school the boy could not help thinking about the lives of many of his schoolmates who were well looked after by their parents. All alone in the boat, with only a *krama* to cover himself, he pondered his future. He felt terribly let down by Prince Sihanouk's government that had not, as his parents explained to him, provided a high school in Kompong Cham, forcing him to be separated from his family, and sending him far upriver to a life of hardship and deprivation. At that time, unknown to the boy, Sihanouk's royal palace came alive every night with champagne parties, and the city's élite jived in the dance halls, while the great mass of people led lives huddled around their bowls of rice and dried fish.

In darkness the boat pulled into a jetty in Phnom Penh. It was 3 am. The passengers went home by cyclo, but Hun Sen walked from the riverside to the pagoda so he could save three riels.

It was fortunate that education was almost free at Lycée Indra Dhevi.

"We paid only for chalk and for sports. But when we enrolled at the school we had to pay 1,800 riel," Hun Sen said, gathering the strands of his past. "It was very difficult for poor children to enter school because 1,800 riel was equal to US$51, which was a lot of money."

The Cambodian riel was fairly strong against the greenback during Sihanouk's rule. Between 1958-68, one US dollar was worth thirty-five riels, according to the Statistical Yearbook for Asia/Far East, 1969. During Lon Nol's régime, in November 1971, the National Bank of Cambodia devalued the riel by 150 per cent.

The little boy's day at the Naga Vann Pagoda began at 5 am, except during examinations when he—then known as Hun Bunall—and the other pagoda boys, had to rise at 4 am. First, he cooked rice porridge for the monks, and then read his textbooks. He sometimes read his lessons while stirring the porridge since time was precious. After that he swept the compound of the pagoda where two huge trees constantly shed leaves and flowers.

"Sometimes I was punished because of these two big trees," he said. "When I took the porridge to the monks they always looked across the compound to check if I had swept it or not. If a lot of leaves and flowers fell from the trees I would be punished."

He walked to school at 6.30 am, taking with him several empty ricebowls, and left school early on the days when it was his turn to collect food in the streets for the monks. The pagoda boys came under pressure to quickly beg for food from door to door because the monks insisted on eating before noon.

"Some monks did not understand the suffering of the others," Hun Sen said. "Sometimes I was punished by the monks if I brought the food late. But if I brought the food before noon they would eat and talk cheerfully, but I also felt very hungry."

To keep the monks in good humour he tried to bring in the food as close to mid-day as possible so that they could eat on time. After they had eaten their fill the boys were given the leftovers. Then they washed the bowls, and it was time to return to school.

In the afternoon the boys fetched water from Kampuchea Krom Street to the pagoda. They found it very difficult to lift the heavy jars. By the time they finished their work for the day it was as late as 7 pm. After that they chanted Buddhist prayers. The ritual was performed twice a day, in the morning while cooking porridge, and at night before retiring.

The pagoda boys did not have the luxury of relaxing on Sundays. The monks ate every day, and the boys had to collect food seven days a week. On Sundays they had to collect food early. And it was on Sundays that Hun Sen learnt to play chess when he stopped over at a barber's shop on his rounds to collect food. The barber, who donated food to the monks, had provided a chessboard for his customers who waited to have their hair cut. Hun Sen joined them in the queue.

"I learnt chess by looking at other people playing," he said.

Back at the pagoda the boys were mere pawns in a simple hierarchy. They were not given rooms. In fact, there were no rooms in the pagoda, in accordance with Khmer tradition.

"I slept in a mobile manner," Hun Sen recollected. "Where there was a vacant space I took it. When it was cold I slept in the space under a monk's bed to keep warm. When there were mosquitoes we asked the monks to let their mosquito nets drape below the bed so we would be protected."

The boys dreaded the monsoon nights when it rained long and hard.

"We had to find a dry place to sleep, a place that did not leak," he said. "When we were young we could sleep anywhere."

Life at the pagoda was shock therapy for Hun Sen whose paternal great-grandparents were rich. They owned about fifteen hectares of land and property in Kompong Cham. His maternal grandparents, however, were not wealthy, but they had a good standing in rural society. His maternal grandmother had a thorough grasp of the local laws, and people flocked to her to seek legal advice.

But his paternal grandparents lost some of their land in a massive erosion along the Mekong river. The financial losses compelled them to leave their village, and move to a village close to where Hun Sen's family lived.

The sudden change in the family's fortunes, combined with the lack of schools in Kompong Cham, made life very difficult for him. Widespread poverty forced thousands of children to leave home, and lead isolated lives in the capital's pagodas.

"I am now determined to build more schools—more than any other Cambodian because I do not want our children to share the same fate as I," Hun Sen said in early-1998 as he looked back at his childhood. "I hated the régimes at that time, even the régime of Sihanouk. It was a régime of injustice that often cheated the people by buying their votes. At the time my father was a propagandist for a politician, but when the politician was elected as a member of parliament he did nothing for the people."

Hun Sen was considered a good student, and wrote letters of application, even love letters, for family and friends. Path Sam, a former teacher at the Lycée Indra Dhevi, said that he had heard one of Hun Sen's teachers remarking that he was a "clever boy, but was very quiet".

Hun Sen did not wear saffron robes, did not shave his head, and was not ordained. The teenager had a keen sense of humour. Another pagoda boy, Ea Samnang, said that one day, just for fun, Hun Sen borrowed a cyclo and a hat from a cyclo driver, and rode the cyclo around the pagoda. But he lost the hat. When he was told to pay thirty riels to its owner, he fetched his clay piggybank that was full of small coins.

"He had to break his piggybank," said Ea Samnang, a close friend of Hun Sen's who lived in the same pagoda.

The two were friends even though Ea Samnang was twenty and Hun Sen was fourteen. Ea Samnang, who later became a teacher at the Bak Touk High School in Phnom Penh, said that Hun Sen's mother visited him at the pagoda frequently.

"She would tell us to study hard because we were poor," said Ea Samnang who studied at the Lycée Sangkum Reastr Niyum, a school named after Sihanouk's régime.

After Hun Sen became the prime minister Ea Samnang went to a public meeting at the Olympic Stadium in Phnom Penh where Hun Sen was attending a ceremony. He sent up a note to Hun Sen with his name on it. The prime minister saw the note, and invited his childhood friend to his residence.

"I went to his house, and we talked about the old days," Ea Samnang said. "He remembered how a friend of ours broke his leg playing football at the pagoda."

Another pagoda boy, Chhim You Teck, who shared the same holy residence with Hun Sen, remembered him as an "ordinary child, who worked very hard, walking from house to house to collect food". Hun Sen said that he knew Chhim You Teck and his family very well, and that they lived on the other side of the Mekong.

Chhim You Teck said: "I was in-charge of the boys, and I used to wait for them to return with the food. I used to collect it, and offer it to the monks."

Hun Sen was one of eight boys given the task of collecting food. Their expeditions usually yielded simple goodies such as sour soup, fish, and bananas.

The boys did not like to bathe, Chhim You Teck said.

"They were too small to draw water from the well," he said. "So, I used to draw the water, and force them to bathe."

The pagoda boys happily played the game of *beth pouk*, a Cambodian version of hide-and-seek, oblivious to the terrible times that lay ahead.

When Kim Chreng, a monk who took care of the boys, passed away in 1990, Hun Sen was aggrieved. But he could not attend the funeral on account of heavy fighting in the Khmer Rouge stronghold of Pailin in the northwest. Hun Sen donated money for the funeral.

Hun Sen quit studying at Lycée Indra Dhevi in 1969, and left before completing his high school examination.

"I left because of the happenings in the pagoda", he said.

Sihanouk's secret agents had entered the pagoda between 1967-69, and rounded up people suspected of harbouring anti-Sihanouk views, he said.

"One of my cousins, Neu Kean, was arrested, and I was afraid I would have to leave the pagoda," Hun Sen said. "I had to leave, but I always wanted to return to the pagoda. In January 1970, my cousin was released from prison, and I intended to return to the pagoda. But the *coup d'état* [in which Sihanouk was overthrown] happened on March 18, 1970, and I could not return."

The *coup* disrupted his education. That singular event transformed a pagoda boy into a guerrilla. All his Buddhist upbringing and fondness for religion was abandoned in the pursuit of a political cause. He wanted nothing more than to restore Sihanouk to power.

"I took to the forest because I saw the clouds of civil war gathering on the horizon," he said with finality.

OVER in Kroch Chhmar, Bun Rany lived the carefree life of a child, happily unaware of the coming conflict, or the existence of Hun Sen.

"I had two brothers and three sisters, and I remember my childhood as a very happy one," said Bun Rany as she delved back in time. "There was no fear, and we all seemed a pretty normal bunch. I was very close to my grandparents on my mother's side. They chatted a lot to me and, without my even knowing it, very gently, they taught me how to live in the Cambodian way, the traditional way. Their advice saw me through much of the hardship I was to suffer later in life."

It would turn out to be a troubled young life—separated for years from her husband, tortured mentally and physically by the Khmer Rouge, going without food or water, bereft of empathy or friendship during a hard and complicated pregnancy.

"It seems to me now, the most precious lessons I put to use in my life were the ones taught to me by my grandparents," she said.

DEEP INSIDE THE MAQUIS

GUERRILLA

He stuffed a small bag with a few shirts and a pair of old shoes, and reported at a jungle base to enlist in the *maquis*, a grand sounding resistance movement started by Sihanouk after he was overthrown in a *coup d'état* in March 1970. The militant movement, officially known as the National United Front for Kampuchea (FUNK), was joined by patriotic Cambodians who lived in the jungle, and waged war against the *coup* leaders commanded by General Lon Nol in an attempt to restore Sihanouk to power. The *maquis* also teamed up with Vietnamese and Laotian communists to struggle against "US imperialism" in Indochina. The Cambodian nationalists borrowed the word *maquis*

HUN SEN: STRONGMAN OF CAMBODIA

from the French Resistance who were named after the underbrush and thickets, or *maquis*, that grew in Europe and served as cover as they fought the German occupying forces in World War II. They transplanted an essentially French idea from thousands of miles away into an Asian country where it took root among the francophone natives.

Penniless and angry, Hun Sen was ripe for the picking. He sensed the onrush of war clouds when Sihanouk was overthrown in a putsch. He saw in their dark eddies a bleak future for himself. With hardly any incentive to attend school he abandoned his studies, and went into the jungle to become a guerrilla. He was eighteen.

"I joined the *maquis* during the Cambodian new year," he said. "I did not know what a soldier's life in the *maquis* would be like. So, I brought along a bag containing shoes and clothes like a person who lives in the city."

The young man wanted to overthrow the Lon Nol régime that had recently toppled Sihanouk. He had grown to admire Sihanouk's efforts to build an urban industry, in spite of his glaring rural shortcomings—his failure to provide education and healthcare, and his failure to orchestrate the agricultural green revolution the farmers pined for, but were unable to achieve due to a lack of modern techniques. Enamoured by the guerrillas he joined the *maquis* on April 14, 1970, less than a month after Sihanouk was removed. Before long he had a new life in the jungle as a member of the *maquis*. But he did not know that Pol Pot and his "Khmers rouges", as Sihanouk called them, were also a part of the *maquis*.

One of the first things he did was to change his name to Hun Samrach to disguise his identity. Two years later the twenty-year-old, then a crack commando, changed his name again, this time to Hun Sen. As he faithfully served the organisation he began to realise that it was under the complete control of the Khmer Rouge. Unperturbed by the Khmer Rouge's bizarre regulations, pathological mistrust for the Cambodian people, and their strictness, Hun Sen worked hard, trained hard, and rapidly climbed up the ranks.

"Not many people from the city or from places of high culture joined the *maquis*," Hun Sen said. "So, in the *maquis* I was called *Lo Kru*."

Even though he was one of the youngest soldiers in his group he was still known as *Lo Kru* which meant teacher or guru. He quickly earned the respect of his colleagues in the area where he carried out his covert activities. He attracted the attention of his leaders who noticed that he spent much of his time teaching the illiterate guerrillas, and making friends.

"This is because besides being a soldier, I was, in a way, an author and an actor," he said. "I was like an author who writes the story, and also like an actor who acts out the story."

He was more than that—a competitive volleyball player, and an attacking soccer player. For all their attempts to restore normalcy to their troubled lives, most Cambodians were irreconcilably divided.

In the depths of the jungle, time hung heavily on him. He spent much of it contemplating the future of his family and his country. He was alarmed at the deep divisions in society. He viewed with dark humour the manner in which Sihanouk had conveniently divided the Cambodians into five camps in the mid-1960s:

- the Khmer Rouge, or the Red Khmers, were essentially communists;
- the Blue Khmers were known as the Khmer Serei, or the Free Khmers movement, that was anti-Sihanouk and pro-America;
- the White Khmers contained elements of the Free Khmers, but were closer to South Vietnam and Thailand;
- the Pink Khmers were the progressives, but did not take to the forest; and,
- the Khmers in power till 1970 were the members of Sihanouk's Sangkum Reastr Niyum (SRN) régime.

After Sihanouk was overthrown both the Blue and the White Khmers cooperated with Lon Nol. The young Hun Sen was disturbed by these sharp divisions that were tearing at the heart of Cambodian society. Responding to an appeal by Sihanouk to the people he initially joined the Pink Khmers during his years in Phnom Penh.

"Among all these groups I hated the Khmer Rouge the most," Hun Sen said in retrospect. "But Sihanouk supported the Khmer Rouge. In those days they [the leaders of the *maquis*] did not mention that the Sihanoukist forces were led by the Khmer Rouge. They only said that the entire movement was led by the Sihanoukist forces. At that time, we had no choice. We were hostage to the war. If I had not joined Sihanouk's side, I would have had to join Lon Nol."

His early political instincts were correct. Later when the bloodshed began he realised that the Sihanoukist forces were, in fact, led by the Khmer Rouge. He was shocked by their brutality. He knew he had committed a big mistake in joining them. He began looking for ways to quit.

JUST when Hun Sen was preparing to join the Sihanoukist forces, a sixteen-year-old girl's life was about to undergo a sweeping change. He did not know Bun Rany then, but the fragile strands of their two lives would soon be woven together in the jungles of the *maquis*.

"It was my seventh year in high school, and it was a year I will not forget," Bun Rany recollected. "My grandparents died that year. It was a terrible blow to me. And then there was the *coup d'état*, which interrupted my education. It was as if my entire life had changed overnight."

"The ousting of Prince Sihanouk by Lon Nol made a deep impact on our young minds," she said. "We were all rebels with a cause and, for the sake of liberating Cambodia, I joined the *maquis*. I was answering Prince Sihanouk's call to join the movement to liberate Cambodia from the Lon Nol régime."

It was all very hush-hush for her at first. She knew that if her parents guessed she was anywhere near the *maquis* they would have been very annoyed.

"A lot of people joined the *maquis* from our village," she said. "In our neighbourhood there were two of us who did not tell our parents that we were joining the *maquis*. I was one of them."

A day later Bun Rany's parents caught on that she was up to something. They followed her into the jungle.

"But they could not reach the spot we were in because it was very deep in the jungle—about two or three kilometres," she said. "There, for the first time, I met the local cadres who were under the command of the Angkar [the political bureau of the central committee of the communist party led by Pol Pot]."

After joining the *maquis* the recruits were asked which part of the organisation they would like to contribute to. The leaders told them that they would be trained in the area they chose. Their attitude in the early days was gentle and very persuasive, Bun Rany said.

She opted for medical training. She was trained by doctors who came from Phnom Penh to lecture the recruits. After six months, the recruits were sent back to the district of Kroch Chhmar to look after the needy and the sick.

"The good thing was that while we were getting theoretical training, we were also encouraged to be hands on, and we got to see the practical side of how to heal and care for the wounded," she said. "Simultaneously, we were trained to be midwives. And after six months' training, we were given the title of public health officers."

When she joined the *maquis* she made it a point to get acquainted with as many people as she could.

"Slowly, as I began to realise that in order to survive I would need all the support I could muster, it became second nature for me to network," she said.

It seemed to work for her in the beginning. The person in charge of the district appeared to care for her, and referred to her as "daughter".

The slip of a girl worked at the hospital for five years before the Khmer Rouge made her the director of that establishment. It was a formula that worked for the Angkar. Catching them young meant they could be brainwashed quickly and easily. It was the fourteen- to twenty-four-year-old, fresh-faced, easily inspired youth that could be persuaded to kill, maim and torture, for a cause.

The Angkar had worked it out pat. The teen years, being the most vulnerable and impressionable, were the perfect time to strike. The responsibility thrust on Bun Rany made her feel proud, but it challenged her a great deal as well.

More than two decades later the overflow of self-confidence was visible as she flashed back twenty-four years.

"I headed all the general fields of medicine," she said. That, without a formal degree, nor even a pass out of high school.

As she rewound the twenty eventful years to her youth her voice became tremulous. A quiver of a smile hovered around her mouth.

It was another world. Spurred by nationalistic idealism she was one of thousands of young people who gave up a normal life—a regular job, an education, a family, liberal thought, in fact all freedom, to join the mass movement so well-orchestrated by the Angkar who had successfully sold starry-eyed youth an empty dream.

Life in the *maquis* was getting to be more and more regimented. Slowly, the patriotic song was beginning to sound like a wake-up bugle in a prison cell. The Khmer Rouge ordered Bun Rany, along with the other young and old female recruits, to cut her dark shoulder-length hair.

"At the time no one was given any wages," she said. "Currency was never used in our area, and the *maquis* provided everything for us to live on."

"We did not realise from 1970 to 75 that there was the Angkar ruling everything in our area," she added. "It was only in 1975, just after the liberation of Phnom Penh, that we realised that the country was divided into regions. After the takeover of Phnom Penh in 1975, the people from other parts of the country were not allowed to come to Phnom Penh."

That severed Bun Rany from her family. When she first joined the *maquis*, she often took leave and returned to her family for a few days. But now, suddenly, all leave was cancelled.

It was as if the organisation had turned into a demonic cult. The recruits who had voluntarily joined it to restore Sihanouk to power, were shocked and dismayed at the brutality. Some senior commanders refused to follow orders because they could not stomach the gratuitous cruelty. Others did what they were told.

Bun Rany wanted to run away. But there was no place to hide from the Khmer Rouge. She stayed to see tragedy unfold before her eyes.

ROMANCING REBELS

It was a rough life deep in the canopy of the jungle where danger lurked in dank trenches, time hung as still as fishing nets put out to dry along the waterways, and loneliness gnawed at young guerrillas.

Separated from his family Hun Sen craved to be loved and cared for. Romance became the forte, even refuge, of the young man who had left home, and now sought the affections of the fairer sex. But the Khmer Rouge frowned upon the pursuit of romance. Young guerrillas were prohibited from developing a relationship with the opposite sex.

"When I say that I was popular with any girl I do not mean that I had a love affair with her," Hun Sen said somewhat defensively. "It was just a normal friendship which I still cherish till today."

An old and faded photograph of a callow nineteen-year-old Hun Sen turned up in 1997. It was the only photograph of him that survived the civil war. It had been preserved by a family in Kompong Cham. In it, the teenager looked lean and handsome. It was apparent why young Khmer women were attracted to him. But he did not develop any serious relationships until he met Bun Rany. She was a director of a Khmer Rouge hospital located about fifty kilometres from the line of fighting against the forces of Lon Nol. The wounded and sick soldiers under Hun Sen's command were sent there for treatment. They playfully addressed her as *sau*, or sister-in-law.

Bun Rany remembered the summer of 1974 as a particularly dry one, with the earth parched over like a jigsaw puzzle. Red dust, like crumbled vermillion, stained clothes, blinded eyes, and filled the nostrils.

Drifting back to 1974, the year of romance, Bun Rany said: "Hun Sen's band of followers played the matchmaking game to perfection. When they met Hun Sen they told him that the beautiful lady director of the hospital sends her regards, and when they met me they said that Hun Sen had sent his regards."

Hun Sen and Bun Rany were left completely in the dark about what was going on. Hun Sen's soldiers wanted them to get married someday when the war ended.

The unspoken, incipient romance soon became known to two of Hun Sen's 'jungle sisters', female Khmer Rouge soldiers who lived nearby.

Hun Sen said: "My sisters started addressing her as *sau* as well. It posed a problem for me to maintain discipline among the soldiers."

It was a year of living dangerously, and of secret courtship, for the pretty Khmer Rouge trainee.

Bun Rany said: "The first time I learnt about Hun Sen was in 1974. His 'jungle brothers' [or comrades] used to come and stay in the hospital and they seemed to like me. It was they who began to fancy being the liaison between him and me."

"In the hospital I was the director, but in the battlefield Hun Sen was a very famous soldier," she said with characteristic pragmatism. "He belonged to a prestigious special unit. So in a way, we were equally matched, and people had a tendency to pair us together."

Whispers reached both parties' ears, and each wanted to get to the bottom of the mystery. The hide-and-seek game finally ended when Bun Rany got her chance to send a message directly to her unseen lover through a health officer from her hospital who was sent to the battlefield to take care of the soldiers under Hun Sen's command.

"I asked this health official to request Hun Sen to come and see me personally, and solve the mystery of the messages being passed back and forth," Bun Rany said. "But I must say I feared his anger because there was so much implied in these messages from other people."

Till then Hun Sen had not seen Bun Rany's face. A silent romance charged the air. He could no longer bear the suspense. Just before the Cambodian new year in 1974 he requested his commander, a woman, to accompany him to meet Bun Rany. He reckoned that he would have easier access to her if he went with a woman.

Hun Sen said: "I only knew that the chief of the hospital was named Rany, but I did not have enough time to see her."

When they arrived at the hospital his commander went to visit a local leader, and Hun Sen was told to wait for her at the hospital.

"At the time Rany did not know me, and neither did I," Hun Sen said. "So I asked her, 'Who is Rany?' She did not tell me the truth, and said that Rany had gone to fetch water. She did not tell me that she was Rany, nor did she know who I was."

For her part, Bun Rany said with a smile: "When he met me he wanted to know where Rany was. I told him that she was out somewhere. Afterwards, he came to my living quarters on the first storey of the building, and we sorted things out."

That night he knew that he was falling in love.

"I thought that if she was so beautiful I should not try to solve the mystery, but just love her," he said. "It was fortunate that after the meeting we continued staying there as it was a bit late, and we could not return to our unit."

They had no pillows and blankets. It was the month of March when the nights were chilly along the Mekong. They were relieved when the local girls brought pillows and blankets for them.

With a giggle Bun Rany said: "The two of them [Hun Sen and his commander] stayed in the hospital. At night we gave them the usual bedding—pillows and blankets—that we provided visitors with. We don't know who took whose blanket, though."

It happened that Hun Sen used the blanket that belonged to Bun Rany.

What attracted Bun Rany to him?

"I've had a great liking for soldiers ever since I was a little girl, and later that feeling grew into a very large envelope of sympathy for the army," she said.

Why the starry-eyed admiration for soldiers?

In her years as the director of the district hospital the sight of the hundreds of wounded, tormented men in uniform, some as young as fourteen, left a deep impression on her, she said.

"They were so brave in the battlefield," she said. "And they suffered so many difficulties. I felt a tug in my heart for them."

Hun Sen lost all contact with Bun Rany for several months. He missed her, he said, and suffered in silence. It was by sheer chance during the rainy season of 1974 that he saw her at Peam-Chi-Laang commune in Tbong Khmum district in Kompong Cham province. She had come to provide treatment to Hun Sen's soldiers who were suffering from malaria.

"I met her by chance when I was travelling with three friends, all of whom died later," he said. "I was travelling by bicycle, and she was travelling in a car with a group of people from the hospital. In order to be close to her I collected money from my friends and invited her, and her girlfriends, to have breakfast with us. We really enjoyed that meal."

Hun Sen was overjoyed to see his beloved.

"Some of our friends still paired us off as husband and wife," he said. "It was an old disease. I was concerned about maintaining discipline, and wanted to stop such talk. I wondered what I should do."

Bun Rany added: "When we'd sorted out all the little glitches between Hun Sen and myself—the details about who was sending love messages to whom— he finally asked the Angkar for permission to marry me."

He took what he thought was the logical step. In late-1974, he submitted a request to marry Bun Rany to his commanders in the Khmer Rouge who controlled even personal matters of love and marriage, and had turned down many applicants.

He was twenty-two when he applied. His request stood a good chance of being approved as he was liked by the commanders at all levels. But now that he had filed his application for marriage he had to work even harder to please many more commanders. At the time he headed a special commando force. He was also an instructor who trained young soldiers to read maps, and use a compass and binoculars. His commanders valued him for his abilities and, as expected, they did not turn down his request outright. But they laid down a condition. They asked him to wait until Phnom Penh was liberated.

"I knew that it was a rejection," he said. "A young man was only allowed to marry at the age of thirty, except the disabled who could marry before that. But I was not disabled yet. My commander was very clever. He did not reject my request, and only said that I should wait until Phnom Penh was liberated. The situation was not good for Bun Rany and me."

One day before the Khmer Rouge captured Phnom Penh Hun Sen was injured in the left eye, and blinded by shrapnel from an artillery shell in Kompong Cham on April 16, 1975. Later, he had an artificial eye fitted at a hospital in Kompong Cham province.

Did it bother the attractive young woman that she was going to marry a disabled man who could see the world with only one eye?

"He was in good condition at the time when we planned to marry," Bun Rany said with a laugh. "Ironically, he was wounded only after he made the formal request to marry me. Eventually, that eye had to be removed, but it wasn't at my hospital that we cut out his eye."

On hearing the news of Hun Sen's plans to marry Bun Rany, her commanders tried to block the marriage. Her world began falling apart when the Angkar produced another suitor.

She related an episode that provided an insight into the passionate young guerrilla. When Hun Sen heard the shocking news that his beloved was going to marry another man, he flew into a rage.

"That really made him very angry, and he fired a few rounds of ammunition wildly," she said. "This is what he told me after we were married."

The blatant interference by the commanders shattered Bun Rany who was deeply in love.

"Imagine my horror when, on my return from a short absence, there were arrangements made for me to marry another man," she said. "As it turned out, he was the director of a printing house."

"When I returned to the hospital I was informed by the people that my marriage with this stranger was fixed by the Angkar to take place within the next three days," she added. "I went straight to the person in charge of the district, and I told him that he could arrange the marriage with anyone else but not me. I did not want to get married to this man."

She encountered new resistance from the most unexpected quarters.

"When I refused to get married to this man, the people in charge of the district—the very same people whom I thought were my well wishers, and had known them for sometime—were extremely angry with me, and they stopped speaking to me," she said with a sigh.

Soon afterwards, there was another twist in the drama. Hun Sen approached the district leadership, and formally asked for permission to marry Bun Rany. Once again, Bun Rany was wrong in believing that she had the support of those who were responsible for social action—the wing of the Khmer Rouge that was supposed to take care of relationship issues. It was not a decision for the lovers to make. It was a matter for the 'teachers' in the Khmer Rouge to deliberate upon.

One of her 'teachers' was very annoyed.

Bun Rany said: "The particular man who handled the request for our wedding was not happy because he had a 'jungle brother' whom he had nearly fixed me up with. It was as if a business deal had fallen through for him, and he sulked, and turned really ugly towards me."

On his side, Hun Sen felt totally helpless. His marriage plans were put on ice by his commanders, and there was nothing he could do about it.

"I was very angry because my request had been accepted when I was healthy, but denied when I was disabled," he said.

Soon afterwards, his commanders lied to him to make him forget Bun Rany. They told him that she was going to marry another man. Hun Sen reacted in anger, and decided to marry another woman. He realised in the nick of time that his commanders had played a dirty trick on him.

"Rany was always waiting for me," he said. "But I was given the wrong information. I acted in haste. I was determined to take revenge, and take a wife from the Kroch Chhmar area, which was my mistake. I made a request to marry this other girl who lived near Rany's unit because I could not accept being discredited in this way. But I was criticised by my friends. They told me that Rany was waiting for me. When I realised the truth, I withdrew the request to marry the other girl, and apologised to Bun Rany."

The lovers faced more heartbreak when the commanders pressured Bun Rany to marry yet another man who worked in the Kroch Chhmar district. She refused.

Next, the commanders turned on Hun Sen. They asked him take another woman as his wife, a woman who was twelve years older than him.

"That woman was a professor, and she had been told to marry a man with the rank of commander," he said. "She later became a member of the national assembly of the Pol Pot régime and used to speak on Khmer Rouge radio. It was very risky for me to reject that proposal, as it would appear that I did not listen to the Angkar. But I rejected it."

Soon afterwards, he faced yet another matrimonial hurdle.

"My commander, named Soeurng, encouraged, and even persuaded me, to marry his daughter," he said. "It was even more difficult because it was not normal for a commander to request his staff to marry his daughter. The only way I could reject the offer was by telling him that I considered him to be my father, and his daughter as my sister. By using this approach he tolerated my reasoning, and I successfully avoided marrying his daughter."

For Bun Rany to have spurned one direct order of her leaders was a dangerous step. Her refusal to follow two consecutive orders to marry men of their choice was an act of extreme provocation.

"And Hun Sen's persistence, coupled with my request to marry him, did not help our image with the leaders either," she said with a smile.

Eventually, they were able to get married when he turned twenty-four, and she was twenty two. They could only do so after he had wriggled out of two unwanted proposals, and she had rejected a couple of men she was being forced to marry. Such were the ways of the Angkar.

In typically collectivist style the Angkar organised a group wedding of thirteen disabled couples instead of going through the trouble of marrying them separately.

"Finally, I could get married along with the disabled," Hun Sen said.

His commander was so displeased at the rejection of his daughter that he refused to provide any assistance to Bun Rany for the marriage. She had to travel alone to the remote place where the wedding was to take place.

Bun Rany said: "At the time of the wedding I was accompanied by one of the cabinet chiefs whom I did not know at all. No one else went with me."

Hun Sen added: "But we got married with the help of the soldiers. It was the first marriage of the disabled, and I was the least disabled among them. I was also the highest-ranking commander among all the thirteen disabled couples who were to marry. We were the thirteenth couple."

The loss of one eye actually helped him win his bride.

Bun Rany said: "It was the first time that the Angkar allowed such a marriage. And, ironically enough it was only the disabled that could have had this privilege— as if being wounded or disabled was like wearing a badge of honour of sorts. We would have liked to get married in the traditional way, and have our own exclusive ceremony, but those were very different circumstances. Just the fact that we were allowed to marry was a great blessing."

Out of the thirteen couples at the mass wedding, eleven matches were arranged by the local Khmer Rouge leaders.

"In the the case of the twelfth couple it was the woman who made the request to the man," Bun Rany said. "For us, the thirteenth couple, it was Hun Sen who made the request."

Many of the couples were fortunate that their relatives attended the mass wedding, but Hun Sen's and Bun Rany's families were not present as they lived very far away.

Couple number thirteen, despite its unfortunate numerological connotation, was in the best physical shape compared to the other couples, many of whom had had their hands or legs blown off in landmine explosions, or in combat.

"The thirteenth couple could be considered the best couple so far as their physical condition and rank was concerned," Hun Sen said with a low laugh.

The marriage ceremonies were conducted in martial style with the brides sitting in a tight row in front, and the grooms sitting right behind them.

"That was the way Pol Pot arranged marriage ceremonies," he said dryly.

Then, the chairman of the ceremonies began reading the résumés of the brides and the grooms. Before the ceremonies began Hun Sen's commander had advised him to delete some points from his résumé, especially his rank, so that the other disabled couples would not be envious. Among them, Hun Sen was the most senior and the best educated.

"According to Pol Pot's system we were classified as being medium-wealthy persons, a class that was disliked by Cambodians at the time," he said.

Before the ceremonies began Hun Sen was asked four questions, and Bun Rany faced three questions. The other couples were asked only one or two questions. One of the questions put to Hun Sen was whether he could turn his wife, who came from a wealthy family, into a proletarian, the class that had no property.

"Only those people who had dark skin were considered to be Cambodians," he said. "My wife had fair skin like the Chinese. So, they did not think that she could be turned into a proletarian, and they questioned me about it."

Was she ever the butt of ridicule, or envy, among the Pol Pot cadres and the guerrillas because of her porcelain skin? The Khmer Rouge's rural chiefs considered only those with dark skin and rough features to be the real Khmers.

Bun Rany said: "In my district there was no such problem. People who lived along the Mekong river had light skin, not dark. But there was a problem after my marriage to Hun Sen when we moved to liv· in Memot, not close to the river. People there were not light-skinned like those of us who came from the river. So, I suppose there was some jealousy there."

After the marriage the Angkar sent Bun Rany to work as a health officer in the districts of Ponhea Krek and Tbong Khmum in Kompong Cham province where irrigation work was being carried out, and Hun Sen was posted to the district of Memot bordering Vietnam.

The troubles of the newly-weds were just beginning. If the wedding was a nightmare, the honeymoon was nothing short of disaster.

Between giggles, Bun Rany recalled how the young couple was separated by villagers who thought that they were unmarried and were indulging in an illicit and clandestine relationship.

"After the marriage ceremony we rested at the village for one night," she said. "After that we took a cyclo-pousse. We knew it would take a long time to reach Hun Sen's home, so on the way we stopped and rested at a village called Ta Hil. Though we were allowed to stay in the village, we were separated at night as the villagers did not believe that we were husband and wife."

The next morning the couple travelled to one of the headquarters of the Angkar, known as Ta Nou. They travelled all of the next day and eventually reached Hun Sen's hometown. But they did not have a place to live. They had to pack their bags, and find a home to move to.

Just one week after she was married she was made to work long hours by the local leaders. She and a woman cook were sent to level the ricefields. The process of levelling the fields was long and arduous as the land had to be raised before it could be ploughed.

Soon afterwards, Hun Sen was transferred to a new headquarters, and was no longer engaged directly in the fighting. Later, the Angkar set up a hospital where Bun Rany was sent to work. Their life was a struggle. The gloom was dispelled with her pregnancy in 1976. The overworked couple was overjoyed at the imminent arrival of their first child.

Distance compounded their troubles. The hospital where she worked was thirty kilometres away from where he was stationed. Although she did not get time off to visit him, he came to see her.

"When I was seven months' pregnant he requested permission to take me with him so I could stay with him for two months," she said.

When the time came to deliver the baby she was sent to the hospital in Memot, but the authorities did not allow Hun Sen to return for the delivery.

She broke down completely as she recalled the tragedy. "I have not spoken about this incident for many years," she said, sobbing inconsolably. It took her a few minutes to compose herself.

"I can see the day as clearly as if it were unfolding right now," she wept. "I really don't know how it could have happened because the midwife had trained with me. She dropped the little baby boy, and his head hit the edge of the bed. The infant bled profusely, and died. But the medical report was made up to present quite another story—it said that the baby had died in the womb, even before he was born!"

How did the twenty-two-year-old and her young husband cope with their baby's death?

"We were hurt very deeply because in the Cambodian tradition, the husband always stands by the wife, literally, when she is pregnant, to give her moral support," she said. "In my case, even when the child died they did not allow Hun Sen to come and visit me. Our first child and his father were separated, never to meet."

Hun Sen described it as one of the greatest tragedies of his life.

"It was one of the earliest tortures I faced," he said. "When the baby was born, the nurse dropped it. The child hit the edge of the bed and broke its spine. It emitted just one wail."

He rushed to the hospital and found the baby bleeding from its mouth. It died soon afterwards.

There was no place for emotions in the Angkar.

"My commander did not allow me to bury the child, or to look after my wife," he said. "He forced me to travel further. Till now I do not know where my child was buried. So I took a place as a symbol of where my child was buried. That influenced me to compose a song entitled, *The Suffering of the Wife being Separated from her Husband,* which narrated the agony of a couple being forced to stay apart."

He began composing in 1989, and wrote the words for more than 100 Cambodian songs. Some of his songs were about his impoverished childhood in the countryside. His favourite was *The Life of the Pagoda Boy.* A line from the song captured his own angst: "Don't be disappointed with the rich children—the pagoda boy will have a bright future." Audio tapes of his sad ballads became hot-sellers in Phnom Penh in the mid-1990s, and the radio channels constantly replayed them.

The loss of her first child made Bun Rany realise that the Angkar was bereft of humanity.

"Slowly, I saw for myself that all the talk about everyone being a part of the revolution was humbug," she said. "There was no equality among us. The commander, or the big boss, as we called him, lived with his wife. But we were not allowed to have a normal family life."

Did the incident sow the seeds of discontent and make her want to leave the Khmer Rouge?

"At the time we did not really have any idea of leaving the organisation, but we began to worry about the future," she said. "We also discovered that some of the good people—the commanders who were of a higher rank than my husband—who were sent for training, did not return. But even then it took us a long time to take stock of what was really happening. It was only several months later, when more people were sent for training and did not return and when this began to happen very regularly, that we realised our lives too may be in grave danger."

The Khmer Rouge executed at least two senior commanders from the Eastern Zone in 1978. They were Chen Sot, the communist party secretary in Region 21, who was also a commander; and, Kun Deth, the chief of military staff in Region 21.

After their first child died, Bun Rany was denied post-natal care, and she developed oedema—a condition which caused her body to retain water and swell. It was only after much pleading with the authorities that Hun Sen was able to take her to his place of residence for two months. But his leaders subjected him to constant criticism, accusing him of being soft and over-concerned about her. He could not stand the incessant barbs, and was forced to send her back.

An exhausted and ailing Bun Rany returned to the hospital where she worked. Fortunately, he was allowed to visit her. Three months later she was pregnant with their second child.

"The men who worked in the hospital were being taken away, so it worried us very much," she said. "You know, one day they were there, the next day they were gone".

The newly-weds pined for each other, but were prised apart. She was prohibited from visiting her husband. In early 1977 things began to get really difficult. When the four midwives who worked at the hospital got pregnant at the same time, their duty roster had to be rotated. After their babies were delivered, there was no medicine for the mothers. They had no ante-natal, or post-natal, care.

When she was pregnant with their second child in June 1977 Hun Sen had to leave her to command the Khmer Rouge forces. She was carrying their eldest son Hun Manet who would later go on to study at the Westpoint Military Academy. But there was not enough food for either mother or son. They lived on maize.

"We would cook the maize like a porridge, pour a lot of water, boil it, and then eat it like a gruel," she said. "For weeks on end this is all we got".

Hun Sen began to view his personal troubles not just as a struggle to be reunited with his wife and children, but as the reunification of the divided nation.

"If I did not wage the struggle, neither my family, nor the nation would have survived," he said. "The difficulties we faced convinced us about the value of national liberation. Whenever I met my wife I was encouraged by her."

BREAKING OFF

He felt the thousand eyes of the Angkar on him at all times. He felt violated. He accepted their strict, inhuman rules for several years until he could take no more. He would pay dearly for challenging their authority when he turned against the organisation. Then they placed his wife under custody. The thousand eyes, which to many Cambodians were like the eyes of a pineapple, were now on her as well.

"I had become the enemy of the Angkar so my wife had to be in prison," Hun Sen said. "No one could be trusted anymore when their husband joined the struggle."

With extreme stealth Hun Sen began a secret rebellion against the Khmer Rouge. But it was not effective. So, on June 20, 1977 he launched an open struggle against their senseless brutality. Before their bloody rule came to an abrupt end two years later they had killed about 1.7 million Cambodians through executions, torture, and starvation.

Even before the killings took on a broad genocidal overtone Hun Sen, as early as 1974, realised and accepted the mistakes committed by the Khmer Rouge.

"At that time we did not know who Pol Pot was," he said. "We only knew Sihanouk and Penn Nouth [a Sihanouk loyalist who served as a minister in the prince's former government]."

His seven years in the Khmer Rouge from April 14, 1970 to June 20, 1977 were not a complete waste. The Khmer Rouge trained him to fight, and think, like a guerrilla. They taught him communist-style military tactics that would later give him an edge over his opponents.

His first post in the Khmer Rouge's Revolutionary Armed Forces was that of a volunteer soldier in what was generally regarded as the "war against American imperialist aggression".

"We were soldiers without any salary," he said. "We lived under great difficulties."

He stood out from the rest. He was noticed by the military high command. On account of his better education he was nicknamed 'guru' by the scores of illiterate volunteer soldiers who looked up to him. The boy who joined the guerrillas together with 500 young people was voted as a member of a leading group and, after being trained, he led a section of forty-eight soldiers.

It was baptism by fire. After being trained for just two weeks the fresh volunteers were divided into units. Hun Sen had been the section leader for only two days when he got his first taste of combat. He was sent to fight the American and South Vietnamese forces that had entered Cambodia's Snoul district, in Kratie province, on May 1, 1970. In a sudden exposure to combat he faced the world's most powerful army, that of the United States. The result was predictable.

The American forces were commanded by Jeoffrey Blume who returned to Cambodia in the 1990s as a businessman and served as the president of the Phnom Penh chapter of the Rotary Club.

"We were defeated by the American forces because we were a new and small group that had to fight against the large-scale forces consisting of tanks and airplanes," Hun Sen said. "Out of forty-eight soldiers in my section there remained only sixteen. Some were killed, some fled home, some ran away to the cities, and one is now living in America."

With a low laugh he remembered the fragile state of his unit.

"The fighting in Snoul depleted my troops so rapidly that from being a chief of a section I became the chief of a small group," he said. "Then we merged with another unit, and I became the chief of a section again."

The military high command then sent him for training to a commando school in a forest. At the commando school soldiers were prepared for higher posts, and they rose up the ranks to become commanders and trainers. When he graduated after a year he was appointed a company commander in charge of more than 130 men. He also served as an instructor, training soldiers to read maps, and use compasses and binoculars. The Angkar reserved such jobs for high school graduates.

"Among the seventy-eight trainees at the time I was the only one who survived," he said. "Some were killed while fighting the Americans, but most were killed during the years when Pol Pot ruled the country. Even I, a survivor, was a disabled person."

Hun Sen's influence in the Khmer Rouge was confined to the military. As an army officer he was not required to develop connections with the ruling political cadres. He never met Pol Pot, Nuon Chea, or Khieu Samphan. But he met Ieng Sary once, in late-1972, when Sary entered the liberated zone. Sary worked as a special overseas envoy of Sihanouk. At the time Hun Sen was being trained at a higher command school where junior officers were groomed to become commanders of battalions and regiments. Throughout his career in the Khmer Rouge he was sent, time and again, to military schools. The Revolutionary Armed Forces, clearly, had big plans for him.

"My expertise and profession is soldiering and intelligence gathering. The basis of being trained as a commander is intelligence," he said. "So, people might say that Hun Sen has a strong intelligence network in the country, and that there are Hun Sen's people [planted] in the other political parties, and that Hun Sen could defeat the Khmer Rouge through the intelligence strategy."

He was promoted to the rank of commander of a 500-strong infantry battalion in 1974. After being wounded in several battles against Lon Nol's forces he was appointed a regimental commander controlling more than 2,000 soldiers. His official posts were: Chief of Special Regimental Staff from 1975, and Deputy Regimental Commander of the Special Regiment from 1977.

"I used this force as an instrument for the struggle [first against Lon Nol, and then against the Khmer Rouge]," he said.

Why did he, and thousands of young people, stay on to serve the Khmer Rouge even though they had come to dislike them?

"But where could we go?" Hun Sen said. "We were hostages to the war. We were convinced of the terrible things Pol Pot did, but even then we did not know where to move to. Those who fled to Vietnam were sent back by Vietnam to Pol Pot, only to be killed by him."

"I hated the Khmer Rouge," he continued. "My anti-Khmer Rouge feelings surfaced when Sihanouk was in power. But I joined the *maquis* for two reasons. First, how could I stand it when America sent its troops into Cambodia, and bombed Cambodia? It was an invasion by a foreign country of a peaceful country."

The second reason, he said, was the irresistible appeal of their charismatic young leader, Sihanouk. Teenagers flocked in numbers to join the *maquis* to ensure that Sihanouk returned to power. Hun Sen had cast his lot with the Khmer

Rouge unknowingly.

"I did not know that all these people belonged to the Khmer Rouge," he said. "I had simply responded to the appeal of Prince Sihanouk. I realised in 1974 that it was not Sihanouk but the Khmer Rouge who ran the show."

Hun Sen and his young compatriots were aware of the crimes that the Khmer Rouge was committing. With Sihanouk lending an aura of respectability to the *maquis* nobody could believe that the top cadres could authorise mass murders, and they were quick to accuse the lower levels. They were wrong. The decisions flowed from the top. In the end, it made no difference which side a young Cambodian joined—be it a Pink Khmer, or a Blue one—because all the Cambodians were hostage to the widening civil war.

As the Lon Nol régime bled from sustained Khmer Rouge attacks it made an effort to recruit better people, and even attempted to woo Hun Sen over to their side.

"I had relatives on Lon Nol's side," Hun Sen said. "One of them was Nou Thol, a two-star general. They asked me to come to the city. They even promised to give me the rank of a colonel."

The two-star general sent a team of officers to talk to Hun Sen and attract him to the city. But he did not go.

"Even if I went to the city I would still have been a soldier," Hun Sen said. "And if I stayed in the liberated zone I would still have been a soldier. So I had no choice. However, I gained more knowledge about the Lon Nol régime through that encounter."

But he could no longer stay where he was. He developed a revulsion for the inhuman practices of the Khmer Rouge, and began devising ways to quit.

When he began his struggle against the Khmer Rouge he was stationed in the eastern part of the Mekong river, close to where his parents lived. The Angkar classified his father as a person with "an old political tendency to hanker after monarchy, private wealth, and rich lifestyle", Hun Sen said. He made up his mind to quit the Khmer Rouge when more than ten of his uncles and nephews were killed by the Khmer Rouge.

The plan to set up a secret network accelerated when Hun Sen was admitted to a field hospital where he had more time to plot his moves. But the network collapsed when out of ten members, eight were arrested.

"Then we decided to take another route," he said. "We would no longer work secretly."

Hun Sen usually did what was asked of him. His days with the Khmer Rouge were spent in military training, and attacking the forces of Lon Nol. But when he was asked by the military high command to carry out a brutal attack on the Cambodian Muslim community, he refused. The incident happened during *Phchum Bun*, a day of mourning, in 1975. Hun Sen was ill and had been admitted to a hospital. He was then working for the chief of general staff in a regiment. A few days after he left the hospital he was seconded to an infantry and artillery battalion that consisted of about 600 and 100 soldiers, respectively.

One day in late-1976 he received an order at 2 am to prepare his forces. Hun Sen guessed that he would be asked to attack Vietnam since his troops were stationed not far from the border with Vietnam. At the eleventh hour he was told that he was being sent to suppress an uprising of the Muslim community in Kroch Chhmar. Pol Pot feared the Muslims who were strong and united as a community, and he was aware that they disapproved of his extreme policies that had caused widespread starvation, disease, and death.

"I was dismayed and disappointed that we would use such a big force against a little Muslim community that was unarmed," he said. "I rejected the order under the pretext that I had to return to the hospital the next day. I advised my assistant that I could not move my forces because more than seventy per cent of the soldiers were suffering from malaria. I returned to the hospital and my forces were not used against the Muslims."

There were other times when he found that the orders of the military high command were impossible to carry out.

Two months before he left the hospital Hun Sen received an order to attack Vietnam on three fronts along a 30-kilometre stretch of the Cambodian-Vietnamese border.

"We were to use one battalion commanded by me, and one battalion led by Heng Samrin," Hun Sen said. "I delayed the fighting until I escaped. We used the pretext that we could not attack because we lacked field intelligence."

The Khmer Rouge Military Commission and the Revolutionary Armed Forces persisted with their designs. Hun Sen was then forced to attack Vietnam in 1977 with the intention of moving the border posts, and encroaching on Vietnamese territory. In the end, he carried out a minor border incursion as a token gesture to satisfy the military high command.

"I moved just one border post, some 200 metres into Vietnam," he said. "This was the place where my forces, and those of Vietnam, were attacking each other."

Questions have lingered about the role played by Hun Sen and his associates. Did he ever attack Vietnam? Did the forces of another Khmer Rouge commander, Heng Samrin, ever attack Vietnam?

"I left the area one year before Heng Samrin and Chea Sim," Hun Sen said. "It is a distortion of facts that I attacked the Vietnamese provinces of Tay Ninh and Song Be, because the forces in the eastern part of the country, including the forces of Heng Samrin, no longer enjoyed the confidence of the Angkar."

As a result, troops commanded by a senior Khmer Rouge commander, Ta Mok, were sent to the eastern Cambodian provinces to suppress Heng Samrin's forces. They forced Heng Samrin to go on the offensive.

Those skirmishes gave Hun Sen a golden opportunity to flee to Vietnam. It had become impossible for him to stay on in Cambodia. It was certain that he would be captured and killed by Pol Pot.

"It is true that Pol Pot sent soldiers to kill me," Hun Sen said. "If I had decided to attack and fight that day I would have become a killer. The day I left for Vietnam in June 1977 my commander was arrested. A motorcycle rider picked me up at the regiment near Memot and took me to the battalion nearby. There, I saw my friends, about thirty of them who held the rank of commanders of regiments and battalions. I knew that they had all been arrested. I found it very difficult to make a decision. What should I do to free them? Then the solution came to me in a flash: the only way was to kill the commander who was talking to me."

Normally, Hun Sen carried two pistols. One was hidden in his bag. The other, a loaded weapon, was strapped on his back.

"I attempted, three times, to remove the gun from my bag in order to kill the commander," Hun Sen said. "The commander was smaller than me, and he had hidden his pistol in his armpit, so I knew that he wouldn't be able to take it out quickly. The first time I reached for my bag I decided not to remove the gun, and instead I took out a book. The second time I hesitated again, and instead of pulling out the gun, I pulled out a pen. The third time I was still indecisive, and I took out a ruler."

Why was he indecisive?

"It was because if I had killed the commander I would have had to order the force to carry out a general offensive," he said. "At that time, there was no clear understanding within the army. If I killed the commander I was not sure whether the soldiers would follow me, or whether some of them would try and kill me. Then, we would certainly have turned ourselves into killers. So, I tried to find a way to get out of that situation by reporting to him about the location of all the forces."

Under pressure Hun Sen told the commander that he still had 1,776 soldiers under his command. Even after he disclosed the information the commander still stayed on. He confiscated all the telephones and equipment, and moved out all the heavy weapons such as DK-75, and 20 mm guns.

Then, Hun Sen was forced to write a letter authorising the arrest of all the local commanders who were his friends and colleagues. At the time most commanders were scared of signing their names on any document, and they wanted others to take the responsibility. This was because if anything went wrong Pol Pot would hold them accountable.

So, Hun Sen was told to write that the commanders, now under arrest, had been summoned by the Angkar for training, and were requested to proceed the same afternoon. But the commander did not pay attention to a sentence that Hun Sen playfully added to the letter: That Hun Sen had asked all the commanders to leave for Vietnam with him.

The idea of escaping to Vietnam was anathema to Hun Sen, in whom a deep mistrust of Vietnam was ingrained. Like most young Cambodians, he was proud of the monarchy and his country's independence, and he viewed Vietnam with suspicion.

"Since I was a child I did not really have good relations with Vietnam," he said with a chuckle. "The young Cambodians and young Vietnamese at school in Phnom Penh were divided, and were not on good terms with each other."

During school holidays he worked as a labourer at a construction site in Phnom Penh where an institute of technology was being built. The Vietnamese and Cambodian workers quarrelled frequently and, as the sparks of nationalism ignited in him, he could not remain on good terms with the Vietnamese workers. He developed a love-hate relationship with them. Soon after joining the *maquis* he briefly lived in the same camp with the North Vietnamese armed forces who were cooperating with the Sihanoukists.

"It was agreed that the Vietnamese would help us, but we also tried to strike against them," Hun Sen said. "The Vietnamese also helped us in 1970 following an appeal made by Sihanouk. The Vietnamese were willing to provide the good quality rice to us, and keep the bad rice for themselves. At the time I used to strike against them, and also steal their weapons from their warehouses when they were away because the Cambodians did not have enough. I also moved the border posts into Vietnam, provoking a lot of fighting between my forces and the Vietnamese army."

There was no premeditated plan for him and his guerrillas to escape to Vietnam.

"We had been thinking the whole night about what we should do before we left for Vietnam," Hun Sen said. "It was at 2 am [on June 20, 1977] that we decided to cross over into Vietnam. We had no plans to do so."

THREE

ESCAPE TO VIETNAM

PRISONER

They waited nervously for the night. As darkness fell around them, four Khmer Rouge soldiers and one commander walked away from their small base near the border with Vietnam. They were escaping from the clutches of the Angkar.

They were running from one enemy straight into the hands of another. From a known devil to the lair of an unknown one. It was a chance they were willing to take. Death by a Vietnamese bullet was preferable to a living death under the Khmer Rouge régime.

They flitted among the tall palm trees that grew sparsely in the flatlands, and advanced perilously close to Vietnam. All they carried in their knapsacks was a very small ration of uncooked rice, cigarettes, and matches.

Hun Sen and four of his trusted soldiers—Nhek Huon, Nuch Than, San Sanh, and Paor Ean—muttered a brief prayer, and started their long trek to Vietnam at 9 pm on June 20, 1977. The five moved one step at a time, picking their way carefully through landmines that had been planted both by the Vietnamese and the Cambodians. When they crossed the Vietnamese border the time on Hun Sen's watch was 2 am. It was June 21. Their crossing point on the Cambodian side was the tiny Koh Thmar village that was a part of Tunloung Commune in Memot district in Kompong Cham province. Just ahead lay the forbidding Vietnamese district of Loc Ninh in the province of Song Be.

They advanced in fear. The darkness made it difficult for them to see where the Vietnamese units were located. After walking some 200 metres into Vietnam Hun Sen advised his men to rest. They cooked some rice porridge. They drank the watery gruel. There was never enough rice to go around as near-famine conditions prevailed under Pol Pot's rule.

"During the small meal I found that all the people who were accompanying me were crying," Hun Sen said. "I also cried, but I had to go and cry in private as I could not allow myself to be seen by the others otherwise they would not have any confidence in me."

After a brief halt they walked four kilometres, and rested again. Once more they cooked half-a-kilogramme of rice porridge. They ate nervously. Hun Sen had decided to take only four people with him. A bigger squad would have increased the risk of being attacked by the Vietnamese, and that would have muddied his plans.

"After finishing the meal we abandoned our weapons, and continued our trip without weapons," Hun Sen said. "As we walked we did not encounter any Vietnamese troops. I felt that the Vietnamese were being a little negligent at a time when Pol Pot was planning to attack them. Pol Pot had said that the Vietnamese had deployed twenty divisions along the border, but when I was fleeing I did not see anyone."

When the sun rose in the clear sky their fears increased. The five Cambodians walked in broad daylight through the day. Not once did they come across Vietnamese border guards. At about 2 pm they reached a Vietnamese village, some twenty kilometres from the border. None of them spoke Vietnamese which made their journey even more hazardous. One of them could speak a few broken sentences, but could not make himself understood.

They ran into a group of Vietnamese rubber plantation workers who were returning home. Hun Sen approached them and found that they could speak a little Cambodian. The plantation workers led the five Cambodians to the village office. After several minutes about twenty soldiers belonging to the Vietnamese self-defense forces arrived on the scene armed with rifles.

"It was the first time that guns were pointed at me," Hun Sen said as he drifted back into the distant past. "But I felt that it was normal for a stranger to be greeted in such a way."

The Vietnamese treated the five Cambodians with extreme suspicion, and detained them for interrogation. They laid out a mat on the floor for them to sit on, in an inferior position. They then arranged three tables in an obviously superior position. The chairman, who posed the questions, sat at the head table, while two note-takers and the interpreters sat at the other two tables. The interrogation lasted about ninety minutes.

"They considered me to be a spy who entered Vietnam to get information," Hun Sen said. "I told them that normally a commander would not undertake intelligence work himself. I said that I had many people to do this kind of work, and that there was no need for me to do it myself. I told them that if we wanted to attack the Vietnamese villages we could have done so easily because we faced no soldiers on the way to Vietnam."

Seemingly convinced by Hun Sen's replies the Vietnamese officials removed the tables, and sat down on the mat with the Cambodian escapees. With that gesture the Cambodians were relieved.

No sooner did they sit together than the Vietnamese hospitality flowed. The Vietnamese cooked rice in 'pot number 10', a pot that was normally used to cook rice for ten to sixteen people. They also prepared a dish of vegetables and pork.

"We finished all the food between the five of us because it was the first time in two years that we were given rice to eat," Hun Sen said. "For two years all we got was porridge."

After the meal, at about 4 pm, they were ordered to travel another four kilometres. He was relieved that the Vietnamese no longer pointed their guns at him, but he remained apprehensive about their immediate future.

He encountered another foreign opponent in the Vietnamese mosquito. He was tortured by malaria during the long march through rubber plantations and down country roads.

"I began shivering, maybe because we had eaten too much, or maybe because of malaria," he said.

Seeing him shiver the military chief of a commune who was accompanying them helped him carry his bags. At the end of the march they arrived at Lang Xinh village, which meant nice village, in the rubber plantation of Loc Ninh.

It was there that the five escapees became a curiosity.

"We were considered to be a type of strange animal that many people wanted to see," Hun Sen said. "The village people gathered to look at us. If they had organised tickets to be sold they would have earned a lot of money."

They were subjected to another round of interrogation by the commander of a Vietnamese battalion. He asked Hun Sen questions through an interpreter, an old lady, who could speak some Khmer and had worked in a rubber plantation in Cambodia.

"They asked us to identify on a map where Pol Pot's forces were located," Hun Sen said. "After I finished telling them, the commander of the battalion shouted at me, but I did not understand what he was saying, as he was shouting in Vietnamese."

Then, the interpreter cut in. He said that the Vietnamese commander had called Hun Sen a liar because he appeared to know more than a person of his rank should know. Hun Sen spoke knowledgeably, and told the commander that he was twenty-five years old. The incredulous commander could not believe that a man so young could hold such a high rank. He thought that generally it was the senior Cambodians who led the struggle, and was unaware that Hun Sen was among a batch of young people, dubbed the Group of March 18, who joined the movement following an appeal by Sihanouk after his removal in the *coup* of 1970.

Soon after the interrogation the five Cambodians were driven by a General Motors truck from Lang Xinh to the district of Loc Ninh. When they arrived they were given another meal of rice, cooked in pot number 10. But this time they were only offered morning glory greens, and rice with fish sauce. The Vietnamese apologised for serving the frugal fare, explaining that it was the best they could do as it was past their meal time.

"We finished all the rice again," Hun Sen said. "We were eating with a vengeance. Within the space of four hours the five of us had finished two enormous quantities of rice cooked twice in pot number 10."

After the meal Hun Sen was separated from the four, and questioned again. The Vietnamese had come to accept, though sceptically, that he held the high rank of a commander.

"The others thought that I would be killed," he said. "The Vietnamese regimental commander who held the rank of a lieutenant colonel questioned me alone from 7.30 am to 12 pm. He was acquainted with me, but he did not reveal that he knew me."

It was a stroke of luck that he had met the commander in 1970. At the time, Hun Sen, a fresh recruit, had travelled to a forest in an area where the Vietnamese commander and his Viet Cong forces were based.

"So, when I refreshed his memory, he realised that I had visited a unit that was stationed close to his unit," he said. "Normally, in such a situation, both the sides know each other's commanders."

The Vietnamese commander was still not convinced. The interrogation was long and exhausting. At 11.30 pm, he was threatened by the commander with dire consequences.

"I told him that I was a commander of a regiment, but the interpreter miscommunicated that I was the commander of a section," Hun Sen said. "I told him that I had more than 2,000 forces under me, but due to battlefield casualties, and imprisonment, there remained only 1,776 troops. Then, the commander shouted, and accused me of lying. I then understood that I had been misinterpreted."

He tried a different approach. He wondered if the ageing Vietnamese commander could speak French as he had served the Vietnamese revolutionary army since the French colonial rule.

"I told him that I was responsible for a regiment, not a section," he said. "The commander then understood, and advised the interpreter to change his terminology from *Trung Doi* (section) to *Trung Doan* (regiment)."

When he returned from the interrogation he found that his four Cambodian compatriots were crying. Hun Sen, the youngest among them, had turned out to be the toughest.

They were kept there for one night. At 3 pm the next day they were bundled into a General Motors truck stacked with firewood. They did not know where they were headed. They feared they were being driven back to Pol Pot, to be killed.

"It was fortunate that I was not handcuffed from the time that I met the Vietnamese till the time that I was interrogated," Hun Sen said. "But after we sat down inside the truck five soldiers pointed their guns at me. I was prepared to commit suicide by slashing my throat with a sewing needle if the Vietnamese sent me back to Pol Pot. So I watched the kilometre posts on the road to see whether we were headed towards Cambodia, or towards Song Be and Ho Chi Minh City. As soldiers, we always carried sewing needles with us in case we needed to mend our clothes."

He was relieved to see from the kilometre posts that they were driving towards Song Be, the lush southern Vietnamese province, and not towards Cambodia.

They arrived at Song Be at about 5 pm, and were taken to the sprawling army headquarters. On the way they were asked to walk about one kilometre through a marketplace and, once again, they became the 'strange animals' that many people stared at. They were herded into a detention centre where indisciplined soldiers were kept in custody and locked into a cell that was ringed on the outside with barbed wire. Soon after they moved in the Vietnamese erected a corrugated iron sheet around the cell to prevent them from looking out.

During the first twenty-two days they were treated like prisoners. Their jailor said that they would be provided with rations worth 6,000 dongs a day. Hun Sen thought that was a lot of money, and imagined that he would spend 3,000 dongs on food, and use the rest to buy cigarettes. But he did not realise that 6,000 dongs of the old South Vietnamese currency that he was familiar with was equivalent to less than a dollar in the new currency of communist Vietnam. Still, the allowance was fairly generous, considering that a Vietnamese soldier received only 7,000 dongs a day.

That first night, Hun Sen and his jittery friends were assaulted by an offensive stench.

"It was a very smelly place because they had kept a group of indisciplined women soldiers in a nearby cell," Hun Sen said. "The smell of their urine was too strong."

To add to their discomfort they were told to sleep on the hard floor, without mats. At 10 pm the chief of the detention centre had a change of heart, and they were provided with beds, mosquito nets, and blankets. But they had to put up with the stench.

Hun Sen was kept in custody in Song Be for twenty-two days until he fell deleriously ill with malaria. Seeing him shiver uncontrollably the Vietnamese moved him to a hospital.

"It was fortunate that I suffered from malaria and grew thinner and thinner," he said. "So, I was sent to one of the military hospitals in the province of Song Be while my four colleagues were still kept in the prison."

The transfer to the hospital was a godsend. He was provided much better rations because the Vietnamese now accepted that his rank was that of a lieutenant colonel. He saved a portion of his daily allowance for his compatriots who were under detention. After he was discharged from the hospital a little more freedom was given to him and his friends.

"But it was freedom within the military compound," Hun Sen said. "We had won their confidence. We were allowed to walk around the camp and talk to the soldiers. Those disciplined and indisciplined Vietnamese soldiers were friendly towards me."

Living conditions improved with the 6,000 dongs in daily allowance, and life became bearable as some of the Vietnamese soldiers shared with them the food their families sent. They even gave Hun Sen clothes to wear.

But Hun Sen was plagued by a constant throbbing fear. Would they remain prisoners forever? Or would they be sent back to Pol Pot to be butchered?

NEWS of his defection soon reached the Angkar's ears. When they realised that Hun Sen had fled to Vietnam they retaliated by forcing Bun Rany to perform hard manual labour. She was made to chop down big trees and clear the land. She was constantly spied on, and her movements were monitored. In a brutal coincidence both husband and wife were prisoners under different circumstances.

"Although I wasn't restricted to a cell, I was guarded all the time," she said. "During the day I was sent to uproot the stems of the trees and big shrubs and bushes in order to clear the land. It was back-breaking work."

The Khmer Rouge worked in very devious ways to erode the self-esteem and confidence of those whom they wanted to punish and torture. They separated the women into two groups of 'widows': a group that had actually lost their husbands in the war; and a second group of 'widows' whose husbands were alive, but the Angkar wanted them killed.

"The fact that our husbands had fled to Vietnam made us damned and punishable criminals in their eyes, and so they tortured us day and night by calling us 'widows'—to ensure we were brainwashed into believing, sooner or later, that our husbands had died," Bun Rany said, her voice breaking a little. "It was horrible, macabre."

The Angkar called her *Kbal Youn Khloun Khmer*, a person who had a Cambodian body and a Vietnamese mind. And when the people around her got to know the reason why she was called a 'widow', they stopped speaking to her.

Hun Sen left for Vietnam when Bun Rany was five months' pregnant with their second child. That was in 1977.

Hun Sen recalled: "Twelve days after she delivered the second child she was put under custody."

She received information that he was alive and well in Vietnam. The knowledge of his well-being gave her the much-needed will to survive. But the

Angkar tried to break his spirit. It spread the word that Bun Rany had died after the birth of her second child as a result of malnutrition and overwork.

She had to overcome all sorts of difficulties. When the 'widows' went to clear the land they had to leave their children under the care of old ladies in an unfamiliar place. It broke her heart to leave her child with someone else. The 'widows' generally ate a gruel made of maize, and it was only on rare occasions that they were given vegetables by some kind-hearted village folk. When she asked for permission to visit her parents she was told that she would only be allowed to see them if they were ill.

Among Bun Rany's group of 'widows' there was a young woman who was married on the same day as her along with the group of thirteen disabled couples. Accompanied by this woman Bun Rany secretly went to visit her parents. She was briefly reunited with her family. But they were advised not to stay at her parents' home. They moved from one friend's house to another.

"We were afraid that if we were discovered by the Angkar as being part of the village they might come after us and kill us," Bun Rany said.

She was temporarily reprieved when the Angkar thought that Hun Sen was dead. They merely monitored her activities.

"There were three of us women whom the Angkar suspected of disloyalty, and we lived together in the same area," she said. "Later when they heard that Hun Sen was still alive they pretended to call us for a meeting with the intention of moving us to another area. From what had happened time and again to our friends and acquaintances who had disappeared I knew that if we were taken in this way, we would certainly be slaughtered."

Even farmers who ventured into the area in search of better living conditions were taken away to be killed. She was tormented by the thought of how the families of her two maternal aunts had been taken away and killed.

. One night Bun Rany overheard two Khmer Rouge chiefs saying that she would be taken away and killed the next morning.

"We planned to flee into the forest that night," she said.

The same night she and a few 'widows' made their getaway. The escapees were tired and thirsty. Although they were near the river they did not dare venture anywhere near the water because it was full of floating corpses.

It was a terrible sight. The Angkar had a grotesque practice—if the starving people stole food, whatever they had stolen would be tied to their hands with a *krama*.

"I shall never forget the sight of a dead child floating on the river, a stolen guava tied to its hand," Bun Rany said.

People were starving, but no one was allowed to touch any of the bananas on the trees that grew around the camp, she said. The Khmer Rouge even confiscated all the dishes, pots, and utensils to prevent people from cooking and eating anything at home. Each person was allowed to keep one plate and one spoon. Like slaves the people in the camp would be summoned by a bell to come and eat the watery broth.

"Even if we found a frog, or a tiny fish, we were not allowed to eat that extra ration," she said.

POLITICAL ASYLUM

The interrogators were bad tempered and aggressive. They bombarded Hun Sen relentlessly with questions. He was on the edge of a breakdown.

The questions were always the same. What is your real name? Which regiment of the Khmer Rouge do you belong to? Where is it located? Why did you come to Vietnam? Were you spying for Pol Pot?

They came up empty-handed after hours of probing. They began to believe that he was no longer loyal to the Khmer Rouge. They appeared to be convinced that his defection was final and irrevocable, that he had burnt all his Cambodian bridges, and that he would be killed if he was sent back.

After spending twenty-two harrowing days in jail in Song Be his detention was extended by three months in the same province. It was then that he requested for political asylum.

The five Cambodians were relocated to another detention centre while the matter of political asylum was being considered. Until it was granted they were kept under custody.

Even so, there were saving graces. Hun Sen was given living expenses worth 21,000 dongs per day, equal to the rations of a Vietnamese government minister. The money, paid at the end of each month, was an indication that he was gradually winning the confidence of the Vietnamese who were making a slow transition from being jailors and interrogators to hosts and, eventually, allies.

"Not only did I have enough to eat, and enough cigarettes to smoke, but I also had some money to spare," he said.

A man of Spartan tastes, Hun Sen did not have a palate for exotic foreign cuisines, and was happiest with an uncomplicated diet of rice and fish. His one passion was cigarettes. When he was denied this indulgence he grew agitated. Throughout his time in assorted Vietnamese prisons he smoked the popular Vietnamese Vam Co brand of cigarettes, and sometimes rolled his own.

"It was hard for me to quit smoking," he said. "In times of difficulty I even smoked papaya leaves. In custody I saved cigarette ends, and used them to make a new cigarette. My theory was that I always tried to find something to smoke in times of scarcity so why stop smoking when there was an abundance?"

After months of living nervously he finally made a breakthrough. As a result of his request for political asylum he was given the rare opportunity to meet General Van Tieng Dung, the chief of the Vietnamese general staff, and other senior army officers, in Ho Chi Minh City on September 30, 1977. The date was significant. On that very day, Pol Pot revisited China, after an earlier trip to Beijing in 1966. As Pol Pot grew closer to the Chinese, Hun Sen was embraced by Hanoi. The Vietnamese needed a Cambodian ally in order to counterbalance the China-Khmer Rouge axis that threatened Vietnam.

The discussions between General Dung, who later became the minister of defence, and Hun Sen were the first flash of the vision he saw of liberating his country. They spoke frankly, and he openly sought his assistance. But he was disheartened by the general's response.

"They told us that they could not help us, and that they would try and solve the problem with Democratic Kampuchea [the formal name of the government of the Khmer Rouge]," Hun Sen said. "Some Vietnamese generals and colonels requested that I should go to Thailand [to seek their assistance]. I told them I could not abandon my people. If they could not help me, I said, 'just give me some weapons, and I will go back to Cambodia and die with my people'."

He did not draw a complete blank. He was granted political asylum, but the Vietnamese denied him military support because they did not wish to get too involved. But he had not come to Vietnam just to seek political asylum; he wanted their help to liberate his country.

"When I requested their assistance I was rejected," he said. "The Vietnamese said that if they acceded to my request for assistance they would be seen as interfering in the affairs of Democratic Kampuchea. The Vietnamese were then trying to negotiate with Democratic Kampuchea to ease the military tensions on their common border."

It was not easy for Hun Sen to convince the Vietnamese to help him liberate Cambodia from the genocidal Khmer Rouge régime that was bolstered by at least 50,000 fanatical fighters. After all, the Vietnamese had traditionally been the Khmer Rouge's staunchest allies. Hanoi trained Pol Pot's forces in the early days of the movement, and the two sides conducted joint operations against the Republican forces of Lon Nol, and the armed forces of South Vietnam and the USA.

"Vietnam always respected the independence and sovereignty of Cambodia, and the Vietnamese leadership rejected my appeal for help, and said that it may harm the relationship between the two countries," Hun Sen said.

Instead, they requested him to go to Thailand, and then travel to a third country. Hun Sen flatly told them that he would not move to Thailand.

Hun Sen profited immensely from a radical shift in regional alliances. He saw that the halcyon days of the friendship between the Khmer Rouge and Vietnam were fast coming to an end as Pol Pot grew closer to China, and hostile to his original friends, the Vietnamese.

A "golden" opportunity appeared when Pol Pot attacked Vietnam in 1977, Hun Sen said. Pol Pot's aggressive behaviour marked the beginning of a change in Vietnamese policy. Hanoi abandoned its non-interference stance, and considered taking revenge.

"If Pol Pot had not attacked Vietnam I don't think we would have got the support of the Vietnamese to overthrow the Khmer Rouge," Hun Sen said. "The mistake Pol Pot made was to kill his own people [including ethnic Vietnamese], and launch attacks on Vietnam."

Political events began moving swiftly in Hun Sen's favour. After being attacked by Pol Pot the Vietnamese felt insulted, and reconsidered their neutrality towards their hotheaded neighbour. When Pol Pot relocated his forces from southwestern Cambodia to eastern Cambodia in readiness to attack Vietnam he forced large numbers of Cambodians to flee to Vietnam.

"That was the golden opportunity for me," he said. "It was then that the Vietnamese decided to help Cambodia. It was an opportunity for us to recruit our armed forces from among the Cambodian refugees who had entered Vietnam. By myself, I could not convince Vietnam. But when Pol Pot attacked then Vietnam retaliated. They felt insulted and decided to help us."

"The Vietnamese began to believe my prediction that Pol Pot had been planning to attack Vietnam," Hun Sen said. "When more and more people fled to Vietnam, the Vietnamese were convinced that there was a grave danger to their security. Then the Vietnamese called me to their headquarters and asked me to pinpoint the places [inside Cambodia] they should attack."

Incensed by the savage attacks launched by Pol Pot, whose forces burnt Vietnamese village homes and occupied parts of Tay Ninh province in September, the Vietnamese struck back against Khmer Rouge forces in Svay Rieng, Prey Veng, Kompong Cham, Kratie, and in some areas of Kandal. In self-defence they attacked Cambodia, in places up to a depth of thirty to seventy kilometres.

"That was the opportunity for me to return to Cambodia, and to try and seek out my wife who had been evacuated to another place," he said.

As the Khmer Rouge grew bolder and launched attacks deep inside Vietnam's Tay Ninh province in January and February 1978, the Vietnamese hit back with awesome firepower. The Vietnam News Agency said that Cambodia turned 130 mm artillery on Tay Ninh, a Cambodian refugee-clogged provincial town, ninety kilometres north of Saigon, killing or wounding thirty civilians. At the same time Vietnamese divisions supported by tanks, artillery and aircraft, penetrated thirty kilometres deep inside Cambodia along the 700 kilometre border, from Ratanakiri in the north to Svay Rieng in the south. Phnom Penh Radio quoted an appeal by head of state Khieu Samphan to troops and civilians to defend themselves against "all enemies" who invaded Cambodia to plunder the rice crop. Samphan accused the Vietnamese forces of destroying rubber plantations, burning down forests and houses, and strafing people. Cambodia severed ties with Vietnam, and snapped air links as well.

Hun Sen urged the Vietnamese to play a more decisive role, but he was disappointed.

"I felt very angry with the Vietnamese because even after attacking Cambodia they decided to withdraw their troops," he said. "They did not create a safe sanctuary for us in Cambodia where we could set up our forces. They withdrew their troops after launching brief attacks for their self-defence. We did not have our own self-defence forces. But I was grateful to them for allowing the Cambodians to move out of their areas which were being attacked, and to come and live in Vietnam. That provided me an opportunity to recruit soldiers for my forces. In this way we could build twenty-eight battalions. Many of the one- and two-star generals who are with me now were recruited by me in 1977."

His recruitment policy would pay dividends. Having handpicked his key generals, colonels, and majors, Hun Sen began building his support base as early as 1977 and, by the 1990s, his recruits controlled the entire country through a vast network that remained loyal to its supreme leader.

As he fashioned a fighting force out of the streaming refugees he emerged as their top leader.

"They called me the commander of the eastern part of the Mekong river," he said. "There were many people who were older than me, but they gave the leadership role to me. The battalions that we raised to fight Pol Pot were mainly built around my forces."

As the Vietnamese generals laid plans to assist him he realised that the West was closely monitoring the development of the Cambodian liberation forces.

While under political asylum Hun Sen gradually developed a durable relationship with Vietnam's top military commanders. After meeting with General Van Tieng Dung he was introduced to General Tran Van Tra who was the commander of the 7th Region and the Ho Chi Minh City area, as well as the deputy commanders of the region. These relationships would prove to be invaluable.

One of the most profitable friendships Hun Sen developed was with General Le Duc Anh who would become one of the most important men in the Vietnamese politico-military establishment. In the early-1990s, General Anh became the president of Vietnam. When Hun Sen crossed over into Vietnam General Anh was the commander of the 9th Region. Later, when General Anh was appointed the commander of the 7th Region, Hun Sen met him at a hospital reserved for medium- and high-ranking officials.

"As I used to fall ill frequently I had to go to the hospital," he said. "I was the youngest person to be admitted to the fourth storey of the hospital which was reserved for generals. I had to disguise myself as a person from Laos."

At the hospital, there was near total disbelief that such a young man could be a senior official. His Vietnamese friends gave him a new identity so that he would not attract attention, or give rise to suspicions.

"They gave my name as Mai Phuc (meaning happiness forever), aged twenty-six, a high-ranking cadre from Region X," Hun Sen said. "Nobody knew where Region X was located. The people in the hospital suspected something because normally in Vietnam only people aged sixty upwards could be considered high-ranking cadres. The people at the fourth storey were aware of my rank, but when I was sent to the X-ray room, the people there wondered 'how could a high-ranking cadre be only twenty-six, and where was he from?' "

It was there that he became acquainted with General Anh.

"He helped me a great deal from his Region 7 resources in building up our Cambodian armed forces," he said. "He also sent several generals and colonels to help me in my work. He was the main person who ensured that the overthrow of the Khmer Rouge was successful."

Till then, the Vietnamese were cautious, even grudging, about how much assistance they would extend to Hun Sen and his band of revolutionaries.

"The Vietnamese rejected giving us political assistance," he said. "But they helped us financially. They gave us weapons and training, and left the work of the political leadership and education to us. Therefore, I knew how to write official documents at the age of twenty-five. I wrote lessons for the [Cambodian] officers and gave lectures myself."

By slow degrees he built his forces from scratch.

Four

TOPPLING POL POT

LIBERATION

A secret plot to overthrow the Pol Pot régime took root on the fertile soil of south Vietnam.

Hun Sen's original plan was to liberate Cambodia in five years. He reckoned that it could not be done sooner even though the Vietnamese had found a reliable ally in him, and had agreed to give him funds and weapons to unshackle his country.

"The idea was to liberate the eastern part of Cambodia, and use it as a springboard to free the western part," Hun Sen said.

The five-year plan involved infiltrating troops into western Cambodia through the Vietnamese province of Ha Tien, to carry out incursions and raids whereas the main forces would attack from the east. The grand liberation would be launched from the Cambodian provinces of Kratie, Stung Treng, Ratanakiri, and Mondulkiri.

"We would disguise our plans by attacking Svay Rieng and Prey Veng provinces, and capturing a part of Kompong Cham," he said. "Then, we would send a force to strengthen our troops in the eastern part of the Mekong river. Later we would enlarge our areas to engulf Svay Rieng and Prey Veng. This was the plan to liberate Cambodia in five years."

As a guerrilla commander he had a sharp military mind. The first step he took was to set up a liberation army, and only then did he think of creating a political organisation.

He suggested to his Cambodian compatriots that their political organisation be named the United Front for the Salvation, Solidarity, and Liberation of Cambodia. It was accepted by the two people closest to him—Sin Song (who was later involved in a failed *coup d'état* in 1994), and Sar Not (who later became Hun Sen's adviser on religious affairs).

The slow-track, five-year plan was speeded up and national liberation took on a sudden urgency when Pol Pot ordered eighteen Khmer Rouge divisions to attack Vietnam. The military action forced the Vietnamese to counterattack swiftly.

"That was not only a golden opportunity, but a diamond opportunity for me because the strongest units of Pol Pot were defeated by the Vietnamese," Hun Sen said. "The decision of the Vietnamese to help us gave us more confidence. The growth of my forces multiplied by three because Pol Pot's strongest forces were depleted."

On a clandestine visit to Cambodia in December 1977 and early 1978, Hun Sen invited some of the top Khmer Rouge commanders to join the front. The need to bolster the liberation forces became even more pressing when he received intelligence information that Pol Pot was planning to send forces led by Ta Mok, an extremely brutal commander, from the southwest to the Vietnamese border. It became imperative for him to make contact with his allies, Heng Samrin and Chea Sim, but it was not easy to communicate with them.

"I tried to get in touch with Heng Samrin who commanded a battalion, and Chea Sim who was the chief of a district but did not control a force," he said.

Gradually, he built up his forces made up of anti-Khmer Rouge nationalists, and infiltrated them into Cambodia.

"When we entered Cambodia there was a big uprising in the eastern part of the country," Hun Sen said. "Our forces made contact with the defectors [who were escaping from the Khmer Rouge régime]. In May 1978 we had set up liberated zones in Kompong Cham and Kratie provinces. Heng Samrin and Chea Sim were the leaders in these liberated areas. At the time we did not have direct contact with them, but we established indirect contact through their forces."

The three men, who had known each other for years, met face to face in November 1978 in Song Be province in south Vietnam. It was their first meeting on Vietnamese soil. But it was not just a meeting between two sides; it involved five factions.

Hun Sen was overjoyed when he met Heng Samrin and Chea Sim, who were his friends although they were older than him. Heng Samrin had escaped from Khmer Rouge purges earlier that year, and sought refuge in Vietnam.

"I was so happy not only to see them, but also to hear the news of the uprising in Cambodia," he said.

The uprising, carried out spontaneously by the liberation forces and the rural people, took place in the eastern regions of Cambodia.

Hun Sen, Heng Samrin, and Chea Sim hammered out the military and political policies of the United Front at the meeting of five rebel parties. One of the parties led by Heng Samrin and Chea Sim had staged an uprising inside Cambodia. A second party under the leadership of Bou Thang had revolted in 1975 in the northeast. The third party were the communists, led by Hanoi-trained intellectual Pen Sovann, and others such as Chea Soth, and Chan Si. The trio had lived in Vietnam for many years since the Geneva conference in 1954. The fourth party were the new forces formed by Hun Sen. And, a fifth party had led the anti-Khmer Rouge resistance in Thailand under the leadership of Say Phuthang and Tea Banh.

Was it difficult for the five rebel parties to work together?

"For Heng Samrin, Chea Sim and I, it was not difficult as we used to be in the eastern region together," Hun Sen said. "Our final goal was to merge. But the high-ranking leaders did not have the time to meet each other. In November

1978 we were very busy setting up the United Front, creating the political programme, and the congress. We declared the formation of the front on December 2, 1978. At the time we had already prepared our forces, food supplies, and weapons for the attack. It was not that we formed the front first and then prepared the army."

The fledgeling group led by Heng Samrin began operating under the name of the United Front for the Salvation, Solidarity, and Liberation of Cambodia.

As Pol Pot made increasingly unreasonable demands on his commanders to attack Vietnam, one by one his eastern commanders broke ranks with him. The biggest blow to his eastern forces was delivered when Heng Samrin and Chea Sim staged a rebellion, and joined the liberation front. A part of Hun Sen's forces entered Cambodia to help the people stage an uprising. For the first time he saw the possibility of overthrowing the Khmer Rouge within a year.

"We were thinking that, at least, we could liberate Cambodia in the new year in 1979," Hun Sen said.

"Then, Heng Samrin and Chea Sim fled into my area with their forces," Hun Sen added. "With our combined forces we set up the liberated zone. We estimated that, at least, we should liberate the country by April 1979. We did not expect that the Pol Pot régime would be so weak, and that the people were only waiting to rise up against it."

IN Hanoi, a crisis-like atmosphere hung over the higher echelons of the Vietnam People's Army (VPA). In 1978, in response to the troubled situation in Cambodia, Hanoi abolished the VPA's General Department of Economic Construction, and redeployed its military units along the Cambodian border. The department, an army wing that supervised the military's involvement in agriculture and industry, was not re-established till 1986, long after the Cambodian war was over, according to Carl Thayer, an Australian defence expert.

By December 1978 a Vietnamese plot to overthrow the Khmer Rouge was carried through. Hanoi Radio announced on December 4 the formation of a Kampuchean United Front, and said that the front had called on the people of Cambodia to "rise up and overthrow the Pol Pot and Ieng Sary clique". Diplomats in Bangkok interpreted the announcement as a decisive step in Vietnam's war against Cambodia, and they predicted a full-scale Vietnamese military and political campaign to eject the Pol Pot régime, and its replacement by a pro-Hanoi régime.

The attack came as expected. The Vietnamese launched a general offensive against the Khmer Rouge on December 25, 1978, backed by the troops of the United Front. A Vietnamese-led force crossed the Mekong river for the first time, and encircled the provincial capital of Kompong Cham, sixty-four kilometres from Phnom Penh, reports said on January 1, 1979. Troops believed to be Vietnamese army regulars invaded Kompong Cham on New Year's Day, with the attackers capturing "thousands of weapons" from Pol Pot's forces, the reports said.

As a military commander Hun Sen knew that the success of any military campaign depended on weapons and food supplies. His forces had been armed by the Vietnamese, and now they were given enough food supplies as well, with a little extra left over for the new recruits that were joining the front inside Cambodia.

The task of raising a massive liberation force consisting of grassroots' Cambodians was daunting. Eventually, some 20,000 Cambodians fought in the grand liberation.

"Our forces were not vanguard units, but they could carry out attacks, occupy land, and motivate people to join us, and thus move our forces forward," Hun Sen said. "We carried on fighting [the Khmer Rouge], while at the same time recruiting new troops."

At times his forces had to await the arrival of the Vietnamese because, by his own admission, "nobody on our side knew how to drive a tank."

In places where his forces encountered strong resistance, they waited for the Vietnamese forces to arrive and punch through Khmer Rouge defenses with tanks and artillery.

"After Pol Pot's border forces were defeated his inland units could not withstand the attacks," he said. "We encountered resistance in Samlaut and Ta Sanh along Cambodia's border with Thailand."

Hun Sen and his cohorts were aware that they could never have overthrown the Khmer Rouge without the military support of Vietnam.

"I do not know, for sure, how many troops the Vietnamese used because the Vietnamese armed forces were very smart in keeping secrets," Hun Sen said. "The Vietnamese do not reveal their cards, even after they finish playing a hand. If they left their cards open, their opponents could estimate their next move. Even if you read the history books you will not come to know how the Vietnamese won the war against the French in Dien Bien Phu. I think there were about 100,000 Vietnamese forces involved in the liberation of Cambodia. The plan was to launch a rapid offensive to liberate the country in a very short time. Therefore, a very large force was used."

"In my understanding the Vietnamese used three key forces—their strongest force was the 4th Army of regular units that was used [later] in the border war against China [in 1979]," he said helpfully. "Their second force was the 7th Army of General Le Duc Anh, and the third force was the 9th Army. They used a variety of tactics. The 4th Army attacked Svay Rieng province, and then moved to station itself in Siem Reap province. When they attacked Pol Pot's troops in Svay Rieng, they chased them all the way to Siem Reap."

"Why didn't the Vietnamese use another army in Siem Reap?" he asked rhetorically. "This was because the 4th Army had carefully studied Pol Pot's units, and knew how to fight them."

Throwing new light on the way the campaign was conducted, he said: "The Vietnamese didn't use many tanks and artillery. They used their experience of attacking from the jungles into the clear areas. They used no airplanes to bombard the enemy, and used them only for transport. They mainly deployed their infantry."

Hun Sen did not take part in the actual fighting as he had done in his early days as a guerrilla. He now played a bigger role. He planned, coordinated, and monitored the movements of his forces.

Faced with the massive onslaught of the Cambodian and Vietnamese forces the Khmer Rouge's defences disintegrated without resistance. The Cambodian and Vietnamese forces closely coordinated their movements, but they attacked separate targets in pursuit of specific objectives. They operated under separate commanders because they did not speak the same language. The Cambodian forces also worked the ground in Cambodia, awakening the people with their political activism.

"Our common target was to oust the Pol Pot régime, yet there were many other military objectives that had to be carried out separately," Hun Sen said. "The Vietnamese could not speak Khmer so the Cambodian forces had to conduct their own operations."

While the Cambodian forces took on the Khmer Rouge in areas where Pol Pot's divisions were relatively weak, the Vietnamese fought the Khmer Rouge in the provinces where they were the strongest. After ejecting the Khmer Rouge from a particular area the Vietnamese army would move on, leaving the Cambodian forces to take over and restore order among the people living in that area.

As the Cambodian liberation army swarmed across the border its numbers grew as more and more people joined it. A keen student of military tactics, Hun Sen said that it was very rare for an army to increase in size after a war.

"We started to liberate the country by using the United Front which had a limited army, but when we finished fighting our army had multiplied many times as more and more people joined it," he said. "When the fighting stopped the 20,000-strong force that we started with ended up as 40,000 as the Pol Pot régime collapsed before the people's forces. When we liberated the people they requested us that they would like to join the armed forces too. When Pol Pot's army fled they left their weapons behind so we acquired new forces with new weapons. My elder brother, Hun Neng, collected 700 pieces of weapons from the fleeing Pol Pot soldiers."

At the end of the war he was surprised to see that his Cambodian forces had grown enormously.

"I asked myself whether we could recruit 28 battalions in order to deploy at least one battalion per province, and we did," he said. "And if it was a big province we deployed two battalions there."

The collapse came sooner than expected, and even surprised Hun Sen. By January 8, Phnom Penh was captured by the Vietnamese and Cambodian rebels. According to the first reports from the news agency of the rebels, Sarpordamean

Kampuchea (SPK), Phnom Penh fell without a fight. The leaders of the Khmer Rouge were evacuated to Beijing in an emergency airlift, and the rebels, who called themselves the "Revolutionary Armed Forces", occupied most of the important buildings. Kampot, on the southern coast, also fell. "The dictatorial and militaristic Pol Pot-Ieng Sary clique has totally collapsed," SPK reported.

WHEN the country had been liberated two American-built Dakota aircraft operated by the Vietnam air force took off from Tan Son Nhat airport in Ho Chi Minh City bound for Pochentong airport in Phnom Penh. One of them carried Hun Sen and Chea Sim, and the other aircraft carried Heng Samrin and Pen Sovann. These were the four main players who had engineered the liberation. Heng Samrin would soon be appointed the president of the new People's Revolutionary Council; Chea Sim would become the interior minister, with a central role played by Pen Sovann as the minister of national defence. Little did Hun Sen know that he would be appointed the foreign minister. In February 1979 they were all coming home to a heroes' welcome.

Since his defection from the Khmer Rouge Hun Sen had stepped onto Cambodian soil only once before, during 1977-78, on a secret reconnaissance mission with the Cambodian infantry. A victorious Hun Sen was returning secure in the knowledge that the Khmer Rouge régime had collapsed, and that his army was occupying Pochentong airport and the capital.

"The liberation forces urgently needed their leaders so I had to come by plane," he said.

At Pochentong airport a welcoming party of Cambodian officials and a few Vietnamese diplomats who travelled to Phnom Penh ahead of them, had gathered to receive the revolutionary leaders. But all eyes were on a fresh-faced young man in his 20s, Hun Sen.

Soon after his arrival in Phnom Penh Hun Sen was taken straight from the airport to the Royal Palace that was once the abode of Sihanouk and his ancestors. It was an honour given to the young leader. He stayed at the palace for two weeks before he was given an official residence.

He was crestfallen when he did not see Bun Rany among the welcoming party at the airport. He had been separated from her for almost two years since May 1977, and had scarcely seen her for the past nine years.

"I thought she was dead because she didn't appear at the airport," he said.

Bun Rany had lived through terrifying times, hiding in villages, living under an assumed identity, alone, without her husband, and not knowing if he was dead or alive.

"She did not dare reveal that she was my wife," he said. "She went and hid in the countryside. After the liberation, my wife, my son, and my relatives stayed in the village, and harvested ears of rice for a living."

The last time he saw her she was five months pregnant, and was living at a hospital run by the Khmer Rouge.

"Fortunately, the Khmer Rouge had announced twice that I had been killed along the Cambodia-Vietnam border, so they did not pay much attention to my wife," he said. "They declared, in June and December 1977, that I was dead. She faced a lot of suffering unlike the other 'widows'. Although the Khmer Rouge said that I had been killed they knew very well that I was alive. When there was an uprising in the eastern region she went into the forest with my son and relatives."

The first piece of disinformation about Hun Sen's death in June coincided with his departure to Vietnam. The second, broadcast in December, was made when he appeared briefly for the first time in a Cambodian village at about the same time as a rapid attack by the Vietnamese on Cambodian settlements near the border.

"When I made my first appearance in the village the Khmer Rouge announced that I was dead," he said. "They said that I was killed by a landmine explosion when I was assisting some Cambodians to seek safe passage to Vietnam. At the time, some Khmer Rouge commanders had also been killed, so the news of my death was connected with this news. My wife was given the news, and she was not killed."

HER heart leapt with joy when she eventually heard he was still alive.

"But he had no clue that I was alive," said Bun Rany who heard the news that her husband was safe soon after the liberation.

Her group of detainees was forced to evacuate twelve days after the liberation of Phnom Penh. They had to walk through the forest for three days and two nights. When they arrived at the designated place they rested for a couple of days. Then she and four other 'widows' were ordered to prepare the staple fish paste to feed the cadres.

"We didn't have anything to eat when Phnom Penh was liberated," she said. "So, we had to cut the rice from the field and eat it."

By this time, news from the front filtered through to her, and she realised that her husband was still alive. But the Khmer Rouge soldiers were still·very powerful in the provinces, and there was no chance for her to escape.

"Even after being liberated we did not dare to speak freely because we had no idea about who were the real soldiers of liberation, and who were the Pol Pot men," she said. "The atmosphere was full of intrigue and you could almost smell the danger all around."

Hun Sen, who had his hands full with the task of rebuilding the foreign ministry went to Chup in Kompong Cham for a meeting. There, he requested the authorities to locate his wife who was believed to be living in the Chup rubber plantation, but they did not oblige.

"He sent my father-in-law and my sister-in-law to locate me," she said. "Even though they stayed for fifteen days in the area they could not find me."

"But it so happened that one of the soldiers accompanying them was eventually able to find me. They returned to pick me up," Bun Rany said, smiling for the first time in the three hours that we had been talking.

Bun Rany and her sister-in-law travelled by motorcycle to Phnom Penh. They took turns to carry the baby. They arrived after driving for one day and one night.

Hun Sen was delerious with joy when he saw her.

"I was in the ministry of foreign affairs when she arrived in Phnom Penh, and somebody told me that she had come to see me," he said. "I didn't believe it. When I came home I saw her. I asked her who was the boy with her. She said, 'he is your son'. The boy didn't call me dad."

With tears welling up in her eyes, Bun Rany added: "My son saw his father for the first time. He called him 'uncle'."

Tragedy struck again. A year later, Pol Pot's soldiers broke into the family's village home and killed Bun Rany's father.

"It was the same day when my mother arrived in Phnom Penh," said Bun Rany, her voice cracking.

Quickly controlling her tears, she added: "When Phnom Penh was liberated we adopted three girls who were orphans of the civil war. They are now all married."

They also gave shelter to an orphan whom they trained as a cook. She remained with the family. They even invited some of their distant relatives into their fold, and lived as an extended family for several years.

After almost nine years of separation she wanted nothing more than to see Hun Sen, and to lead a regular life as a family.

"I thought I'd help him set up a farm," she said. "Politics was the last thing on my mind. I was completely fed up with my life between 1970 and 1979, when I hardly got to see him. But the winds changed, and he had to take care of the country because there was no one else to do it."

When she first arrived in the city there was not much food for the people, and no water. People starved, lived on leaves and roots, and rarely ate maize and rice.

Bun Rany had participated in Pol Pot's failed experiment, and was deeply hurt by it. She never met Pol Pot, but she came across another Khmer Rouge leader, Hou Youn, who had passed through her hospital, and she had provided his meals. But in the end she was left with nothing except deep pain.

Her wounds healed as she settled down to a new life as the wife of the young foreign minister. Even then, they faced difficulties. Hun Sen was not paid a salary.

"We had nothing," she said. "We had only maize and rice to eat, and the maize was not Cambodian-grown maize. It was food sent as aid by Vietnam. For those of us who have experienced the generosity of Vietnam, we know that it would have been very difficult to survive without their help. Those who did not know the reality doubted the real story."

The young Hun family lived in the same house in Phnom Penh for ten years, until they moved into their new home in Takhmau.

"And I still cook for the family," she said with a laugh.

Her life remained simple even though her husband was in the limelight.

"I hardly met any celebrities because I mostly stayed at home to look after the children," she said.

THE oppressed people welcomed the Vietnamese forces. They were even grateful to them for putting an end to the Khmer Rouge massacres. They believed that the days of peace and plenty were about to return. Their initial euphoria evaporated about a year later when many Cambodians felt that the Vietnamese liberators had turned into occupiers.

Was the Heng Samrin government created under Vietnam's guidance, or was it an independent Cambodian initiative?

"Even though we had some assistance from foreign countries, it [the government] was our idea," Hun Sen said. "We were more independent than the tripartite coalition government [formed soon afterwards by Sihanouk, Son Sann, and the Khmer Rouge]."

"When Sihanouk, Son Sann, and Khieu Samphan organised a meeting in Singapore [in September 1981], they had no agreement, and tremendous pressure was put on them by Asean [Association of Southeast Asian Nations] and, as a result, they could form their government in Kuala Lumpur," he said. "We were much more independent than these people. We arranged that Heng Samrin would be the chairman of the front, as well as the party. Pen Sovann would be the prime minister and minister of defence. Chea Sim would be the minister of interior, and I was the foreign minister. We made the arrangement in the manner of an integrated force."

Looking back, he said: "I underestimated the idea of the Asean leaders in forming the tripartite government. They told us that our Heng Samrin government, created by the Vietnamese, was meaningless. We knew well what they had been doing with Sihanouk, Son Sann, and Khieu Samphan, and what these people had been receiving from them [in terms of lethal and non-lethal aid]. We knew who was independent, and who was under commission. There were no foreigners close to me. Whereas the rest were working with foreigners."

At this stage of the exhaustive interview with Hun Sen in December 1997, we referred to the liberation of Cambodia as an "invasion". The *faux pax* instantly drew an outraged response.

"May I correct the word you used. We were liberating the country, not invading," he said. "You can see whether there is any form of foreign invasion in Cambodia. The question of foreign troops coming to Cambodia is not new. There were the French and the Japanese. Then, there were forces from the US, South Vietnam, the Philippines, Thailand, and Australia. In short, the Asean countries invaded Cambodia, and they helped the tripartite coalition, and the Khmer Rouge, to fight against us."

The Vietnamese, he said, played a liberating role in Cambodia in 1978, a role markedly different from the South Vietnamese forces that pillaged and destroyed Cambodia in the early 1970s. "Without the Vietnamese armed forces we would die," he said.

· Blaming America and Asean for fuelling the fire in Cambodia, he said: "There is no way that Asean and America could teach Cambodia. They are the cause of the violation of human rights and the destruction in Cambodia. We want to be polite to the new generation, and we don't want to use such words. Would you like us to motivate three million people to stage demonstrations seeking compensation for the war? We cannot accept the word invasion," he said.

"Without Pol Pot there wouldn't be any Vietnamese armed forces in Cambodia," he added. "And without Asean and the American invasion in Cambodia there would be no Pol Pot. Today, [December 6, 1997] I have rejected a meeting with an American delegation because I don't want to be advised. Or else, I will advise them in return. It is better not to have any strong words against each other. It is better not to meet each other."

"Why do they advise us about human rights?" he said. "When we realised that there was no good word from Washington I just cancelled the meeting. I am a nation. I cannot listen to anyone's advice. I am not a tripartite coalition that seeks advise from Asean. I am young, but I am equal to those people who worked with us like [Vietnamese leaders] Le Duc Anh, Le Duc Tho, and Nguyen Van Linh. When I asked them [Vietnam] to withdraw their experts, they did. We do not owe any debt to these people."

THE VIETNAMESE ROLE

With his seven eyes, it was said, Hun Sen could foresee every move his enemies were planning to make.

"I have one Cambodian eye and six Japanese eyes," he said about the various glass eyes that were fitted by Japan and the Soviet Union after he was blinded in his left eye in heavy fighting just before Phnom Penh fell in 1975.

When the combined forces of the resistance—Pol Pot, Sihanouk, and Son Sann—failed to overthrow the Heng Samrin government and its later incarnation, the Hun Sen administration, they grew frustrated and resorted to petty name-calling, even abuse. Hun Sen and his government suffered the indignity of being called, among other things, "Vietnam's lackey", "stooge", "puppet", "quisling", and "one-eyed Hun Sen". The presence of Vietnamese soldiers in Cambodia was a "military occupation", his critics charged. Retold hundreds of times these fighting words soon became ideological jargon that clouded the real issues of the genocide and the civil war. These words were used to admonish the liberators of the country from the murderous Khmer Rouge and, in turn, anoint the Khmer Rouge as the legitimate representative of Cambodia at the United Nations.

The West, and most of non-communist Asia, supported the Khmer Rouge. They glossed over the genocide, and were deaf to the rising cries within Cambodia for justice and the need to punish the perpetrators. These countries were immune to this rage, beyond its reach. The resistance knew that it could indulge itself only because the West and non-communist Asia would continue to hold these views unchanged. This fuelled Hun Sen's anger. His rage, temporarily contained by the hope that some day the Khmer Rouge would be brought to justice, flared quietly.

Alarmed at the unreasonable and unconscionable support for the Khmer Rouge, the Vietnamese decided to stay on in Cambodia to prevent them from recapturing power. From the start Hun Sen knew the answers to two critical questions: how long did the Vietnamese plan to stay in Cambodia? Was "occupation" ever a part of the plan to liberate the country?

"According to the discussions, we planned that the Vietnamese would attack, and then withdraw immediately in 1979," Hun Sen said. "It was I who talked with Le Duc Tho [a member of the Vietnamese Communist Party politburo] and others. I told them that if they withdrew, and Pol Pot returned, more people would be killed. At the time, the Cambodian forces were not able to handle Pol Pot, and we needed time to strengthen our forces, and our economy."

Without Vietnam's help the Phnom Penh government would not have survived. Fortunately for Hun Sen Hanoi never vacillated in its support. Vietnam's foreign minister, Nguyen Co Thach, said in June 1983 that his country would only withdraw its forces from Cambodia after a political settlement was reached between his country and China. That pact would ensure that China stopped aiding and arming the Khmer Rouge, and that Vietnam withdrew its 140,000 forces from Cambodia. Hun Sen, then playing the crucial role of foreign minister, did not want to be left isolated in a situation where the Vietnamese withdrew their forces, but China continued arming Pol Pot.

"The Vietnamese did not want to stay," he added. "It was our side that made such a request. We then agreed that they would try to reduce their forces in 1982. The Vietnamese would decrease their numbers, and we would increase our forces. Even as a foreign minister I was involved in such a strategy. I still remember the meeting of the foreign ministers of Cambodia, Laos, and Vietnam in Hanoi in 1985 where we agreed that the Vietnamese forces would be withdrawn in ten to fifteen years. But owing to the progress of [developing] the Cambodian armed forces, and the [peace] talks between Sihanouk and me, we withdrew the Vietnamese forces earlier."

But fears persisted that Vietnam was turning Cambodia into its colony. A report in the *Bangkok Post* in June 1983 said that Hanoi had set up "development villages" in Cambodia where one out of every five families was Vietnamese. Quoting "highly reliable military documents", the newspaper said that such villages had been created in Battambang and Koh Kong, and in provinces along Cambodia's border with Vietnam. It said that Vietnam was trying to achieve a twenty per cent mix of Vietnamese at all levels. The central Cambodian administration was being strictly controlled by Vietnamese experts who had been inducted into the higher levels of the administration to oversee and guide the officials of the Phnom Penh government, it said.

Three years later, in May 1986, the New China News Agency said that the Cambodian government was backed by a code-numbered committee of Vietnamese advisors and specialists, without whom it could not survive a single day. It said that Hanoi had set up a "Cambodia working committee" code-numbered 478, the unseen backstage ruler of the country. The Chinese agency said that this committee had been manipulating the Heng Samrin government, and its army, through its advisors.

Hun Sen was realistic about the necessity of having Vietnamese troops based on Cambodian soil. They were there to fight and mop up the Khmer Rouge. They were not there as colonisers.

"Without Vietnam's help we would die," he said.

For its part Vietnam miscalculated the reaction of the world to its Cambodian adventure. It was counting on the support of the major powers for having overthrown a genocidal régime, but when the support did not come through, and the international community nursed the Khmer Rouge back to life and helped develop the resistance forces, Hanoi realised that it had been sucked into a long and costly conflict. Once it was committed, Vietnam raised its troop strength in Cambodia to as many as 180,000 to 200,000.

In the early 1980s Vietnamese General Le Duc Anh's "Cambodianization Plan" was enforced. According to Australian defence expert Carl Thayer, it involved attacks on the Cambodian resistance positions along the border under a five-phased plan code-named "K-5" (ke hoach nam in Vietnamese). In its totality the plan included sealing the border with Thailand, destroying the resistance fighters, and building up the forces of Phnom Penh. It was an expensive adventure. Hanoi admitted that the Cambodian drama was bleeding it white, and began devising ways of getting out.

One of the earliest indications that the Vietnamese were serious about pulling out came from Hun Sen's friend and ally, Indian prime minister Rajiv Gandhi, who visited Vietnam in November 1985. Rajiv confirmed that Hanoi had agreed to withdraw its troops from Cambodia by 1990, and might do so even sooner. At any rate, the withdrawals had started even earlier, in 1982, when Hanoi conducted a series of troop withdrawals, although some military observers dismissed them as troop rotations. Still, outside observers saw the Vietnamese strength decline from 140,000 in 1987 to 100,000 in 1988, and eventually to 60,000 in 1989.

A Vietnamese withdrawal seemed possible when Soviet foreign minister Eduard Shevardnadze said in May 1987 that the Soviet model of withdrawal from Afghanistan in twenty-two months might become a model in solving the Cambodian conflict. The most definitive statement came from Hun Sen who declared in Paris in 1989 that, whether or not the Cambodian problem was resolved, Vietnam would withdraw its troops from Cambodia in September 1989.

"We withdrew the [Vietnamese] forces even before the [Paris peace] accord was signed [in 1991]," he said.

He still remained concerned that his government would face a major test of survival after Vietnam withdrew its forces. Diplomats speculated that Hun Sen would not survive long, and that the Khmer Rouge would recapture power. They joked that he would last in power only for as long as it took a Khmer Rouge tank to drive from the Thai border to Phnom Penh.

But he was confident that his country would be stable after the final withdrawal, as it had remained secure after six previous partial pullouts. Reporting on a partial Vietnamese withdrawal in May 1983, United Press International correspondent Paul Anderson wrote: "After witnessing the departure of the Vietnamese troops from Phnom Penh, journalists had the option of flying to the Vietnamese border in helicopters at US$220 each, or travelling by bus to see the soldiers cross the frontier. Only the first of two helicopters managed to arrive for the gala ceremonies. The buses were the victim of disorganisation and late starts. The second helicopter was the victim of greed. Eager for hard currency, the Cambodians had oversold the second 'copter, causing such a delay in Phnom Penh that the ceremonies were over before the journalists even departed."

The Vietnamese withdrawal in September 1989 turned into a major media event with many reporters camping in open parks in Phnom Penh because the few hotels were full. As their newspapers published pictures of smiling Vietnamese soldiers sitting atop departing battle-tanks, it appeared that the Vietnamese had indeed gone home for good, a decade after they arrived. Did some Vietnamese experts stay back to advise the Cambodians?

"That is a wrong impression," Hun Sen said. "We had prepared ourselves to become self-reliant. The military, economic, and political advisors of Vietnam were withdrawn in 1988—one year before the withdrawal of the Vietnamese armed forces."

"Why did we do it this way?" he asked, putting a rhetorical spin on it. "We could benefit from the Vietnamese units who helped us in fighting, but we could not rely on the Vietnamese thinking."

A very worried Hun Sen stopped over in Vietnam en route to the second round of peace talks with Sihanouk in Saint Germain, France, in February 1988. He expressed his concerns to Nguyen Van Linh, the Vietnamese Communist Party general-secretary, and they struck a deal to repatriate the advisors ahead of the pullout of the armed forces. The Vietnamese advisors, who arrived in 1979, were withdrawn in phases between June and August 1988.

But according to the Cambodian resistance about 70,000 to 80,000 Vietnamese troops disguised as Cambodians stayed behind. They claimed that Vietnamese civilian advisors continued their attachment with various ministries in Phnom Penh, and that Cambodian officers received training in Vietnam for two more years.

"The role of the Vietnamese advisors was the same as that of the foreign advisors [in the embassies and in foreign organisations] who worked in Cambodia through the 1990s," Hun Sen said. "I have the impression that these foreign advisors were interfering much more in the internal affairs of Cambodia than the Vietnamese advisors. They only agreed to advise us, and left it to us, the Cambodians, to make the decisions."

Like many Asian leaders Hun Sen could not tolerate being lectured by Western governments and their area experts.

"The foreign advisors to Cambodia—if we don't listen to them—threaten to cut assistance to us," he said. "The foreign advisors were doing what they accused the Vietnamese of doing. They were behaving like the masters of Cambodia. They said that Vietnam occupied Cambodia, but in reality Vietnam did a lot for us. Vietnam was good to us. The most important role the Vietnamese played was to prevent the Pol Pot régime from returning. On the political side it was the Cambodians who made the decisions."

. Before they left the Vietnamese built up a large stockpile of weapons for the Phnom Penh government. The Soviet Union also contributed to the supplies. General Vu Xuan Vinh, the chief of the Vietnamese defence ministry's international relations department, said that Hanoi advised Cambodia not to launch any major offensive as that would drain the stock of weapons, and instead to pursue a policy of attacking the resistance forces only when attacked.

United Nations' military observers claimed that Vietnamese special forces continued limited operations inside Cambodia. Élite Vietnamese troops were based in Siem Reap till early 1992, they said. According to press reports, Vietnamese troops entered Kampot province in March 1991 to repulse a Khmer Rouge attack. Richard Solomon, an assistant US secretary of state, told a senate hearing in April 1991 that the Vietnamese had left in place thousands of military advisors, in the 5,000 to 10,000 range. The Vietnamese had sent their forces in and out of Cambodia to deal with specific engagements, he added.

Heng Samrin and Hun Sen were accused of setting up a communist-style economic system by giving the state a disproportionately large share in the economy and, in doing so, blindly following Vietnam.

"The economic systems of Vietnam and Cambodia are different," Hun Sen argued. "We had some Vietnamese economic advisors, but the economy of Cambodia is different from Vietnam. We listened to their [Vietnamese] opinions, but we made the decisions. But now, if we do not follow what they [the West] say they will threaten to cut assistance, or raise an outcry in the newspapers."

It was speculated that the Vietnamese had carted away millions of dollars worth of natural resources from Cambodia, and that they took timber and rubber during their long stay in the country. Hun Sen rejected the allegation.

"It is not true," he said. "The trade between our countries was a normal affair. Vietnam could buy timber and rubber from Cambodia at the same price as other countries bought these commodities from us."

Vietnam paid for its Cambodian adventure in blood. After withdrawing their forces in 1989, Vietnamese officials released conflicting reports on their human losses. According to one estimate between 40,000 and 50,000 Vietnamese troops were killed, or wounded, in Cambodia during 1978-88. A study that was presented to the national assembly in Hanoi said that some 67,000 Vietnamese were killed, or wounded, during the ten-year campaign in Cambodia. The highest numbers were claimed by Major-General Nguyen Van Thai who said that about 55,300 Vietnamese were killed, 110,000 seriously wounded, and 55,000 slightly injured, making a total of 220,300 war casualties.

The Phnom Penh government felt indebted to the Vietnamese. General secretary Heng Samrin said in his report to the fifth congress of the Kampuchean People's Revolutionary Party in October 1985 that Cambodia must strengthen its alliance with Vietnam, Laos, and the Soviet Union, because such an alliance was a "law" that would guarantee the success of the Cambodian revolution. Heng Samrin tried to change the mindset of the people who were suspicious of the presence of the Vietnamese forces. He urged them to give up their "narrow-minded chauvinism" that infringed on the friendship between Cambodia and Vietnam.

But many Cambodians watched with a feeling of dismay and disgust as Hanoi stamped its authority. Ministries and departments were headed by Cambodian and Vietnamese officials. Resentment mounted when, in 1985, people spoke out about being forcibly conscripted into the Cambodian army by the Vietnamese. However, even the most critical Cambodians realised that it was Hanoi's experts who had helped re-create the education system that had been completely destroyed by the Khmer Rouge.

An anti-Vietnam motif remained a dark shadow that deepened the mistrust between the two countries.

FIVE

REBEL'S RISE

GROOMING THE GUERRILLA

The Hun family and friends watched the rapid political rise of Hun Sen with a mixture of disbelief, amazement, and admiration. Elsewhere, the once-powerful Norodom family and the Khmer Rouge, still lusting for power, were shocked and confounded. A peasant lad without formal higher education was emerging as the most powerful leader in post-independence Cambodia. He was rewriting the power equation, and erasing painful memories of the autocratic rule of Sihanouk whose monumental foreign policy mistakes in the 1970s led to the US aerial bombardment of Cambodia, and the holocaust that followed.

His political ascent began long before he became the foreign minister at the age of twenty-seven. His first political post was that of a founding member of the United Front that was created on December 2, 1978.

"Before the birth of the front I was already the leader of the resistance movement on the east side of the Mekong river ever since I broke away from the Pol Pot clique," he said. "I was a military commander and a political leader with the task of building both the military and political forces."

But he was reluctant to step into active politics. When the top members of the communist Kampuchean People's Revolutionary Council—formed in Phnom Penh after the Khmer Rouge was overthrown—asked him to become the foreign minister he refused to take the job. He was aware of his shortcomings and realised that he was out of his depth. However, when the senior leaders persuaded him to reconsider he reluctantly agreed, and was appointed the foreign minister on January 7, 1979.

"I agreed to accept the post for a trial period of three months because I had never received any training for this kind of work," Hun Sen said. "I was given a monthly remuneration of sixteen kilogrammes of foodgrains, of which ten kilogrammes was rice and six kilogrammes was maize."

Overnight, the revolutionary became a member of the establishment. In his own words the new responsibilities that came with the ministerial position were often too much to cope with.

"I faced lots of difficulties in understanding and grasping the complex issues of international affairs because I had no expertise," he said. "But, through training I learnt how to deal with these complexities. That is why I refused to be the foreign minister initially, and took on the post for a three-month probation period. I was fortunate that several Cambodian leaders who had a great deal of experience and knowledge of diplomatic affairs helped me constantly. I, too, made a determined effort to study and research world affairs."

Hun Sen made his international debut at a ministerial meeting of the non-aligned countries in Colombo, Sri Lanka, in June 1979. He took to his new job with aplomb.

"Like Cambodia, Sri Lanka was also a place of intense struggle," he said. "At the time we still occupied the Cambodian seat at the meetings of the non-aligned countries," he added.

On his way to Sri Lanka he flew to the two countries that were Cambodia's strongest allies in order to get their blessings and support—he first went to Vietnam, and then the Soviet Union. At the Sri Lanka meeting Cambodia did not have diplomatic relations with the major South Asian power, India, whose prime minister Morarji Desai refused to recognise the Phnom Penh government unless Vietnam withdrew its forces.

"Although we did not have diplomatic relations, India did not object to our presence," Hun Sen said. "After Mrs Indira Gandhi came to power in 1980 India eventually recognised Cambodia, and forged diplomatic relations."

The Morarji government unexpectedly weighed in to support Cambodia at the United Nations in November 1979. India suggested that a proposed conference on Cambodia should be attended by Asean and the Indochinese states, and that the outside powers be kept out to minimise interference. Asean did not support the proposal because a smaller forum could easily be stage-managed by Hanoi to its advantage.

The India card was important to Cambodia. It was the only non-communist country willing to support the isolated Phnom Penh government. But Cambodia's hopes were dashed when the new Indian prime minister Indira Gandhi rebuffed Vietnamese prime minister Pham Van Dong's proposal for India to extend diplomatic recognition to the Phnom Penh government. Gandhi's reluctance stemmed from her concern that she would be seen to have been pressured by the Vietnamese premier to recognise Cambodia. However, Dong did manage to extract one important concession during his visit to New Delhi in April 1980—Gandhi dropped the precondition of her predecessor, Morarji, who had demanded that the Vietnamese withdraw their forces before India recognised Phnom Penh.

Just three months after Dong's visit India established diplomatic relations with Cambodia in July 1980. Indian foreign minister Narasimha Rao said that Cambodia needed all possible assistance from the international community after the "terrible ordeals". The announcement did not come as a surprise as the Gandhi government had given an earlier assurance that it would recognise the new rulers of Phnom Penh.

The most significant victory of the new Cambodian government was winning diplomatic recognition from India which became the first non-communist country to break the cordon of isolation that the West and non-communist Asia had thrown around Phnom Penh. The Indians had relented after being pressured by Vietnam and its staunch ally, the Soviet Union.

While Cambodia's campaign to win friends came up against roadblocks in Southeast Asia and everywhere in the West, Hun Sen was cutting his diplomatic teeth. According to the daily bulletin of the Cambodian news agency, Sarpordamean Kampuchea, dated June 14, 1979, he held talks with Sri Lankan officials on his first visit to that country. There, he met officials from Vietnam, Laos, Cuba, and several non-aligned states, many of whom launched a scathing attack on the Khmer Rouge régime.

Taking the cue, he spoke to reporters from the *Far Eastern Economic Review*, an official Cambodian newspaper, and correspondents from several countries. He related to them the story of the liberation of Cambodia, the long struggle, and the overthrow of the Pol Pot clique. In colourful language he condemned Pol Pot and Ieng Sary as being the "slaves of the Chinese emperor who invaded and killed more than three million Cambodians, and tortured and punished the remaining four million people who survived the genocide". After the briefing Hun Sen showed the press a documentary film on the crimes of the Khmer Rouge.

At home, life for Hun Sen's young family was, for the first time, entering a harmonious phase. His wife, however, had her reservations about his new job as the foreign minister.

"She was unhappy because she didn't want me to enter politics," he said. "She persuaded me to abandon the post, and go back to the countryside to work as a farmer. I didn't agree with her because, at the time, I was working for the nation. But she was fed up with the suffering."

The reunited family was allotted a house fronting the Independence Monument in Phnom Penh, and they quickly settled down there.

"At that time there was no residence for a foreign minister, but there were so many empty houses in Phnom Penh—everybody could choose one," he said. "I could get 300 houses if I wanted."

Outwardly, very little changed in his lifestyle. He received a meagre parliamentary salary, and lived in the same house for several years. Later, in the 1990s, as a resurgent Cambodian press went on the offensive, among other things it criticised his State of Cambodia government for illegally occupying the homes and property that belonged to others. Hun Sen explained that the issue of overlapping property claims was a legacy of the Pol Pot régime that drove city dwellers from their homes, and overturned the social structure.

"After liberation on January 7, 1979 Phnom Penh was a ghost city without people," he said. "Many home owners lost their lives. Nobody possessed their home ownership documents. When the people returned to the city they chose to live in houses which were situated near their place of work. As the liberated people returned, one by one, they were resettled. This process resulted in an irreversible situation which required us to implement the principle of non-revision of borders as n the African countries after gaining independence from the colonialists. It would bring about a dangerous war between the newcomers and the previous owners if the ownership was revised, and would cause another evacuation of people across the country."

His job was never easy. His country desperately needed loans, but he could not get through the stiff-hinged door at the World Bank. Cambodia was ringed by an economic embargo enforced by most non-communist countries that wanted to punish the Heng Samrin government because it was supported by Vietnam. The chief enemy of the non-communist world was communist Vietnam, a country that had defeated the French and American forces. When Hun Sen found it impossible to get international loans his government came to depend completely on the Soviet Union, Cuba, Vietnam and, to some extent, India.

"It was a period of the Cold War, ideological warfare, and a struggle between the two blocs, the West and the East," he said. "The West had imposed unjust punishment on us, while the socialist countries extended their hand to help us economically and militarily in order to prevent the Pol Pot régime from returning."

Trying to gain entry into the United Nations was like talking to a stone wall.

"We made every effort to request the UN to give justice to the Cambodian people who had survived the genocide," he said. "On the contrary, due to the pressure exerted by a number of countries, the representatives of Pol Pot could occupy the Cambodian seat at the UN."

Tragedy degenerated into farce. The West and the non-communist Asian countries, in order to punish Vietnam, penalised Cambodia largely because it was supported by Vietnam. In the process these countries thought it morally acceptable to have a genocidal régime warm the Cambodian seat at the UN in the name of Democratic Kampuchea, the official name of the Khmer Rouge.

At home, the rotten core of the economy that the Khmer Rouge had bequeathed to the nation lay exposed. In early March 1979 residents of Phnom Penh were forced to survive by eating roots, wild fruit, and leaves. Millions of hectares of ricefields were temporarily abandoned due to the war. There was no drinking water, telephone service, mail, transport, markets, and no money. To ease the situation the new government sometimes distributed rice and flour. It was only in August that news filtered out that the Heng Samrin government was preparing to revive the use of money, and create a cash-based economy before the end of the year. Communication lines were severed. Cambodia was unreachable.

Soon after Hun Sen became the foreign minister Cambodia's first newspaper since 1975 made an appearance. The state-owned paper consisted of eight pages, four of which were filled with pictures, and four with articles on the policies of the new government. Just what these policies were became apparent a month later when president Heng Samrin said in an interview that his immediate tasks were to supply the basic needs of the people, and mop up the remnants of the Khmer Rouge. The interview was released by the government to coincide with a visit to Phnom Penh by Vietnamese prime minister Pham Van Dong who became the first foreign head of government to travel to the country to meet its leaders in a public display of solidarity. But Heng Samrin had other concerns. His immediate tasks were to provide food, housing, clothing, and health services to the millions of displaced people who were returning to their homes after the genocide.

The first sign that Sihanouk was determined to fight his way back to power became apparent in July 1979 when the powerless prince said in Paris that he would create a parallel Cambodian government in exile. The Phnom Penh government labelled Sihanouk's proposed alliance with the Khmer Rouge and

Son Sann as a front led by "a puppet—no more, no less".

Hun Sen had not forgotten that Sihanouk had briefly served as a puppet head of state of the Pol Pot régime, and had played a crucial hand in the development of the Khmer Rouge. Hun Sen, then a hard line figure, rejected any idea of a dialogue with Sihanouk or Son Sann, the two exiled leaders who were on the verge of forming an alliance with the Khmer Rouge.

By this time, Hun Sen had become a fluent and forceful exponent of Cambodian foreign policy. His rapid progress did not go unnoticed by his political bosses, Heng Samrin, Pen Sovann, and Chea Sim. In 1981, he was rewarded with the post of vice-prime minister, in addition to his role as foreign minister. A more confident Hun Sen began travelling further afield to what would later become his favourite city, New Delhi. It was in the company of Indian political leaders, and foreign office bureaucrats, that he felt most at ease and among friends. On a six-day visit to New Delhi in August 1981 he unveiled a two-stage plan to resolve the Cambodian problem through a regional conference among the three Indochinese states and Asean, and later an international conference bringing together the major powers, particularly the USA and China.

One month later Sihanouk flew to Singapore where he met Son Sann and Khieu Samphan at their first formal meeting to create a united force against the Phnom Penh government and its Vietnamese backers. Phnom Penh dismissed the meeting as "only a new piece of theatre created by Beijing and Washington". It added: "The haggling among Mr Son Sann, Mr Sihanouk, and Mr Khieu Samphan, traitors to the Kampuchean people, will come to nothing because they are working in their own interests."

Hun Sen quickly became the public face, and the voice, of the Phnom Penh government, and played the lead in countering Sihanouk's propaganda. The youngest foreign minister in the world, at the time, did not have the faintest idea that he was about to become the youngest prime minister in the world.

PEAKING AT THIRTY-THREE

It was the death of prime minister Chan Si that cleared the way for Hun Sen to take his post. In a stunningly rapid ascent up the pyramid slope of the communist party he was elected prime minister in January 1985, two weeks after Chan Si died of a heart attack, and just six years after becoming foreign minister.

The new prime minister was just thirty-three, and ranked fifth in the seven-member politburo of the ruling Kampuchean People's Revolutionary Party (KPRP). The relatively inexperienced ex-guerrilla was elected unanimously at a plenary session of the national assembly. He described his ascent as being the logical culmination of his leadership roles as a guerrilla, a commander, and later as an organiser of the united front.

"Brothers in the party leadership entrusted me with the post of the prime minister when prime minister Chan Si passed away at the end of 1984," he said.

His rise would have been inconceivable without the support of an assortment of veteran party leaders such as Heng Samrin, Chea Sim, Say Phuthang, Chea Soth, Bou Thang, Tea Banh, Sai Chhum, and Sar Kheng, as well as a group whom Hun Sen dubbed the "senior" intellectuals such as Hor Nam Hong, Chem Snguon, Phlek Phirun, and My Samedi, and a cabal whom he called the "junior intellectuals".

He set two records: one for the world, another for Cambodia. At thirty-three he became the youngest prime minister in the world at that time, winning all the votes that were cast in a secret ballot in the national assembly in early 1985.

"It was the only instance in Cambodian history when a Cambodian leader got 100 per cent of the secret votes of confidence in the national assembly," he said. "This never happened in the case of [former] prime ministers Pen Sovann and Chan Si, my predecessors, who had lost a number of votes of confidence."

Hun Sen was referring to the vote to elect Pen Sovann as the prime minister in July 1981, and Chan Si the next year. A pro-Hanoi communist, Pen Sovann was sacked after having served for six months as secretary-general of the ruling party. At other times he was the vice president, defence minister, and president of the council of ministers. It was believed that he was the victim of a personality clash with Heng Samrin following deep ideological differences.

Pen Sovann was a stalwart of the KPRP, an offshoot of the Indochinese Communist Party (ICP) that played a vital role against the French colonial rule and the Japanese occupation of Cambodia. The KPRP was formed in 1951 after the ICP was dissolved and reorganised into three communist parties for Vietnam, Laos, and Cambodia. The party in Cambodia split in 1962 into pro-China and pro-Soviet Union factions. Pol Pot led the pro-Chinese group that was vehemently anti-Soviet. In January 1979, the division became permanent when the pro-Soviet and pro-Vietnamese faction under Pen Sovann replaced Pol Pot as the leader in Phnom Penh. Pen Sovann was elected the first secretary of the KPRP's central committee at a time when the party had about sixty-five regular members.

Pen Sovann distanced the party from Pol Pot's communist group, whom he castigated for being traitors, at the KPRP's fourth party congress from May 26-29, 1981. The congress resolved to wipe out Pol Pot's "reactionary ultra-nationalist doctrine", erase personality cults, and develop a strong Marxist-Leninist party.

When Heng Samrin suddenly replaced Pen Sovann as the party leader on December 4, 1981, the KPRP's pro-Vietnamese stance became even more pronounced. Pen Sovann was ated in a purge, arrested in December, and virtually exiled to Hanoi because he was seen as not being loyal enough to the Vietnamese. Under Vietnamese guard he was flown to Hanoi where he spent seven years in jail, and another three under house arrest.

"I was in a fifteen square metre cell. I was cut off from the outside world, and they only gave me five dollars a month to live," Pen Sovann told the *Phnom Penh Post* in an interview in May 1997.

"Hun Sen and [fellow senior communist party official] Say Phuthang were responsible for my imprisonment," he said.

Over in Phnom Penh the national assembly voted to elect Chan Si as prime minister in early-1982. At the time Hun Sen was visiting France as foreign minister. The same year he also travelled to the Soviet Union, and took a vacation on the Black Sea.

When Pen Sovann inquired why he had been jailed in Vietnam he received a letter signed by Say Phuthang on February 12, 1982. The letter accused him of being "narrow-minded, extremely nationalistic, and against the Vietnamese". As a result, the KPRP could not let him return to Cambodia, the letter said.

After Pen Sovann was thought to be sufficiently re-educated, he was allowed to return home in 1992. He then applied for a post in the Cambodian People's

Party (CPP), the successor to the KPRP, but was not accepted because he was not trusted. His repeated requests to join the party were denied. Finally, in 1994, he was appointed as an advisor to the CPP's branch in Takeo. But the CPP began doubting his loyalty when it was rumoured that he might join the Khmer Nation Party founded the following year by a French-educated company executive named Sam Rainsy who was a son of Sam Sary, a senior official in the government of Sihanouk in the 1960s. As a result Pen Sovann lost his post. He alleged that Hun Sen had threatened to confiscate his house in Takeo, and his car. Then he made several requests to the CPP to allow him to rejoin the party.

"I kneel and beg to join [the CPP] by writing once or twice a year to Hun Sen and Chea Sim. Recently, I asked Chea Sim whether I could serve the CPP," he said.

A desperate Pen Sovann then turned to Ranariddh's Funcinpec party, only to be spurned on account of his former Marxist-Leninist tendencies. He remained in the margins of Phnom Penh politics, harbouring feeble hopes of starting his own political party.

AFTER the exile of Pen Sovann, the new prime minister, Chan Si, did not last long. His death, in October 1984, opened the way for another election. With two stalwarts out of the way the party was led by a third stalwart, Heng Samrin. Suddenly, the elevation of Hun Sen, a longstanding friend and ally of Heng Samrin, was both possible and plausible. At the time of Chan Si's death Hun Sen was in Hanoi where he was briefing Vietnamese officials on Cambodian affairs. Soon afterwards, Hun Sen was appointed acting prime minister by the party leadership in Phnom Penh. The prime ministership was only inches away.

The party nominated just one candidate, Hun Sen, in the secret vote to elect a new premier. The five top leaders who vetted and shortlisted the candidates for premiership were Heng Samrin, Chea Sim, Say Phuthang, Chea Soth, and Bou Thang. They were Hun Sen's five godfathers. Without the support of these party veterans he would have had no future. None of the five stood as candidates for premiership because they already occupied the highest posts within the state and the party. Heng Samrin was the head of state; Chea Sim was the chairman of the national assembly; Chea Soth and Bou Thang were deputy prime ministers in charge of the economy and national defence; and Say Phuthang was a key member of the politburo.

While Say Phuthang proposed Hun Sen's name within the communist party, Heng Samrin did so in the national assembly, and Chea Sim supervised the vote.

"Although I was not eager for the top job I had to accept it because their confidence had been entrusted in me," Hun Sen said.

How did a man so young and inexperienced win the confidence of the Cambodian leaders who seemed willing to take a risk by nominating him as the prime minister?

"They reposed a lot of confidence in me," he said. "At that time among the members of the government and the party I was the youngest. They were aware of my capabilities which I had demonstrated as the foreign minister."

The novice foreign minister was aware that his KPRP was a house built on sand, a weak and wobbly entity with a few branches, and a membership of less than 1,000 people. The largest province, Kompong Cham, had as few as thirty regular members. After he became the prime minister the KPRP held its fifth congress from October 13-16, 1985, a major event when party membership rose to more than 7,000.

But Heng Samrin admitted that the economy had remained stunted and unbalanced, and industries suffered from a lack of fuel, spare-parts, and raw materials. He warned that a transition to socialism would take "dozens of years". The congress unveiled the country's First Plan (1986-90) that added the private economy to the three sectors mentioned in the Constitution—the state sector, collective sector, and family sector. It was the private sector that would play a central role in helping Hun Sen's government survive its years in isolation.

The media saw cracks in the party. Chea Sim's unwavering support and personal friendship with Hun Sen came under attack from diplomats and observers who speculated that there was an intense rivalry between the two men. Such rumours had persisted since they first surfaced in the early 1980s. First hints of the supposed rivalry became apparent when Chea Sim was believed to have engineered the dismissal of Khieu Kanharith as the editor of the party's newspaper.

Kanharith was one of Hun Sen's closest friends and allies. Chea Sim, apparently, frowned upon Kanharith's frequent criticisms of government policy, and his proximity to Western reporters who sought him out for comments on the secretive party. Diplomats wagered that Chea Sim was behind the dismissal of Kanharith and that, by sacking a person close to Hun Sen, he wanted to send a message of his disapproval indirectly, without publicly confronting Prime Minister Hun Sen.

The spat between Chea Sim and Hun Sen was believed to hark back to the peace talks in Tokyo when Hun Sen is understood to have named all six members of the Supreme National Council, the body that was to run Cambodia until elections could be held. Hun Sen did so without seeking the approval of his party colleagues in Phnom Penh, the story went. Worse, diplomats said that there were factions within the CPP that thought Hun Sen to be extremely pro-West, and viewed him as having made too many concessions to those countries. From this, conclusions were hastily drawn that the CPP, far from being united, was badly split. Beneath it all ran swift undercurrents of the rumoured Hun Sen-Chea Sim rivalry.

"This speculation has been going on for more than fifteen years," Hun Sen said with a wide grin. "Before 1984 they said that there was rivalry between Heng Samrin and Sai Phuthang, and between Heng Samrin and Chea Sim. A rivalry between Chea Sim and I is a no-win rivalry. If there was a no-win situation it meant that there was no rivalry. What was the rivalry for? Chea Sim is the head of the CPP and the chairman of the national assembly—both very senior positions. What's the use for him to take the post of prime minister? Now, I am a powerful prime minister, so what is the use for me to take the post of the head of the party, and that of the national assembly?"

Who was more powerful—Hun Sen or Chea Sim?

"I don't want to say who is more powerful. But everybody has their own obligation. If Chea Sim takes the post of prime minister maybe he would do better than Hun Sen," he said.

When the rumours of a split between the two leaders first began doing the rounds of the capital in the late-1980s Hun Sen was seen as a reformist and Chea Sim, a hardliner. As he spearheaded the reforms he set a collision course with the conservatives within the communist party. It was rumoured that a long-simmering rivalry went on the boil. While Chea Sim wanted Hun Sen to make no concessions to the non-communist factions at the peace talks, Hun Sen pursued a policy of reconciliation, and played a decisive role in achieving peace. All sorts of horror stories swirled around Phnom Penh's bars. Some said that a difference of opinion between Hun Sen and Chea Sim arose because the former was reputed to have the best team of economic advisors in town, and they were running rings around Chea Sim's boys. One of the best informed analysts, Soviet embassy counsellor V. Loukianov, dismissed the bar gossip, and said that Chea Sim was not after Hun Sen's job.

"There's no question of it. Mr Chea Sim is senior to Mr Hun Sen in the government and in the party's politburo," Loukianov said. "So, Mr Chea Sim would gain nothing by toppling Mr Hun Sen who is his political junior."

In 1998 we told Hun Sen about the comments that Loukianov made in 1990.

"He was right because Chea Sim has always been my boss," Hun Sen responded. "Even now, both Heng Samrin and Chea Sim are my bosses. There are two more people who are my bosses—Chea Soth and Sai Phuthang. We can compare the CPP to a football team. The most important person in the team is the coach. If the coach is not effective then the team cannot win. Chea Soth is a very good coach. When the German football team was defeated they did not blame the players. They blamed the coach. It is the same for the party. There is only one kind of rivalry between Chea Sim and me—golf. He has played golf for a long time, and I cannot defeat him. I am trying to beat him at the game."

The gossip of a split between Hun Sen and Chea Sim hounded them through 1992. Perturbed by the negative publicity, the CPP urged its members to close ranks and forge a united front ahead of elections the following year. Diplomats in the capital insisted that a power struggle raged between a hard line Chea Sim, who was the party's president, and a reformist Hun Sen, the party's vice-president. The story went that Chea Sim had gained the upper hand in a power struggle following a constitutional amendment in April which allowed him to act as the president in the absence, or illness, of President Heng Samrin. The pecking order now was Chea Sim, Heng Samrin, and then, Hun Sen. While Hun Sen had elevated his close associates to ministerial posts, Chea Sim appointed his brother-in-law, Sar Kheng, as a deputy prime minister and the minister of interior.

A senior Cambodian government official confided that the political trio of Hun Sen, Chea Sim, and Heng Samrin that ran Cambodia were not just comrades but were close friends who liked to share a bottle of cognac.

"Sometimes Hun Sen walks into Chea Sim's house, or Heng Samrin walks into Hun Sen's house, and they eat and drink together. They are the best of friends," the official said.

The ruling party said in May 1992 that there was no basis to the "rumours" of a power struggle, and that the party was united. But sceptical diplomats wagered that the power struggle would hurt the party in the elections.

Hun Sen had been a member of the KPRP's original politburo ever since its formation in exile. When the central committee and the politburo was set up, his godfathers ensured a place for him. Almost a year after becoming the prime minister, he gave up the post of foreign minister in December 1986, in order to concentrate his energies on running the country and, in particular, to manage the military campaign against the Khmer Rouge.

Ringed by a crippling American trade embargo and a ban on World Bank and International Monetary Fund loans to Cambodia, the ex-guerrilla found himself clamped in a vice of economic and diplomatic challenges. By his own admission he found some of these issues "quite complicated", especially the management of the painful transition from a planned economy to a mixed economy and, ultimately, to an open economy.

"It was imperative to find a political solution through negotiations," Hun Sen said. "Economic reforms went along with political reforms. However, political stability had to be maintained so the economic reforms could be carried out together with the search for a political solution to end the war and bring about peace."

He paused to drag long and hard on a cigarette, then took a sip of Chinese tea, before saying: "I will write a book about these complicated issues."

The stigma of being labelled in the foreign press as a "Vietnam-installed puppet régime" made it even more difficult for him to ease his isolated country onto the path of economic reform. Although it did bother him, there was little he could do to mould world opinion at the time. He could not fathom why the world had forgotten the hard-earned liberation of Cambodia and the removal of the Khmer Rouge by the Cambodian rebels and the Vietnamese army.

"Justice was still prevalent in the world," Hun Sen said. "Therefore, I did not pay much attention to what [issues] were raised. I devoted much of my time to help the people to be free from poverty, our real enemy, rather than quarrelling with the press."

"It was a very complicated period. So, when I became the prime minister I continued to be the foreign minister," he said. "From 1979 to 1983 it was a state of total confrontation. From 1984 we entered a new phase of confrontation and negotiation. I still remember two very important men from Asean: the foreign ministers—M ichtar Kusumaatmadja of Indonesia, and Ghazalie Shafie of Malaysia. From the Indochinese countries, we had Nguyen Co Thach of Vietnam We had two groups of countries—the Asean six and the Indochinese three. So, we had to speed up the process of negotiation."

To prevent Thailand from interfering in Cambodian affairs, and urge it to end its support of the Khmer Rouge, the Hun Sen government proposed that the Thai military play a neutral role in order to avoid confrontation. In the end, Hun Sen had a secret meeting with Thai General Chavalit Yongchaiyudh in Vientiane in late-1988, and he met Prime Minister Chatichai Choonhavan in 1989. It was futile. Thailand continued supporting the Khmer Rouge.

Nurtured by his party bosses Hun Sen adopted a hard line against the resistance led by Sihanouk, while his army fought the remnants of the Khmer Rouge along the border with Thailand. Unlike democracies where fledgeling prime ministers were made insecure, and then toppled, the young Cambodian premier could count on the unstinting backing of his communist party chiefs. The party evolved a consensus on its domestic and foreign policy, and Hun Sen fine-tuned it. In May 1987 he rejected an overture for peace made by Sihanouk as "not new and not realistic". But by October he softened his stand, and offered the top three positions to Sihanouk in a future coalition government—head of state, deputy head of state, and prime minister. Sihanouk rejected the offer out of hand in December 1987.

"I would rather die in Beijing or Pyongyang than be a puppet president in Phnom Penh, a stooge of Hanoi," Sihanouk said in France.

Sihanouk was willing, however, to return as the head of a new state run by his three-party opposition and the Hun Sen government.

The angry young man gradually saw sense in the search for peace, and agreed to start talks with Sihanouk who lived in exile in Beijing, and occasionally travelled to Pyongyang and Paris.

"I did consider achieving a peaceful solution, especially with Sihanouk, since the early-1980s after the first partial withdrawal of the Vietnamese troops from Cambodia in 1982," Hun Sen said.

The breakthrough occurred on December 2, 1987 when Hun Sen met Sihanouk at a neutral location at a 13th century renaissance chateau in Fère-en-Tardenois, a wooded village northeast of Paris, France. It was the first dialogue between the sixty-five-year-old prince and the thirty-five-year-old peasant. It soon became apparent that it was a dialogue of equals, between an urbane champagne-swilling prince and a hard-bitten nationalist schooled in the jungles of Indochina.

"The decision to hold the talks was based on the view that military power could not solve the Cambodian problem, and only negotiations and national reconciliation could bring peace," Hun Sen said.

Although the two adversaries had serious differences, during their talks Hun Sen put them all behind him. At Fère-en-Tardenois, after six hours of eyeballing each other, the two men reached a tentative agreement on a four-point plan to end the bloody nine-year civil war. Hun Sen made it clear that he was not in France just to meet Sihanouk. He left the talks to attend a French Communist Party congress, making his political leanings quite apparent.

After three days of talks at the historic chateau they agreed to ask North Korean strongman, Kim Il Sung, to mediate between China and Vietnam, the main backers of the Khmer Rouge and the Phnom Penh government respectively. The fact that a communiqué, issued at the end of the talks, made no mention of the controversial presence of some 140,000 Vietnamese troops in Cambodia, spoke volumes for Hun Sen's dexterity as a negotiator. The two leaders agreed to pursue talks in Pyongyang a month later.

."The significance of the agreement between Sihanouk and me was to seek a peaceful solution," he said.

Just six days after their landmark talks the mercurial Sihanouk suddenly changed his mind, and cancelled further peace talks with Hun Sen, calling him a "lackey of the Vietnamese" who arrived at the talks "empty-handed and sought to score propaganda points". Sihanouk's flip-flops delayed the return of peace to his country. It showed that he remained hostage to the Khmer Rouge, a guerrilla outfit that he encouraged in the 1970s in the desperate hope that it would restore him to power. In the end, Sihanouk was disappointed when the Khmer Rouge captured power after capitalising on Sihanouk's popularity with the people, and then kept him virtually imprisoned in the Royal Palace in Phnom Penh.

Hun Sen did not have a stomach for insults, or for foreign food. On his travels, particularly to France, he could not eat the local fare. Norodom Ranariddh, a son of Sihanouk, recalled a story of how he would not eat French food during the Paris talks, and that Asian food had to be arranged for him.

"I do not like foreign food, except Chinese food," Hun Sen said. "The Cambodian nationals who lived in Paris helped cook Khmer food for me. When I travel abroad I always carry dried fish and fish sauce, which are my familiar foods."

Under pressure and intense criticism from the Khmer Rouge, Sihanouk called off the Pyongyang talks. Sihanouk argued that he had asked Hun Sen to include the withdrawal of the Vietnamese troops in the final communiqué, but Hun Sen responded that "such references were useless". Sihanouk set preconditions—he would not meet Hun Sen again unless, first, the Vietnamese negotiated directly with Sihanouk and, secondly, if the Khmer Rouge and Son Sann did not agree to meet Hun Sen. With the talks broken off Hun Sen told the Cambodians to "fight and negotiate simultaneously".

The loudest and harshest exchanges were those between Hun Sen and the Khmer Rouge.

."The Khmer Rouge and I never agreed with each other," Hun Sen said. "I often got into arguments with the Khmer Rouge during the negotiations. I was always optimistic, and that was why I continued with the negotiations. There were lots of difficulties, but it was better than fighting."

As the peace talks loomed ahead Hun Sen took back the post of foreign minister in late-1987 in order to stamp his personal style on the foreign affairs portfolio, a department that would play a critical role in managing the negotiations. He dropped the former foreign minister, Kong Korm, who had warmed the seat for him, to the job as his assistant. The move enhanced his stature while he was preparing for a second round of talks with Sihanouk.

Throwing the schedule into utter confusion Sihanouk once again performed a flip-flop. He asked Hun Sen to meet him, this time, in St-Germain-en-Laye in France on January 20-21, 1988.

The rapidly maturing Hun Sen knew who his friends were. Before meeting Sihanouk he stopped over in New Delhi to talk to his ally, the Indian Prime Minister Rajiv Gandhi who had inherited his mother's warmth and affection for the Cambodians that went beyond the compulsions of their political alliance. The two countries were bound by the threads of a common Hindu culture, and the Pali-Sanskrit script that the language of the Khmers was based on. Rajiv and Hun Sen met for more than an hour, and discussed ways of finding peace.

In the wintering French retreat of St Germain-en-Laye he met Sihanouk for a second round of talks. Hun Sen quickly proved his sharpness as a negotiator when, using a gently chiding but respectful tone, he succeeded in getting Sihanouk to agree to form a two-party coalition government between the prince and himself, leaving out the Khmer Rouge and Son Sann. The final session of their two-day talks stretched to almost five hours. In the end, Sihanouk was persuaded to drop his previous insistence on forming a four-party government that also included the Khmer Rouge. But Sihanouk rejected Hun Sen's demand that the Khmer Rouge be disbanded after Hun Sen linked the withdrawal of the Vietnamese from Cambodia to the demobilisation of Pol Pot's forces.

Although younger in years than his political rivals such as Sihanouk, Son Sann, and Pol Pot, all in their sixties, Hun Sen grew in political stature through his participation in the peace talks. Even though Sihanouk was older Hun Sen negotiated with him from a position of strength and equality. He presented the reformist face of the State of Cambodia, and regularly came out with a string of strong and clever statements that were crafted to make sensational newspaper headlines.

As Hun Sen left a deep impression at the peace talks, Sihanouk's son, Ranariddh, a new political recruit, was also trying to make an impact.

"Often some people forget the historical reality," Hun Sen said. "My counterpart in the peace talks was not Ranariddh, not Khieu Samphan, not Son Sann. Please remember that it was a negotiation between Hun Sen and Sihanouk that began on December 18, 1987 in France. At that time Ranariddh was a note-taking man, and was equal to Cham Prasidh, who was my personal secretary. During the negotiations those present were Sihanouk, his wife [Monique], and Ranariddh; and on my side I had Dith Munthy, and Cham Prasidh. So, they should not forget the history."

At that time, Cambodia had two governments—Hun Sen was the head of the government that ran the country, and Sihanouk was the head of a coalition government in exile that took the form of a resistance force.

"But we did not recognise the factions in his three-party government," Hun Sen said. "So, besides Sihanouk the others were not my counterparts. When writing the history of Cambodia please don't forget this point. Some people want to promote the note-taking secretary in the meeting to a negotiator. History is history. We cannot readjust it."

Comparisons between Hun Sen and Ranariddh were, nevertheless, drawn.

"Whether he was capable or incapable I don't want to judge him," Hun Sen said. "I was born in a village. He [Ranariddh] was born in a royal palace. He got a doctorate in France. I got a doctorate in Vietnam. More people were born in villages than in the palace. If he looks down on Hun Sen he will look down on millions of people who are poorer than himself. He should not forget that I used to confront his father. When they look down on me they fall into their own trap."

From St-Germain-en-Laye the sputtering "on-now, off-again" talks and their tired participants lurched to places such as Bogor and Jakarta in Indonesia, and to Tokyo. But as the factions were still trading artillery fire, peace was in jeopardy.

The vitiated atmosphere led to an escalation of tensions. To make matters worse Sihanouk urged China not to end its assistance to the Khmer Rouge. On the other side, the Soviet Union did not stint on spending its roubles to arm the Phnom Penh government.

In June 1989 the first squadron of Soviet-built MiG-21 fighter jets, flown by Cambodian pilots trained in the Soviet Union, touched down at Pochentong airport in Phnom Penh. The Soviet military build-up was a part of a plan to strengthen Cambodian defenses ahead of a planned withdrawal of Vietnamese troops in September. Just before the arrival of the fighters, Moscow had delivered tanks, armoured personnel carriers, and artillery to Phnom Penh.

The unpredictable Sihanouk sprang yet another surprise. In August he stepped down as the head of his political party, Funcinpec, and appointed Ranariddh as its new secretary-general. Sihanouk relinquished his post in order to project himself as a non-partisan supreme leader of Cambodia, and thereby hasten the process of achieving peace.

After the withdrawal of the Vietnamese forces from Cambodia in September 1989 the Phnom Penh government eventually began winning new friends. Cracks appeared in the Western policy to isolate Cambodia. By November the Sihanouk-led resistance was alarmed, and the USA and Asean countries watched with concern as Britain, Canada, France, New Zealand, and Australia began a dialogue with the Hun Sen government.

France, a former colonial ruler of Cambodia, was ready to open an *Alliance Française* in Phnom Penh to serve as an official cultural mission. Canada and Britain sent diplomats on a fact-finding trip to Cambodia. The same month, New Zealand's foreign minister, Russell Marshall, met Hun Sen in Ho Chi Minh City during his trip through Southeast Asia.

Hun Sen was overjoyed when the European parliament in Strasbourg urged member states of the European Community in November to extend *de facto* recognition to his government. It called for an end to all military aid to the Sihanouk-led opposition factions and "deplored the Chinese government's continued political, military, and economic support of the Khmer Rouge". While urging the twelve European states to intensify humanitarian aid to the Cambodian people, it told them to isolate the Khmer Rouge army and its leaders "diplomatically and militarily", particularly in the UN. A diplomat in Phnom Penh commented: "In Washington, they're not happy with it. But on the other hand it was not unexpected, and nobody has moved towards recognition of Phnom Penh."

Ultimately, a durable peace accord was signed in Paris in October 1991. It called on the four factions to cooperate, and hold elections in 1993. Even though the Khmer Rouge signed on the dotted line, it boycotted the polls.

"But this [my differences with the Khmer Rouge] was not the cause of the boycott of the elections by the Khmer Rouge in 1993," Hun Sen said. "They did not honour any of their commitments as they were required by the Paris peace accord."

When Sihanouk returned home to Cambodia in November 1991, after twelve years in exile, his tune had changed again.

"Hun Sen is a remarkable leader," Sihanouk said. "He is young, intelligent, and experienced in the affairs of state. He is patriotic, and has a genuine love for his people. He has national pride. When I was young I was like him—energetic, tempestuous, violent with words. But that's youth. We all mellow with age. Cambodia is lucky to have Hun Sen. We need several Hun Sens."

From calling him a "bad son", Sihanouk now referred to Hun Sen as his "adopted son". But an attack on Khmer Rouge leader, Khieu Samphan, by an enraged Phnom Penh mob altered some of Sihanouk's perceptions. As a part of the peace plan Samphan had been allowed to return to Phnom Penh where he was relegated to live in an abandoned outhouse at the Royal Palace. When he was attacked by a large mob that was thirsty for his blood, diplomats alleged that the Phnom Penh government might have been behind it because it did little to stop the assault. Sihanouk commented that he now trusted Hun Sen "only fifty per cent".

For his part, Hun Sen added another item to his impressive *curriculum-vitae*. He made up for a lack of formal education by completing a 172-page thesis entitled, "The Characteristics of Cambodian Politics". A doctoral degree was awarded to him by Vietnam's National Institute of Politics in 1991. The poor pagoda boy who could not complete his studies now had the highest academic honours.

THE FOUR ESCAPEES

As silently as the creeping moonshadows, the four Khmer Rouge guerrillas walked close behind their leader, Hun Sen, as he led them deeper and deeper into Vietnamese territory. The four were frightened, more frightened than their leader. They feared they would be shot dead by the Vietnamese border guards.

It was a risk worth taking. They were escaping from Pol Pot's clutches into the jaws of communist Vietnam. The four men—Nhek Huon, Nuch Than, San Sanh, and Paor Ean—wept as they crossed the tense border on June 21, 1977. They left their lives in the hands of their leader, Hun Sen.

Their worst fears came true: they were incessantly interrogated by the Vietnamese military authorities; they were thrown into jail in the Vietnamese province of Song Be. They were prepared to die.

But then, Hun Sen prevailed. He was able to convince the Vietnamese to help him raise a liberation force.

When the Khmer Rouge was overthrown in 1979 the four men drove into Phnom Penh victoriously as war heroes. Their hardship and suffering did not go unrewarded by their mentor. In spite of the great gulf created by the passage of time, Hun Sen still remained friends with the four. Old camaraderie did not die.

One of the escapees, Nhek Huon, was elevated to a senior post in the military in Phnom Penh in 1979 where he stayed till the early-1980s. He was then moved to take command of the western battlefield between 1983-85, but was recalled after suffering a severe attack of malaria. He was transferred to the Second Regional Military command in Kompong Cham as the second-in-command. But because of failing health he was reassigned to a desk job in Phnom Penh where he formulated military strategy.

A second defector, Nuch Than, was appointed the head of the youth wing of the Cambodian People's Party, a post that Hun Sen had relinquished in his favour. Afterwards, Nuch Than was appointed the deputy general-director of a state-owned rubber plantation, but he did not last long in the job.

Talking about the third follower, San Sanh, Hun Sen said: "In the assault against the Khmer Rouge in 1979, San Sanh was the head of a battalion that confronted the Khmer Rouge in the front lines in Battambang province."

San Sanh was transferred to the ministry of commerce in 1980, and rose to become a director in the inspection department.

The fourth escapee, Paor Ean, was rewarded with the post of the head of military logistics in Phnom Penh. Later he left the country for the West.

Even though these four men, who rallied behind Hun Sen in his time of need, were no longer a part of the power structure, they would always have a special place in Hun Sen's heart. Hun Sen's style of command and control was based on camaraderie, friendship, and loyalty. On these principles he built up a vast network of supporters who were ready to die for him.

DEFEAT

To his parents he would always be a carefree pagoda boy even though, now at age thirty-nine, he had played many dangerous roles—that of a Khmer Rouge guerrilla, a liberator, a communist, and a peace negotiator. He had always managed to snatch victory at the end of each act of the political drama. None of it had prepared him for rejection and defeat.

As he learnt the intricacies of his trade he made up for a lack of formal education with earthy, rustic common sense, and a strong belief in what was right for his country. The political maturing of Hun Sen culminated in the signing of the Paris peace accords in 1991 which brought in their wake 22,000 peacekeepers of the United Nations Transitional Authority in Cambodia (Untac). They arrived in Cambodia in late-1991 to organise the general election in May 1993, the first in more than two decades. Dozens of political parties mushroomed in the summer sun, and took to the campaign trail. As they worked the ground, allegations flew that Hun Sen's Cambodian People's Party (CPP) was intimidating the other parties, even killing their workers.

"This was just not true," Hun Sen said sharply. "I would like to ask why, after the elections, did they consider it a free and fair poll? Because the CPP lost, they no longer used the word 'intimidation'. But if the CPP had won they would have retained this word. What an injustice against us."

He added presciently: "The same thing will happen to us in the next election in 1998."

In the thick of the 1993 election Untac official Reginald Austin, who was in charge of organising the poll, said that the CPP and the Khmer Rouge were behind most of the political violence and intimidation. Things were quiet until the royalist Funcinpec began opening its party offices across the land.

Austin, who installed Western-style elections in authoritarian Cambodia, said: "As Funcinpec made headway with voters in areas controlled by the CPP, the CPP grew suspicious and began harassing the other parties. The worst political violence happened in Prey Veng province which used to be a very peaceful place."

Till that time Untac lacked hard evidence to nail the CPP which deflected the blame for many violent incidents onto the Khmer Rouge. The true extent of the political murders would only emerge months later, seriously implicating both the CPP and the Khmer Rouge and, to a lesser extent, Funcinpec.

When the results of the poll were announced in early-June 1993 the royalist Funcinpec won fifty-eight seats, and the CPP fifty-one seats. CPP stalwart Chea Sim cried foul, and wrote a series of stinging letters to the UN complaining about electoral fraud that involved the breaking of padlocks on the ballot boxes. Untac disputed some of the charges, accepted others, and claimed broad success for its mammoth election.

For Hun Sen it was the first taste of defeat in a devastating, yet truthful and telling, verdict delivered by the people. It was not outright rejection though. The people still trusted him and his party enough to give them fifty-one seats in the assembly, and viewed him as their saviour from the genocide. But they also wanted to give Ranariddh's royalists a chance to rule and improve their lives. They sent Hun Sen a crushing message that he had not done enough to extricate them from appalling poverty.

For the new democrat the political reality was sobering, and brought with it a sense of being wronged. The old rage was ignited.

"About 1,000 ballot boxes had their padlocks broken, and a large number of ballots were found scattered outside the boxes," Hun Sen said. "These irregularities led to the conclusion that the elections were not fair."

He felt that Untac's policies had loaded the dice against his party.

"The Untac had made two amendments to the electoral law without consulting the Supreme National Council [the SNC, a body that consisted of the four main Cambodian political factions, and represented Cambodian sovereignty]," he said.

These amendments gave the political parties the right to sign and seal the ballot boxes, and set up safe havens to store the boxes at night. As a result the parties may have been given ample opportunity to cheat by exchanging the ballot boxes.

Hun Sen accepted defeat. He saw in his loss the imprint of his past mistakes. He knew that he would have to turn his failure into success by working harder to help the rural poor. He became a sort of Robin Hood figure, taking contributions from lavish donors and investing the money, in desperate haste, in building schools, roads, and irrigation canals throughout the country. They came to be known as "Hun Sen road", "Hun Sen school", and "Hun Sen canal".

His charitable deeds drew uncharitable protests from Ranariddh's royalists who lacked the stamina to keep up with Hun Sen's reconstruction programme that changed the face of entire villages. Ranariddh's work in the villages paled by comparison. The royalists debased the reconstruction process, accusing Hun Sen of buying entire villages with his largesse. Their cynicism, however, did not convince the poor villagers who had come to regard Hun Sen as one of their own.

THE REAL POWER

From the tears of defeat flowed the rage and the power of a strongman.

When his party lost the general election in 1993 Hun Sen was, to all eyes, a loser. But things in Cambodia were not always what they seemed. Although Ranariddh took charge as the first prime minister he could not control the vast provincial administration that was run by second prime minister Hun Sen's party. Too small and too thin on the ground Ranariddh's party lacked the manpower. Hun Sen's party, in contrast, controlled the administration through its network of army commanders, police chiefs, and governors, most of whom had fought alongside their prime minister in the war of liberation against the Khmer Rouge. The powerful provincial figures were handpicked by Hun Sen, and they remained loyal to him. Ranariddh's partymen generally held foreign passports, and did not appear to have the stomach for the heat and dust of the poverty-stricken countryside, or the bullets that flew out of the tall grass. Compared to the CPP, Funcinpec was minuscule.

Soon after the elections Ranariddh and Hun Sen worked hard at building and polishing the façade of a cohesive government and, for a time, they succeeded in presenting a united front. The first and second prime ministers even went abroad on joint official visits, and praised each other unstintingly. But it was just a brittle façade, doomed to crack under pressure. Ranariddh grew increasingly frustrated with the awesome power of the CPP which his Funcinpec could not match.

Their insecurities stemmed from size. Hun Sen was always on edge because he had to control a vast country on a shoestring budget; Ranariddh was concerned that his party was unable to manage its own affairs, let alone run the country.

One of Ranariddh's complaints was that, as the first prime minister, he could not get his partymen appointed to posts in the ministry of information, or as judges—two departments that were stacked by the CPP.

But Hun Sen said: "Ranariddh forgot the difference between public and political functions. These officials work for the public, which is neutral. They do not serve the policy of a political party. They serve the policy of the royal government as a whole. Further, the judges should be independent, and should not be appointed by political parties, or the government."

It sounded like a self-serving argument. Nevertheless, within the government Hun Sen's power was at its peak, though within his own party his authority and political style was questioned and criticised. A congress of the CPP, held in 1996, generated speculation that factions existed within the party. Hun Sen quickly scotched the rumours.

"The CPP is a most democratic party," he said. "Party members dare to express their opinions, and criticise other party members who commit mistakes. We cannot say that there are divisions in the CPP, but we can say that there are people who dare to express their opinions. The CPP is more democratic than other political parties."

It was alleged that the CPP was funded by rich Cambodian businessmen, but Hun Sen dismissed these suggestions as well.

"The CPP gets its funds from the donations and contributions made by a large number of party members," he said. "This kind of an allegation is slanderous."

As these controversies boiled over, a falling-out between the two prime ministers seemed imminent. How did relations with Ranariddh sour?

"Tension in the coalition government broke out when Ranariddh decided to seek a military balance between Funcinpec and the CPP on January 20, 1996, and [made inflammatory statements] at the Funcinpec congress in March 1996," Hun Sen said. "I did not have any personal contradictions with Ranariddh, but Ranariddh did betray his partners in the royal government by illegally smuggling weapons, clandestinely building up his forces, holding secret talks with the outlawed Khmer Rouge, and infiltrating troops, many of whom were Khmer Rouge soldiers, into Phnom Penh."

The final provocation was a secret pact between Ranariddh and the Khmer Rouge that was signed in early-July 1997. The dangerous alliance could not go unanswered, Hun Sen said. On July 4, his forces moved against troops loyal to Ranariddh, and destroyed them in short order.

What was till then a strong suspicion stood confirmed—that Hun Sen had become the most powerful man in Cambodia. Many voters, the more than thirty-eight per cent who voted for the CPP in the 1993 elections, felt that only a strong leader like Hun Sen could hold the fractured country together. Equally, the forty-five per cent who voted for Ranariddh disagreed vociferously. They wanted democracy of the freewheeling kind to be introduced into a country that had seen only various shades of authoritarian government.

STRONGMAN

The news always arrived late in Vung Tau.

A quiet beach resort in south Vietnam, Vung Tau, known as *Cap Saint Jacques* during the French colonial rule, was swept by cool seabreezes blowing in from the South China Sea the year round. Vung Tau's beaches were undiscovered and unspoilt by tourists. Only a few Russian oil-rig workers and their wives lounged on deckchairs. Time stood perfectly still. The newspapers were a day old, sometimes two, which added to the resort's remoteness. And it was not too far from Cambodia. For these reasons it was Hun Sen's preferred holiday spot.

Hun Sen, Bun Rany, and their children were sleeping in their suite after a relaxing day on the beach, when, in the early hours of July 5, 1997 the ringing of the mobile phone woke him up. Groggily Hun Sen picked up the phone. The caller was a member of his staff in Phnom Penh who informed him that Ranariddh's troops were digging in for an offensive against the government's forces. For Hun Sen the news came early while Vung Tau slept. Cutting short the family vacation he flew back on his helicopter to his country residence in Takhmau near Phnom Penh at about 10 am the same day.

Unlike Vung Tau the news arrived early in Phnom Penh. When Hun Sen listened to the Voice of America that day, and rifled through the news reports over the following days, he was surprised and bemused that the media had suddenly elevated him to the status of a "strongman".

"It is not yet correct to call me a strongman," he told the authors after the event. "I will recognise that I am a strongman when I succeed in eliminating the poverty of the Cambodian people and bring peace, economic development, and security to Cambodia. In the near future I will make every effort to have the forthcoming elections held in a free, fair, and democratic manner, and without intimidation."

Hun Sen's holiday in Vung Tau was not a state secret. As had been the practice, the two prime ministers, Ranariddh and Hun Sen, were expected to inform each other, and the council of ministers, in advance about their travel plans. Hun Sen notified the government that he would be on vacation in Vung Tau from July 1-7. Accompanying him and Bun Rany were their children who were studying in the USA, Singapore, and France. It was a family reunion till it was cut short.

Ranariddh did not tell the government when exactly he would go abroad. He originally said that he would depart for France on July 9, but he abruptly left the country, in secret, on July 4 just before the fighting began. Even before gunfire rattled the streets of Phnom Penh, Ranariddh had been given advance warning of trouble, and had hurriedly taken a flight out to Bangkok.

In swift moves Hun Sen effectively overthrew Ranariddh when his forces attacked and destroyed his rival's army in clashes on July 4 and 5. Phnom Penh burned, people ran from their homes, and the sound of artillery, mortar, and automatic weapons shattered the serenity of the slow-paced capital.

The people could not understand why the fighting had broken out. They feared that civil war had returned like some unwanted ghost from the past. Cambodians who tuned into the Voice of America listened to Ranariddh accusing Hun Sen of launching a *coup d'état* against him. The government dismissed the charges. It said that if Hun Sen had intended to stage a *coup* he would not have been holidaying abroad, and that he would have been present in the capital to manage the action. Rather, the fighting was orchestrated, and launched, by Ranariddh who was in Phnom Penh on the eve of the clashes while Hun Sen was abroad, it said. And, having done so, Ranariddh fled to safety in Bangkok just hours before the fighting broke out. Ranariddh's version of events was the exact opposite: that he had done nothing illegal or provocative, and that Hun Sen's forces had launched the attack first.

The prelude to the clashes, the government said, was the "illegal" formation of two Funcinpec military strongholds—a garrison at Wat Phniet in Kompong Speu province, and the gathering of forces around the residence of General Chao Sambath, a senior Funcinpec commander.

When the government received complaints from officials in Kompong Speu that an "illegal" garrison had been set up there, it asked Funcinpec General Nhiek Bun Chhay to relocate his troops to the barracks at the Tang Krasang base in Phnom Penh. But he refused. All the troops belonging to the Cambodian factions were supposed to have been merged with the Royal Cambodian Armed Forces (RCAF), but this understanding was often breached. On the night of July 4 the RCAF chief of staff, General Ke Kim Yan, tried to get Nhiek Bun Chhay to shut down the illegal garrison, and move his troops. The latter kept stalling. An ultimatum was issued to Nhiek Bun Chhay to shut his base by 5.30 am on July 5.

There were no signs of closure. At 6 am, Ke Kim Yan ordered that the base be surrounded, and at 6.30 am RCAF troops entered and disarmed the illegally recruited troops.

At the same time the residence of General Chao Sambath had turned into a mini-garrison. Repeated attempts to get his troops to surrender their weapons failed. After the illegal forces in Kompong Speu were disarmed, troops under Nhiek Bun Chhay's command, based at Pochentong Airport, seized the airport on July 5, and shut it down. They arrested several airport officials. At about 5 pm reinforcements from Nhiek Bun Chhay's Tang Krasang military base moved to the airport to reinforce their position. The seizure of the airport was seen by the government as a hostile act aimed at preventing Hun Sen from returning from Vung Tau.

The same morning Hun Sen appeared on state television. He told the people to remain calm, and urged the troops to return to their barracks. At about 3 pm peace in Phnom Penh was shattered for the first time since the liberation of Cambodia in 1979. As the military police approached the residence of Chao Sambath they came under fire from within, and from nearby buildings. The military police then used a T-55 tank in a show of force, but the rebels blew up its treads with an anti-tank rocket. As the area was heavily populated with civilians, the military police could not retaliate until the residents left their homes.

Soon afterwards, the two sides clashed at three places: the residence of Nhiek Bun Chhay, at Pochentong Airport, and at Tang Krasang military base. People cowered in fear as their city resounded with the deep bass of DK-82 mortars, the booming of DK-75 guns mounted on armoured personnel carriers, and the rattling of 100 mm guns mounted on tanks. As night fell over the burning city, and the thundery sounds of gunfire stopped, the stunned city dwellers breathed a sigh of relief.

Hun Sen and his national commanders did not sleep that night. They hunkered down to review the situation. Hun Sen's training as a guerrilla commander was put to use as he took charge. In the early hours of the morning of July 6 the decision was taken to launch mopping-up operations.

But Ranariddh's forces did not give up. They went on the offensive. Two columns of Funcinpec tanks and troops moved out of the Tang Krasang base at

4 am, and rolled towards the capital. The government reacted by throwing a cordon around the house of Chao Sambath, and tried to prevent the two tank columns from entering the city.

. On the way to the city Nhiek Bun Chhay's forces captured an arms warehouse where most of the weapons imported by Ranariddh were stored. When his forces reached the outer limits of the city their advance was blocked by government forces. The superior forces of Nhiek Bun Chhay were pitted against the military police.

In this perilous situation Hun Sen ordered his élite bodyguards to rush from Takhmau to join the combat because the other RCAF units were already deployed in the city, and the provincial units were too far away to be recalled in time. At 9.30 am bodyguards attached to Regiment 70, backed by three tanks and three armoured personnel carriers, reached the line of fighting to support the military police and the special forces. Two government tanks were destroyed in the morning battles.

A new front opened up in the afternoon. The forces deployed at Ranariddh's residence and its periphery began firing. Forces belonging to Funcinpec General Serey Kosal attacked the house of government minister Sok An, but were repulsed. Next, the government forces attacked Ranariddh's residence and forced the troops holed up inside to surrender.

At 2.30 pm Ranariddh's forces, positioned within his Funcinpec party headquarters near the Chroy Changva bridge, fired on government forces that were deployed close by. Ranariddh's forces were overwhelmed in quick time.

The final assault on the Tang Krasang base began around 3.30 pm when reinforcements were rushed to assist Hun Sen's bodyguards. Forces from Military Region 2 arrived after completing their operations against the Funcinpec party headquarters. Brigade 444 from Military Region 3, backed by six tanks, drove down from Kompong Speu. Together they attacked Nhiek Bun Chhay's position from the rear, inflicting heavy casualties on their adversary. By 6 pm, troops of Brigade 444 captured the residence of Chao Sambath, and by 7 pm Ranariddh's forces were in scattered retreat.

In the coming days Hun Sen explained why he took tough pre-emptive action against Ranariddh's military commanders who had embarked on a secret military build-up, and moved their forces to Phnom Penh without the approval of the ministry of defence. To add to the provocation Ranariddh imported a huge cache of weapons without the consent of the ministry of defence. His generals strengthened their units by inducting Khmer Rouge soldiers. Ranariddh's secret negotiations with the Khmer Rouge, aimed at forging an alliance, was seen as a declaration of war. The moderate Ranariddh was replaced by a politician hungry for military parity with Hun Sen, and driven by a desire to safeguard his position by using armed force. It was a fatal mistake to directly challenge the emerging strongman.

When Ranariddh saw that Hun Sen had succeeded in getting Khmer Rouge leader Ieng Sary to break away from Pol Pot in 1996, the royalists tried to forge an alliance with other guerrilla factions. But there was a difference. Hun Sen did not induct the Khmer Rouge into his forces, whereas Ranariddh's alliance was aimed at using the Khmer Rouge to strengthen his own forces, a motive that was not lost on the Khmer Rouge.

A secret Khmer Rouge meeting that was exposed by the *Phnom Penh Post* in its May 22-June 4, 1998 edition, confirmed suspicions that Ranariddh was again joining forces with his old battlefield allies. The report said that the Khmer Rouge had accepted Ranariddh's overtures to join his National United Front, but only to strengthen itself to later betray Ranariddh, and take power to complete its aborted peasant revolution.

These disclosures suggested that Ranariddh's claims, that he had never cooperated with the Khmer Rouge, were false. They also served to justify Hun Sen's action to destroy Ranariddh's military. The Khmer Rouge papers were obtained by the *Post* reporters on May 15, 1998 in Choam, some fourteen kilometres from Anlong Veng, at a house next to Pol Pot's, and near the burnt out remains of his funeral pyre. The documents were authenticated on May 19 by Pich Chheang, a former Khmer Rouge ambassador to China, and by Yim San, a commander of the Khmer Rouge Division 980.

One of the entries in the seized documents said: "Ranariddh's boat is sinking in the sea, but our boat is not. We have to help him but the way we help is to offer him a stick—not a hand, not an embrace, not to let him cling to our boat, or we all die. We have to play a trick."

A Khmer Rouge official, Ta Tem, was quoted as saying: "The Front is not important. Signing to join the Front obtains us legitimacy. Once we are legitimate the world will want to help us...The Front is only a transition to grab forces, not to go to die, but to grab forces and fight the *yuon*."(A pejorative word for the Vietnamese).

As he lost influence within his government, and among his partymen who could not tolerate his authoritarian style, Ranariddh grew frustrated and needed to forge an alliance with other Cambodians to shore up his political base and recruit troops that could stand up to the forces loyal to Hun Sen. There was only one way to accomplish this impossible task. He had to turn to the Khmer Rouge for help.

By 1996 Ranariddh's Funcinpec was a pale shadow of its former self. The party was weakened with the sacking of finance minister Sam Rainsy from the government in 1994, and from the party in 1995, as well as the arrest and exile of foreign minister Norodom Sirivudh in 1995. At the time, Ranariddh denounced Sirivudh for plotting to kill Hun Sen. Worse, his Funcinpec party was plagued by the fear that the CPP might win the election in 1998.

For his part, Ranariddh was frustrated at every step. He was unable to get his people appointed to posts in the ministry of information, or as judges to the law courts. He felt overwhelmed by the awesome power and reach of the CPP's civilian administration. As a result, Ranariddh mounted a scathing attack on his coalition partner, the CPP, at Funcinpec's party congress in March 1996.

The congress began on a harmonious note. Ranariddh even invited Hun Sen to attend the opening session where banners in the meeting hall proclaimed, "Long live the Funcinpec-CPP alliance". No sooner had Hun Sen departed from the session than Ranariddh ripped apart the idea of sharing power, and accused the government of being a puppet of the Vietnamese. He then threatened to withdraw from the coalition.

A weakened Ranariddh began making overtures to Sirivudh. The CPP saw in this a double game that was intended to destabilise the coalition. As Funcinpec built up its forces, Ranariddh imported almost three tonnes of weapons to arm his soldiers. The weapons were secretly imported in Ranariddh's name as "spare parts". When the container was inspected at the southern Sihanoukville port, the authorities found rockets, AK-47 assault rifles, hand guns, and ammunition. General Choa Phirun, the chief of the department of material and technique of the ministry of national defence, said that Ranariddh's "spare parts" were imported without the knowledge of his department, and without the approval of the general staff, the ministry of defence, the commanders-in-chief, or the royal government.

As Ranariddh grew more radical he promoted hardliners such as Serey Kosal and Nhiek Bun Chhay to higher posts in his military. When a state-owned television station refused to air a broadcast by Serey Kosal it was attacked with rockets and assault rifles. These isolated events eventually erupted in the outbreak of fighting, and the overthrow of Ranariddh.

Although Ranariddh sought refuge in Bangkok he still faced criminal charges for illegally importing the weapons. Ranariddh was loath to face charges in a Phnom Penh military court. After months of uncertainty, during which Hun Sen insisted that if Ranariddh returned he would be taken straight from the airport to jail, Hun Sen relented and proposed an amnesty for him. Ranariddh was ultimately given a royal amnesty by Sihanouk.

But politically Ranariddh was weakened, and his party had split into at least nine factions. He was stripped of his parliamentary immunity, and replaced as the first prime minister in an August 6, 1997 vote in the national assembly.

After the military takeover Hun Sen told us: "Ranariddh is in conflict with the law. The court will have to decide his case according to the law. I have never considered Ranariddh my enemy, therefore I proposed an amnesty for him over the sentence that was passed by the court."

"We did not take strong action against Funcinpec but against an extremist group led by Ranariddh, and a number of his generals," he added.

But several ominous questions remained. Surely, the killing of more than forty Ranariddh supporters could have been avoided.

"I did not want the fighting to happen, but Ranariddh and his generals did not give us any other option," Hun Sen said. "It was inevitable that there would be casualties on both sides, as well as among the people."

. Was the destruction of Ranariddh's residence an intentional act, or did the troops get carried away in the heat of the moment?

"Fighting always causes damage to human life and property, whether it belongs to individuals, or to political parties," Hun Sen said. "It is better not to cause the fighting."

Hun Sen's calculated gamble had shown that he could defy the USA and Asean, even if it meant being denied aid by the former, or membership of the regional grouping in the short term. He counted on winning both those objectives as early as 1998.

Not a single country labelled Hun Sen's action a *coup*. But Ranariddh said: "We must call a cat a cat. It was a *coup*, of course."

For his part, Hun Sen told us: "I was displeased when people said that I had staged a coup because, at the time, all my children had come back home from New York and Singapore, and my mother was with me. If I was to stage a *coup* I would not call my children back home, and keep my mother in the house around which the fighting was going on."

The USA merely suspended two-thirds of its US$35 million in annual aid, but the Clinton administration stopped short of calling it a *coup*. Doing so would have rendered any future aid to Cambodia illegal under US law which bans funds to a régime that results from a putsch. The process of resuming aid would have become tangled in endless congressional debates, and the ultimate sufferers would have been the Cambodian people. Japan refused to cut its US$70 million in aid, while China, Asean, Australia, and the European Union were not entirely averse to the emergence of a strong leader who would, they hoped, finally stop a protracted civil war. A major setback to Hun Sen was the refusal by Asean to admit Cambodia into its ranks at its ministerial meeting on July 10, 1997.

Visibly disappointed by Asean's double standards in admitting Myanmar despite the human rights abuses committed by its military junta, while denying membership to Cambodia, Hun Sen turned towards China for support. He paid obeisance to Beijing by shutting down Taiwan's representative office in Phnom

Penh after accusing it of supporting Ranariddh. China's embassy in Phnom Penh said that it appreciated the shift to a one-China policy.

With Ranariddh in self-imposed exile, Sihanouk lent his support to the duo of Hun Sen, who remained the second prime minister, and Ung Huot, who was appointed the first prime minister by a vote in the national assembly on August 6. Sihanouk did not endorse his son Ranariddh's bid to represent the country at the United Nations as he was not too close to him, and instead approved the names of officials appointed by the powerful Phnom Penh pair. Sihanouk, earlier, did not condemn the military clashes that led to Ranariddh's overthrow. His refusal to support Ranariddh, therefore, revealed the tensions in the royal family.

"The king is neutral, and above all political parties," Hun Sen said. "Furthermore, their majesties, the king and queen, have as many as eleven million children who have always called on them as father and mother, grandfather and grandmother. Therefore, it is certain that the king will not take sides with one man against another. It is the generous heart of the king that I clearly understand."

While France and Japan supported Hun Sen, the USA wanted to see the return of Ranariddh.

"The current tendency is to open the door for all political parties and politicians, including Ranariddh, to participate in the polls," Hun Sen said. "The royal government has done everything possible in this direction."

Even as thirty-nine political parties registered to contest the general election in July 1998, the most powerful personality was clearly Hun Sen who appeared to have positioned himself to lead his country well into the next century. Backed by his military, supported by a huge administrative network, and protected by his bodyguards, the youthful leader seemed impervious to any future *coup d'état* as a tight cordon of handpicked military and civilian leaders was fiercely loyal to him.

"It was on this basis that I advised Ranariddh, and all the leaders, that if they would like to topple me militarily they would have to wait for ten or fifteen years," Hun Sen said. "They would have to wait until the people I recruited had retired because ninety per cent of the generals, and the young officers, are my people. The deputy governor of Siem Reap is a two-star general, whom I recruited.

The people who have been sharing [power] with me, are now spread throughout the country."

"They could not turn the gun against me," he continued. "They would not refuse to carry out an order if Hun Sen gave that order. It's a big mistake on the part of Ranariddh. I advised Ranariddh that if he would like to score a victory over Hun Sen he would have to play smarter politics than Hun Sen. It would be dangerous for him if he launches any military adventure. Out of twenty-four hours in a day we needed only eleven hours to put an end to the incident."

The people who have been sharing power [with me] are now spread throughout the country.

They would not turn the gun against their... he continued. They would not refuse to carry out an order if Imp Sen gave that order. It is his privilege on the part of Ranariddh backed Ranariddh that I he would like to seize a victory everything Sen he would have to play smarter politics than Hun Sen. I would be dangerous for him if he launches any military adventure. Out of twenty-four hours in a day we reflected only about three hours on end to the problem.

Six

RED RUBBLE

PHNOM PENH'S COMMUNISTS

His political bosses in the Kampuchean People's Revolutionary Party (KPRP) told him to win friends abroad, and put an end to the country's isolation. It was a difficult task for the newly-installed prime minister who, in 1985, had doors slammed on him and his KPRP by the non-communist countries in Asia and the West.

Four years later the situation remained just as grim for the People's Republic of Kampuchea (PRK) despite its attempt to whitewash its image by changing its name to the State of Cambodia (SOC). But it would not wash. Hun Sen spent nights in his Takhmau home worrying about these matters. There was little he could do to counter the press reports that routinely called his government a "pariah state". The SOC needed just about everything—foreign investments and aid to develop the country, and weapons to arm the military. Hun Sen's main ally, the rapidly fragmenting Soviet Union, could no longer be counted on to supply weapons free of cost.

Hun Sen scanned the map of the world. His country was ringed by an embargo. The only non-communist country that supported his government was India.

Hun Sen did not waste his India card. He played it whenever he could. On a visit to New Delhi in October 1990 he asked the Indian government to help find a solution to the civil war. Hun Sen and the Indian Minister for External Affairs, Inder Kumar Gujral, discussed the prospects for peace in Cambodia that the Indian officials said was almost within grasp. But they did not reveal much else.

In private Hun Sen asked Gujral for military aid. The request stayed secret.

On a visit to Singapore in 1993, Gujral, who was no longer the foreign minister but remained a member of parliament, told us that Hun Sen had, in fact, asked India during the October 1990 meeting to supply arms to Cambodia so that it could defend itself against its enemies, principally the Khmer Rouge.

"I didn't know how to respond to Hun Sen's request because I did not know whether he had made this kind of a request to my predecessor," Gujral said.

In the end, Gujral did not make a commitment to supply arms. But that did not jeopardise the closeness between India and Cambodia—Indian army troops that served as United Nations' peacekeepers during the elections in 1993 were injured fighting the Khmer Rouge.

In some respects the country's isolation was self-imposed by the SOC. In 1990 there was a ban on the import of most foreign newspapers. As far as the vice-minister of culture Pen Yet was concerned the only newspapers permitted to enter the country were those from the socialist countries.

The socialist bearhug had smothered Cambodia in other ways as well. There were just nine foreign embassies in the capital, eight from the socialist bloc alone. Diplomats from the Soviet Union, Cuba, Hungary, Bulgaria, Poland, Czechoslovakia, Laos, and Vietnam were honoured guests who had access to the top leadership. In return, the communists who ran Cambodia were able to extract financial aid from the European socialist bloc. But as the decade of the 1990s began, the devastated socialist bloc economies were in no shape to bail out Cambodia. Efforts by Phnom Penh's communists to look for other sources of aid were rebuffed.

Cambodia's only non-communist ally, India, had shut down its embassy along with a mass exodus of foreign missions when the Khmer Rouge overthrew the Lon Nol régime in 1975, and captured power. When the Khmer Rouge was, in turn, ousted by the military forces of Vietnam and Cambodian rebels in 1979, India was the first non-communist country to recognise Phnom Penh the very next year.

The socialist bloc diplomats, too, returned to a friendlier Phnom Penh to open large missions. At the time the Indian mission attracted a lot of attention, but did little else. Indian diplomats hardly boosted trade between the two countries; their presence was more a show of solidarity with another Indian ally, the Vietnamese, for having liberated Cambodia from the Khmer Rouge. The existence of the Indian embassy in Phnom Penh was proof of New Delhi's closeness to Vietnam and Cambodia at a time when both these countries were considered parlahs by the non-communist world.

The most powerful embassy in the capital was that of the Soviet Union whose run down compound was at odds with the fact that it was the most influential entity in the city, next only to the Hun Sen government. As we approached the electrically-operated wrought iron embassy gate in May 1990, it swung open by itself. More Cold War stereotypes lay ahead. We were met by a sullen Russian woman who asked us to wait for the only official who had been authorised to speak on behalf of the embassy. His name was V. Loukianov. Although he wore formal office attire, Loukianov was completely relaxed and, with his David Niven moustache, was so unlike the typical Soviet diplomat. In his clipped British accent, acquired at a Moscow language course, he was willing to talk about Cambodia with rare candour. We agreed to meet for dinner at the Mekong restaurant of the Cambodiana Hotel.

'This is a wild place," said Loukianov, carving a piece of prime rib. "A few people have become rich overnight. They are driving around town signing deals by the dozen, but many are signed and forgotten."

Hun Sen's Phnom Penh was a city of a million aberrations. While a rich minority of Cambodians signed business deals with its foreign partners, and treated itself to sumptuous ten-course Chinese banquets, an unfortunate eighty per cent of the people seldom had meat, or their favourite *pra hok,* on their tables.

"There are some truly bizarre things going on," Loukianov said. "At this very hotel, a Cambodian flush with cash flung US$500 at the feet of a singer for singing his favourite Chinese song."

Loukianov was aware of the embarrassing similarities between communist Cambodia and the Leninists who ran the Soviet Union, bonded as they were in a socialist alliance that had spread itself rather thickly over Cambodia, and neighbouring Vietnam and Laos. Sadly for isolated Cambodia, the Soviets had by 1990 cut back severely on their trade credits, and in another bizarre display of camaraderie, Moscow had decided to help the poor country by training Cambodians to set up a circus. It did not make the Cambodians smile. Neither did liberal supplies of free Cuban sugar sweeten things. The Cubans went one better. They sent a boxer to train them in the art of pugilism. The Cambodians were not amused.

Those were hard times. The Soviet government was in bad odour at home and in Cambodia. Mikhail Gorbachev's efforts to reform the bankrupt Soviet economy were faltering, making it convenient for the Cambodians to blame the Soviets, in part, for their economic problems. The Soviet commercial officer in Phnom Penh, Nikolay Orekhov, told us that his country could no longer finance the construction of ports, roads, and bridges, but would continue to construct printing presses free of cost, and help Cambodia set up its own circus.

To top it all, a Cuban junior diplomat we met, proudly said that Cuba's relations with Cambodia had improved. Havana had not only sent a boxing coach, but had also dispatched a Hispanic professor to Phnom Penh.

"A little knowledge of Spanish may help Cambodia improve its relations with the Spanish-speaking world," he said, sipping lime juice at his residence-cum-embassy.

Some Soviet and Cuban policies were irrelevant to the point of being farcical.

While a handful of people in Phnom Penh would have turned up for practice sessions with the boxing coach, or for Spanish lessons, the vast majority of huddled Cambodians, living in scattered villages in their fragile wooden huts on stilts, did not need lectures. They urgently wanted shelter, drinking water, and electricity.

Cambodians were a sad and broken people eager to impress outsiders, but their brave smiles could not conceal the wounds within. Many remembered the holocaust. How thousands of people living in Phnom Penh, women and children included, were tortured. Scorpions were set upon womens' breasts, their nails extracted, and, if they were lucky, death came quickly by the gun. Those who survived these indignities were herded cattle-like into communes. Times had changed. Pol Pot's Maoist communists were now replaced by Soviet-style communists.

"LOOK around you, and you will see many communist party men sitting around the bars and enjoying their whiskies," said Vanna, our taxidriver. The communists had begun coming out into the open in their frumpy business suits tailored in Phnom Penh, and were openly striking business deals with Chinese businessmen from Singapore and Thailand.

"Look at them, their salary is less than US$25 a month, and yet they own houses and cars, and they dine out," .

Much later, Mam Sophana, a Cambodian architect who was trained in America, and returned to help rebuild his country, gently admonished us for our haste to label Cambodian officials as corrupt.

Sophana said: "Outsiders are stupid if they point a finger at the Hun Sen government, and say 'you are corrupt, you are no good'. They should see the reality before they talk. If these people, Heng Samrin and Hun Sen, were not brave enough they would have given up long ago. Corruption is a very complicated word. You have to know the roots. How much salary does a civil servant get? Just US$20 a month. The government does not have the money to pay higher salaries. So, how can they survive? Let those people who say 'Cambodians are corrupt' live in Cambodia for a month, and they will know they are not corrupt."

Pen Yet, the softspoken, moustachioed vice-minister of culture and information, threw up his hands in a grand gesture of helplessness at another form of corruption where the worst offenders were not the impoverished Cambodians, but rich antique dealers who were stripping the Angkor temples off their ancient sculptures.

"Cambodia has lost about twenty per cent of her ancient treasures to smugglers, and we plan to enlist the services of Interpol to catch them," Pen Yet said. "London is the main destination for the Cambodian treasures which are sold at auctions. We are now making a list of the antique objects we have lost, and the list will be given to Interpol for action."

The country, Pen Yet said, had more than 1,000 ancient monuments, and it was these places the smugglers were raiding. Shaking his head, he said that Cambodians stole antiques, and sold them to foreigners who made a killing on the world markets. Smugglers were not the only threat. The civil war had taken its toll as well, with militant factions stealing antiques to buy weapons. The Khmer Rouge had been blamed for decamping with gold and silver antiques from the Silver Pagoda, located within the Royal Palace in Phnom Penh. Some Cambodians dismissed the allegation that the Khmer Rouge had pilfered the antiques. The guerrillas, they said, were disciplined and completely incorruptible. There were exceptions: a Khmer Rouge leader, Ta Mok, was found in possession of rare sculptures taken from Angkor Wat. When the Cambodian army attacked Ta Mok's residence in 1993, it found a treasure trove he had left behind in the hurry to escape.

Sophana's absurd logic made perfect sense to those who were capable of twisting the system for their own ends, but left the whimpering masses, the ninety per cent of the country's estimated nine million people, on the edge of poverty. There were no reliable statistics on national population as the last census, in 1962, had recorded a population of 5.72 million. It was only in mid-1998 that a new census would reveal that the population had grown to 11.42 million.

The communist government led by Hun Sen was in a cleft-stick. Shunned by the non-communist world as an illegitimate pariah government installed by Vietnam, Phnom Penh was denied recognition and international loans. The state lurched from financial crisis to crisis, and came to rely excessively on the Soviet

Union for gasoline and fertiliser, and on Cuba for necessities like sugar. There was simply no money to pay salaries to civil servants. As a result, the state did what all parlous communist governments had done at one time or another: it decided to provide state employees with subsidised goods every month—eighteen kilogrammes of rice, two bars of Soviet-made soap, and one kilogramme of sugar. All other Cambodians were left to fend for themselves. Paupers and prime ministers alike were at the mercy of a rotten system.

Two years later, in 1992, when we met Hun Sen for the first time, he said: "When I began as a foreign minister in 1979, my salary was in the form of rations—sixteen kilogrammes of rice and six kilogrammes of maize. Nowadays, the situation is not as pessimistic as in 1979. That is why we should not be too pessimistic, or optimistic."

As Phnom Penh's rich communists drank themselves into a stupor every night, the capital's poor children took to begging. The madness and the logic of the jungle economy and the cruel contradictions of Cambodian life did not go unnoticed by the Khmer Rouge. Those who tuned into the guerrillas' clandestine radio station were entertained by hysterical broadcasters lambasting the Phnom Penh communists for selling the Cambodian economy to foreign speculators.

The Khmer Rouge, who had banned money and enterprise during their bizarre rule, had not changed. They ridiculed the lopsided economic structure where just one per cent of the people ate well, and the rest were deprived. Khmer Rouge leaders we had met, such as Mak Ben, a former military commander, spoke scathingly of the Phnom Penh communists. But Mak Ben had forgotten that life during the Khmer Rouge's so-called egalitarian society had been much worse as the poorest people became even poorer after Pol Pot shut down the economy.

Hun Sen's administration, strapped for funds, came up against a brick wall. With development arrested and the country still isolated, the Cambodians lived in a bygone age. The only shop that stocked books in the capital was the *Librairie d'Etat* at 224 Achar Mean Boulevard, proud stockists of several Soviet pamphlets, but not a word in English, or French.

The truth emerged that all foreign publications were banned except a few

Soviet journals. But even if foreign papers had been allowed to circulate, who would have read them? Few tourists were visible on the streets, and nobody could give a straight answer as to how many had been bold enough to set foot in the war-torn land.

A few months later the dapper Sam Promonea, the general-director of tourism, told us that 16,993 tourists visited Cambodia in 1990, most of whom were Japanese, followed by the French, Germans, Swiss, and Italians. These were not rich business-class travellers, he said; most were backpackers who were quite happy living in cheap guesthouses.

The ban on foreign newspapers was broken at the newly-opened Cambodiana Hotel in November 1990, and a few other establishments. Stacks of the *Bangkok Post,* a daily newspaper published in Thailand, were delivered to hotel guests in their rooms, a day late because of a delay in transportation from Bangkok.

The real Cambodia went to bed hungry, and limped in the streets of Siem Reap. Yim Sokan, an eleven-year-old who worked at a petrol kiosk in the city, said that he was forced to work because his father, whose legs were blown off by a landmine planted by the Khmer Rouge guerrillas, could not find a job. So, young Sokan had to support a family of six. For every unlettered Sokan in Siem Reap there was a child, just as unfortunate of circumstance, just as poor and deprived, but blessed by an ability to speak English, and a little French.

"C'est très difficile," Sokan said about his life, and added: *"Je travaille beaucoup et je suis fatigué."*

Under the communist régime English remained a less spoken language because most of the scholarships were provided by the Soviet Union and the socialist bloc. But in July 1993, the new royal government that came to power following elections in May that year, openly supported the use of French, and abandoned the Russian language. The reason was simple. France, having reopened its embassy earlier, had offered to rebuild the educational system, provided the medium of instruction was French. But France's campaign to put the Gallic language on Cambodian tongues foundered.

Over 1,000 students staged a protest against the use of French as a medium of instruction for courses at the Institute of Technology in the capital. The students said that a knowledge of French would not help them find jobs. One of Sihanouk's sons, Ranariddh, a former professor at a university in France who had just become the first prime minister, told the students that they had no choice but to study French.

By December 1993, Sihanouk had jumped into the fray. From his hospital bed in Beijing where he had been undergoing treatment for cancer, Sihanouk wrote a paper called *National Education: To Learn French or English?* Curiously, he wrote the paper in French, but argued in support of the use of English.

"This support is legitimate, logical, and realistic because in today's and tomorrow's world, English—as the language of communication and international study—has become, and will inevitably remain, a quasi-universal language," Sihanouk wrote. "Even the young Chinese nurses in the hospital where I am staying are conscientiously learning English."

Cambodian students had nothing personal against French, or any other foreign language. The fact was that they felt cheated. First, they were made to learn Russian by the pro-Soviet governments of Pen Sovann, Chan Si, Heng Samrin, and Hun Sen between 1979-91. At the same time the Vietnamese backers of the régime ensured that Vietnamese was a compulsory subject. Others learnt Romanian because there were Romanian scholarships up for grabs. Now, the students realised that their learning of Russian, Vietnamese, and Romanian had been a waste, and they did not want to speak French either. By 1994 an enterprising Westerner opened a small institute to teach English. It was called the Banana Centre, and residents of the capital were certainly taking to it with a relish.

BY September 1991 Hun Sen's communist government was gripped by a sense of paralysis. It was uncertain about its fate after Sihanouk returned to the Royal Palace in November, twenty-one years after he was overthrown in a palace *coup*. In anticipation of the return of the prince, Cambodian workmen burned skin in the hot sun as they repaired and whitewashed the royal residence. Numbed by decades of civil war, genocide, and poverty, there was no great mood of expectation, no talk of a grand homecoming party for the god-prince who would come back to a vastly improved country. Sihanouk did not have good memories of Phnom Penh because Pol Pot had kept him a prisoner inside his own palace, and restricted his movements. As a result, he could only imagine the kind of destruction that Pol Pot had unleashed. Just before the Vietnamese forces rolled into the capital in 1979, Sihanouk escaped by plane to Beijing. He left behind a city that was turned into a ghost town by the Khmer Rouge.

During Sihanouk's rule the capital resembled a balmy French provincial town with broad boulevards, dance halls, French restaurants, and a gracious lifestyle. Phnom Penh called itself the pearl of Southeast Asia, although Saigon also laid claim to the same status. All that was gone, wiped out by the Khmer Rouge who banned enterprise and money, and turned the country into a concentration camp. Attempts by Hun Sen to revamp the economy ended in failure because of a near total lack of international support. Cambodia was still a pariah. Not only was the Hun Sen government worried about its political future after the prince, considered a master tactician and manipulator, returned to head the Supreme National Council (SNC), made up of all the warring factions, but the very future of Cambodian communism was in danger.

Soviet embassy counsellor Loukianov stroked his David Niven moustache, and said: "Communism in Cambodia is under threat, and that is a source of worry to the leaders in the government."

After decades of abysmal failure Cambodian communism took its last gasps. The ruling party's leaders shudder d in the face of an uncertain future. Realising that the Cambodians would not to erate being ruled by a cabal of Marxists, Hun Sen began earnest preparations to vhitewash the party and the state with a coat of democracy. The government hurriedly drafted a new Constitution, watering down communism as a state ideology. Change was forced upon the Hun Sen government by the sheer pressure of circumstance. The communist party knew it had to change with the times because an historic peace accord to end the civil war would be signed in October 1991. The next step would be the general election, supervised by the United Nations. The government realised that its eleven years of isolated misrule would consign it to oblivion at the elections; it knew that it could not possibly take on the democratic political parties headed by the

Cambodian princes and their supporters.

For all their camaraderie the whitewashed communists who had defected from the Khmer Rouge more than a decade earlier were no match for Sihanouk's personal style. But few in Cambodia seemed worried about the prince's return; they realised that the benign prince could only provide free entertainment with his water festivals, jazz soirées, and unpredictability. Real power would still reside with the communists who had earlier adopted a new name, Cambodian People's Party, or CPP.

It would be a gross injustice to heap all the blame for Cambodia's monumental failures at the CPP's doorstep. The real damage was wreaked by the Khmer Rouge who dismantled the economy, shut down businesses and factories, and systematically murdered Western-trained Cambodian intellectuals, doctors, teachers, and scientists in their mad zeal to build a new Cambodia, a country without any Western influences and imbued with Maoist ideals of an agriculture-based society. Their dislike for money was so extreme that they actually blew up the central bank building at Tou Samouth Boulevard.

After the elections in May 1993 we asked a senior central banker, Tioulong Saumura, why the Khmer Rouge had behaved the way they did. Saumura, a daughter of former Cambodian army chief Nhiek Tioulong who served Sihanouk, had given up her six-figure salary in Paris for a job as the deputy governor of the National Bank of Cambodia that paid merely US$50 a month.

"It has been such a trauma," she said. "When the Khmer Rouge seized power, one building they totally blew up was this one, the central bank, because it was a symbol of capitalism. They wanted to show their hostility against the free market. This building is three years old, and it was rebuilt by the Hun Sen government exactly as it was before."

What a comedown for a country whose treasury buildings had covered a vast area during the reign of the Angkor kings. With an impatient flick of her wrist, Paris-educated Saumura said in strongly French-accented tones: "We want to turn the page. We want to write a good story, and it has to be a good story."

Hun Sen had exactly the same thoughts. He wanted to see his country rise, and take its place among the prosperous economies of Southeast Asia. He spoke about his plans incessantly. He had the power to do it. Alas, he lacked international support.

In the fading evening light, the restored pink-painted National Bank of Cambodia looked like a headless ghost from a savage past come back to haunt a present that seemed no less brutal.

THE EMBARGO

The outsized condor-winged Soviet Ilyushin jet touched down at Phnom Penh's Pochentong Airport. A group of Soviet diplomats stepped off the aircraft. Baggage handlers offloaded crates of vodka, and smaller packages of caviar. There was an even more important piece of cargo aboard—a secret consignment of Cambodian currency notes, the riel.

The bills were printed in Moscow, and flown to Cambodia about once every two months. The Phnom Penh government lacked printing presses. The cash deliveries helped the government survive its isolation until the early 1990s. The Soviets replenished the currency, and maintained the monetary system.

The money would quickly be injected into the market as fresh fuel to the inflationary fire. Michael Ward, a World Bank official stationed in Cambodia as a member of the United Nations Transitional Authority in Cambodia (Untac), said: "As the government's deficit rises, it prints more money."

The state simply printed money to finance the budget, as did many governments, sending inflation spiralling upwards to triple digits. Not only did the government print money, Ward said, the Khmer Rouge, too, issued xeroxed coupons which passed for money in the northwestern zones it controlled.

After Untac took charge of the finances of the Hun Sen government it ordered the state to stop printing its currency in the Soviet Union. But Phnom Penh would not admit that it flew in bills pressed in the Soviet Union.

The minister concerned with the issue was evasive. Prince Norodom Chakrapong, a son of Sihanouk, who joined Hun Sen's government in 1992 as a vice-prime minister in charge of civil aviation, denied a report that Untac had prevented a plane-load of riels, printed in Moscow, from being circulated in Cambodia in order to control inflation which was then running at about 150 per cent.

Chakrapong said: "There are many other reasons for inflation, including the heavy spending by Untac staff which has sent the price of food soaring."

After surviving for several indistinguished years as a country without currency—the Khmer Rouge had banned the use of money—the state reintroduced the riel in 1980. But in 1979 the new government did not have the wherewithal to issue currency, and it paid state employees in kind—sixteen to twenty-four kilogrammes of rice per month. Employees were given essential goods at subsidised prices. Salaries for civil servants were introduced only in 1983, and raised to 6,600 riels in 1988 to allow for the higher cost of living. The emptiness of the state coffers, and the reckless tinkering by untrained financial managers, conspired to cause the riel to plunge from 4 riels to the US dollar to 880 riels to the dollar in 1992, and hit an historic low of 5,000 riels to the dollar in mid-1993, before recovering to 2,500 riels in October 1994. With planned expenditure of 186 billion riels (less than US$100 million) in 1992, and a deficit of 83 billion riels, the government could do precious little to develop the country.

As a result of the withdrawal of the Vietnamese forces from Cambodia in 1989, and the collapse of the Soviet Union soon afterwards, the Hun Sen government was denied direct military support by Hanoi, and economic aid by Moscow. It was a tremendous squeeze on the budget, eighty per cent of which was being funnelled into the armed forces. The government did not have the luxury of being able to buy military hardware because of a lack of funds. Most of the defence budget was spent on salaries for the army, for one good reason: if the army was not paid, it would turn against its own government and, worse, break away to form an organised force of bandits.

The poor people of Cambodia, in silence, endured the bizarre policies of their rulers. Just as some peculiar events came in the shape of a secret cargo of money flown in from Moscow, so at other times odd things had happened on the banks of the Tonle Sap.

The brown banks of the mighty river lay exposed as the water level dropped in the dry season, leaving fish and vegetation to rot under an unforgiving sun. A taxidriver pointed at a disused building on the river bank, and said: "That Sihanouk casino house. Now closing down."

Norodom Sihanouk, god-prince, film-maker, saxophone player, jazz singer, party lover, author, and forever mercurial, came up with an eccentric scheme in the late-1960s to set up a casino in his poor country. That way, he reckoned, his people would grow richer, and the state would earn a windfall. The prince commissioned a Khmer-style building on the banks of the Tonle Sap where a casino began operating. The clatter of the roulette tables was silenced soon enough when the prince was removed in a *coup* in 1970. Some damage had been done anyway. The casino impoverished hundreds of people in Phnom Penh who could not resist a flutter, driving a few to suicide. The prince cut a ridiculous and slightly arch figure.

Soon after Cambodians started gambling with a vengeance, Sihanouk had the slightly better idea of opening a five-star hotel located right next to the ill-starred casino. The *coup* put paid to his scheme. In the end, it took a Singapore company to make the prince's dream a reality. An enormous old building on the banks of the Tonle Sap was refurbished by two Singaporean businessmen and a Cambodian-Chinese named Hui Keung, who divided his time between Phnom Penh and Hong Kong and represented the new breed of Cambodian entrepreneur to emerge after the destruction of the business community by the Khmer Rouge. The trio was among the early risk-takers. They went ahead and invested capital to restore the Cambodiana Hotel, defying an investment embargo by the government of Singapore. They also sloughed off the attendant risks, and made a long-term commitment to a country most businessmen were giving a miss. A spiffy looking hotel opened in June 1990 at a time when the USA, too, had enforced a trade embargo against Cambodia. For its part, Singapore banned its firms from investing capital in Cambodia, but allowed them to trade in goods. Singapore did not want investments to strengthen the Vietnam-backed Hun Sen government in its fight against the resistance forces of Sihanouk, former premier Son Sann, and the Khmer Rouge. The strategy was to keep Cambodia as isolated as possible, and to make Hun Sen's government look, and feel, like a pariah. The embargo gradually crumbled the way embargoes have in other countries that faced them, principally South Africa.

It was a time when politics of the most bizarre kind was played by Southeast Asia's non-communist countries, and the USA. In order to create an international groundswell against the Hun Sen government and its Vietnamese patrons, these countries ensured that Cambodia's United Nations' seat was occupied by the Khmer Rouge, whose officials sat in the general assembly even before the blood of about 1.7 million dead Cambodians could dry on their hands. The guerrillas had been legitimised.

Later, the world would be shocked and dismayed when the same guerrillas whom it supported, murdered three young male tourists from Britain, France, and Australia. They were travelling by train from Phnom Penh to the southern port city of Sihanoukville in July 1994 when the guerrillas raided the train and captured them. When ham-fisted negotiations to obtain their release were ultimately botched, the Cambodian army launched military operations against the guerrilla base, and that failed as well. The remains of the three were found in shallow graves in the countryside, in November.

The Hun Sen government capitalised on the growing presence of foreign businessmen in Phnom Penh, a bustling city which, in 1990, bore scant resemblance to a communist country, even less to a country at war with itself. Lunch at the Mekong restaurant of the Cambodiana Hotel had a carnival feel about it as foreign businessmen, diplomats, journalists, and hordes of Japanese and European tourists laid siege to a French-style buffet spread. A mini-economic boom in the capital seemed set to continue. Michel Horn, the French general manager of the hotel, said that his company would invest even more money in the hotel.

Hun Sen meant business, and enacted a foreign investment law on July 26, 1989, years ahead of many other Asian countries. By 1992 about US$300 million had actually been invested in the country. Coca-Cola had set up a bottling plant in Phnom Penh, and Australian businessmen were brewing Angkor beer in the southern port city of Sihanoukville. A jungle economy took root courtesy of the investment law that bore the seal of President Heng Samrin. The passage of the law provided guarantees that the state would not nationalise or expropriate foreign investments. It was a promise the state would keep, even though no formal courts of appeal existed where foreign firms could take their grievances in case of a dispute. Although the law spelt out the level of taxes foreign firms would pay, some firms circumvented the rules by paying whatever they chose.

Desperate to break free of the noose of the embargoes, the Hun Sen government began hawking the national assets. It awarded six oilfields near the Gulf of Thailand to foreign firms even before the peace accord was signed in October 1991. The firms made substantial investments to explore for oil in offshore Cambodia in the Khmer Trough, close to the Thailand-owned Pattani Trough that supplied most of Thailand's oil. These deals netted an income of US$6 million in 1991, and US$20 million by 1992. Even earlier, a Japanese sawmiller, Okada, had inked a deal to invest US$16 million to set up mills in a venture that further denuded the endangered forests.

As government officials and their foreign business partners felled trees, forest cover in the provinces of Kandal and Takeo near Phnom Penh shrank from fifteen per cent in the early 1960s to zero in the 1980s. Even the Khmer Rouge sold timber concessions to Thai traders with close links to the Thai military. A report by the international law firm Baker & McKenzie advised businessmen who were keen to trade with the Khmer Rouge to fill in a standard business form issued by the guerrillas.

Australian state-run telecommunications firm, OTC International, on cue, signed a deal with the Hun Sen government. It marked a significant breakthrough for Hun Sen as the firm helped pull his government, and his country, out of isolation.

OTC's operations manager in Phnom Penh, Lindsay Harradine, said: "When we came to Cambodia in 1990 there were less than ten operator-assisted lines via Moscow."

That meant if you wanted to call London your call would go through three operators, and it could take forever to get a connection.

"First, you'd call the local operator in Phnom Penh who would call the operator in Moscow, who would in turn call the operator in London, who would finally connect you," Harradine said with a tired smile.

Diplomats spent hours waiting by the phone. Each morning, Western diplomats would pray that a Soviet-supplied Intersputnik satellite dish—which linked Cambodia to the outside world via Moscow—would perform. Throwing caution to the winds and treating the embargo with contempt, OTC signed a ten-year business deal in early 1990 with the Cambodian Directorate of Posts and Telecommunications. In effect, firms like OTC and the dozens of other foreign investors, were following a policy of constructive engagement, rather than a negative policy of isolating the Hun Sen government, whom many businessmen viewed as the grand liberators from the terrible genocide.

The giant Australian firm was helpless when confronted by the lumbering Cambodian bureaucracy. Back then it was no secret that the phone lines were usually dead. What was not known was that the bureaucracy had virtually killed off the telecommunications system. Over time it became apparent that the Department of Posts and Telecommunications, which ran the network, had been hamstrung by governmental meddling. It was a small miracle that the system worked at all.

Curiously, the department remained in deep financial trouble despite turning a profit of 150 million riels (US$96,000) in 1990. The heart of the problem was that government offices and state-run firms—which accounted for eighty per cent of the subscribers—were reluctant to pay their phone bills. It was the same story for the other government utilities, such as the water and electricity departments.

The critics of the Hun Sen government overlooked its economic contributions. The task of rebuilding the country from the millions of broken bits that the Khmer Rouge had left behind fell on the Hun Sen government. Politics aside, the government had a moral obligation to the millions whose lives had been shattered emotionally by the deaths of their loved ones, the loss of their property, and the shutting down of the economy by the guerrillas. For a government that faced a barrage of embargoes, it was a tall order, but a task that Hun Sen and his team did not shrink from.

His government took control of a state where private property rights had been abolished, and property records burnt by the Khmer Rouge, businessmen and intellectuals killed, and factories and banks shut down. Staking a claim to property was a nightmare for the people. All too often as many as three or four families squabbled over the same house whose original owners may have been killed, or were in exile. The communist government, therefore, found it convenient to solve the problem by nationalising land and factories. It later realised its folly, and allowed private ownership of agricultural land.

At the same time the government began leasing factories and land in the cities to foreign investors. Later, Prince Sihanouk would allege that officials of the Hun Sen government had embezzled the money from the leases, and were selling the entire country. Besides having to face these charges, Hun Sen's economic reforms were stymied by internal compulsions to stretch the budget to fight the Khmer Rouge and the forces of Prince Sihanouk and Son Sann along the Thai border.

What kept the penniless country from falling apart? What kept the poor people from marching up to the council of ministers building, where Hun Sen's office was located, and letting loose their anger? After all, the people living in serried little wooden huts balanced precariously on stilts in parched villages, or in boxy slums in the cities, had a long list of complaints. The answer was simply this—the Hun Sen government may not have delivered the basic services such as water, electricity, or even basic housing, but it spared no effort to ensure that by the mid-1980s the country had enough rice.

But the year 1979 was a disaster. As the Khmer Rouge had just been overthrown, and the people newly liberated, there was chaos in the farms, and much of the rice crop was not harvested. As a result famine broke out that year. Rice stocks accumulated by the Khmer Rouge were quickly used up, and the famine was worsened by a severe drought. But the farmers were able to do the impossible. They actually managed to double the rice crop the following year. While people could not afford to eat chicken and pork, there was no shortage of cheap and freely available rice, which was sometimes supplemented by small rice shipments from abroad.

Rice was a time-bomb that could explode if the government failed to sever the link between unscrupulous Cambodian businessmen and their Thai counterparts. Traditionally, local businessmen in cahoots with Thai traders were responsible for creating shortages of rice by selling it just across the border in Thailand where it fetched a price thirty per cent higher than the price fixed by the Cambodian government. The effect of the artificially-created shortage of rice was that it pushed up the price in Cambodia, making it too expensive for the masses. It was nothing new for Asia. From the last days of Mao Zedong to the Deng Xiaoping régime, rice was smuggled out of China to places where it fetched a higher price.

All hell could break loose if the rain gods were unkind to farmers, and a drought came to pass. A bad harvest would spell political disaster for any government that ruled Cambodia. A full blown rice riot would ensure that the party in power would not be re-elected. Australian Lieutenant-General John Sanderson, who served as the force commander of the UN peacekeeping forces in Cambodia, once told us that the nexus between rice traders and Thailand ought to be cut once and for all, for the sake of stability. One way to do that was to erect roadblocks on the highway to Thailand

Roadblocks were needed. But so were motorable roads. There was no blacktop road to the killing fields of Choeung Ek, just a thirty minute drive from Phnom Penh. There was only a dirt-track over which bullock carts, trucks, and cars squeezed past each other, whipping up a screen of dust.

Virtually no roads were built after the 1930s, and the old roads were subjected to incessant bombardment by the Khmer Rouge. The guerrillas resorted to literally cutting away sections of a road to make it impossible to drive. Travel by rail was possible, but not plausible. The more adventurous among the droves of backpackers did not think twice before taking a train journey. Anything could happen, from a raid by bandits, to a Khmer Rouge attack, or an explosion set off by a landmine. There were just two rail lines, each of one-metre gauge. One was the 385 kilometre line from Phnom Penh to the Thai border town of Poipet, built in the 1940s by the former French colonial rulers, and the other was a 263 kilometre line from Phnom Penh to the port of Sihanoukville, built in post-independence Cambodia in the 1960s. On the Sihanoukville line the engine did not lead the train; it came behind a wagon meant to take the brunt of an explosion. A diplomat quipped darkly that those who travelled on the lead wagon travelled free as a concession to the risk they took.

The heavily-armed guards who hung about vacantly in the compartments did not inspire much confidence either, and they were eyed with deep mistrust by the travellers.

Air travel in the 1980s carried similar risks to the trains. Though there were fears that the little Russian-built aircraft could be hit by sniper fire as it made the final approach to land at Siem Reap, a more real danger was the technical safety of the aircraft itself. The minuscule fleet was maintained by slovenly Russians who were notorious for underpaying their technical workers. Kampuchea Airlines, the flag carrier, operated a fleet of three Russian Antonov-24 propeller aircraft, two Tupolev-134 jets, and three MI-8 helicopters. The airline, based at a patio-sized airport in Phnom Penh, valiantly operated regular flights to Siem Reap and Stung Treng, and twice-weekly to Hanoi and Ho Chi Minh City. Travelling from Ho Chi Minh City to Phnom Penh was inconvenient because the twice-weekly flights were almost always full, forcing travellers to undertake an eight-hour journey by taxi, driving through the border at Bavet, surviving a river crossing, armed guards, and sullen immigration officials.

The prevalent perception of Cambodia was of a country where bullock-carts were the preferred mode of transportation. But not many villagers could afford to buy a bullock, or a cart. Still, bicycles and motorcycles were becoming more visible. There were more than 5,000 cars in the cities by 1989, and as many as 60,000 motorcycles. By 1992, the car population had leapt to 40,000, most of which had been brought into the country by the 22,000 UN troops, and the *nouveau riche*.

One of the nastier aspects of living in Cambodia at that time, tourists and residents discovered, was its foul water. The five-star Cambodiana Hotel did not provide potable water in its rooms. The water, pumped from the silted Mekong, ran red—the colour of the government.

The city of Phnom Penh drew its drinking water from the Tonle Sap and Tonle Bassac rivers. The city, unconscionably, pumped raw sewage into the very water it drank. The river water was filtered at three very old French-built treatment plants that often ran out of chemicals, and when that happened, water was simply released to the city without being treated. Till the mid-1990s, a mere twenty per cent of the urban population could turn on a tap, and get treated water. The rest had to use wells, ponds, and streams which posed a serious health hazard. Children suffered acute diarrhea eight times a year, on average. Like the telephone company, the water and electricity departments were cash-strapped because government offices and companies that used the services would not pay their bills.

One of the most absurd acts in the Khmer Rouge burlesque was its decision, between 1975-79, to abolish schools coupled with a brutal pogrom against teachers, academics, artists, writers, and intellectuals, many of whom were killed. Only a lucky few could use Vietnam or Thailand as an escape route to a better life in the West. When the Heng Samrin régime took control it grappled with the impossible task of rebuilding an education system literally out of the graves of dead teachers—an entire teaching profession had been put to the sword. Students had lost four years of education, and would lose several more as the entire system had been laid to waste.

As expected the socialist bloc countries rushed to Cambodia's side, bringing funds and technical assistance to set up new schools, and reviving older ones. Some of the aid came in the shape of training for Cambodian government officials at Moscow's institutes of higher learning. As a result, Cambodian economic officials returned with their heads stuffed with outdated ideas of centralised planning and the supremacy of a command economy, just at the time when neighbouring Thailand and Singapore were vigorously opening their markets to foreign capital.

With just thirty per cent of the people literate, and an average lifespan of a mere fifty years, Cambodia could not possibly slip any lower into the morass of stagnation. Vietnam, which suffered a much longer war against the Chinese, French, and Americans, had done much better with a literacy rate of over eighty per cent, and an average lifespan of sixty-five years. But to give Cambodia its due, the five years of compulsory education had worked wonders. A group of children in Siem Reap amazed visitors with its fluency in English learnt at a local school. They even related a fairly accurate history of Angkor Wat in six minutes, which usually got them a well-earned dollar.

The Moscow-trained officials were, predictably, finding themselves out of sync. The country was welcoming Cambodian scholars, trained in the West, who were coming back to their homeland and uplifting the academic standards.

"The day is not far," commented a Canadian academic on attachment to the government, "when foreign students will come to the University of Phnom Penh to study Khmer history, rather than go to Yale University in the USA."

It was the well-heeled Cambodians who were filling in a shortage caused by the withdrawal in 1990 of Soviet teachers as a result of a cutback in Moscow's aid. A supreme irony was that teachers were playing truant. Many took part-time jobs to make ends meet when salary payments became irregular.

The killing of an entire academic fraternity was rivalled, in savagery, only by the systematic annihilation of the medical profession by a truculent Khmer Rouge. Meas Kim Suon, a doctor-turned-journalist, told us that when the Khmer Rouge had completed the destruction, there were less than fifty doctors left in the entire country. At a time when economists measured the sophistication of an economy by the number of doctors that served the population, the Khmer Rouge was busy erasing the medical profession. On April 17, 1975 the Khmer Rouge invaded the capital, and converged on the hospitals. Doctors and nurses were forced to march towards the countryside, where they were killed.

Eyewitness accounts documented by the Heng Samrin régime have it that Dr Phlek Chhat, resident physician at the Preah Ket Mealea hospital, was arrested in Kompong Thom province. A burning torch was thrust into his mouth, and he was killed. Like Dr Phlek, hundreds of doctors never saw their families again after they were snatched that morning. With the closure of hospitals, a Cambodian's lifespan had shrunk to just thirty-one years when Heng Samrin took charge in 1979. An effort to produce doctors was launched and, by 1991, the medical colleges had churned out over 700 of them.

Meas Kim Suon was one of the mass-produced doctors. Soon after he graduated in the mid-1980s, he was attached as a field doctor to the Cambodian army that was fighting a guerrilla war against the Khmer Rouge and the Sihanoukists along the Thai border. Kim Suon worked under malarial conditions, removing bullets and shrapnel from soldiers' bodies, amputating limbs, and sewing gaping holes.

He worked day and night until he grew tired of life in the jungle, and chose to become a journalist. He took a regular job as a guide for foreign journalists in the ministry of information and, during the run-up to the May 1993 elections, began reporting for a Japanese daily newspaper, the *Mainichi Daily News*. Kim Suon had done his bit for the country, and was now doing what he liked best, said his boss at the ministry, Leng Sochea.

Having worked with two generations of the Meas family—Kim Suon and his elder brother, Meas Kim Heng, who was a senior official in the ministry of foreign affairs—we were aware of the homegrown talent Cambodia was able to produce in times of adversity. Kim Heng was later sent to Washington, DC on a diplomatic posting.

Like his junior, Leng Sochea was a rising star in the ministry. We first met Sochea in 1990 when he was a guide in the ministry of foreign affairs. We worked together in the capital and the provinces where his array of contacts and ability to think on his feet helped enormously. After the elections, Sochea was promoted as the director of press in the ministry of information, and then he moved further up, becoming the deputy director-general of information.

Both Kim Suon and Sochea were fair-skinned owing to their Chinese ancestry. "I am a half-blood," Kim Suon liked to say with a goodnatured grin.

Even though Cambodia succeeded somewhat in rebuilding its medical force, less than half the population had access to medical care, and only twenty per cent of the medicines needed were produced locally. The government, in the mid-1980s, began importing essential drugs which were sold at highly inflated prices in the local market, further hurting a long-suffering people. While in principle health services were free at the time, government doctors were unscrupulous enough to charge money. A twenty-year civil war extracted a heavy toll on families, with limbless men numbering over 41,000, and skewing the population mix: it was believed that about sixty-five per cent of the adult population consisted of women who were having to shoulder the burden of singlehandedly raising a family.

For the newly-rich Cambodians the picture was not as bleak. Prime Minister Hun Sen must have done something right when, ten years after the Khmer Rouge were booted out, the economy grew by a modest 2.4 per cent in 1989. In those days Phnom Penh was a peaceful place where canny foreign businessmen made hay. We have not forgotten the response we got from a Singaporean businessman when we mentioned the need for caution before investing in Cambodia.

"The more dangerous it gets the more business I do," he said, flashing a knowing smile. "I made most of my money in the most dangerous times before the peace accord was signed in October 1991."

The economy, according to the UN's own estimates, posted negative growth in 1990 as a direct result of a cutback in Soviet trade credits, but rebounded with an amazing 13.5 per cent growth in 1991, a sober 6.5 per cent in 1992, more than 8 per cent in 1994, and was forecast to maintain a 7 per cent pace till the end of the century. But the Asian economic crisis that broke in 1997 dampened Cambodia's growth prospects.

It was odd, even unfair, that the newspapers seemed to focus on the negative aspects, with reporters acting more like body counters, instead of probing deeper into a society in irrevocable change. The news that the economy had grown by 6.5 per cent in 1992 was generally ignored by the world's press which was primarily expending its energies in attacking Hun Sen's administration. What lent credibility to the country's achievement was that the remarkable growth rate was announced by the UN which was mandated to run the country from late-1991 through 1993. Not only did the 6.5 per cent figure go missing in action, so did the 13.5 per cent number. When the UN said nice things about Cambodia's economic prospects, journalists believed whatever was said, but when the Hun Sen government said the same positive things about its performance a year earlier, its claims were disbelieved.

Even in those days Phnom Penh, and the ninety per cent of the country under the control of the Hun Sen government, was relatively safe for foreign investors to operate in. Cambodia was more hospitable than Bosnia. No foreign businessman had been killed in Cambodia, aside from an attack on a Taiwanese businessman by bandits in the countryside, but a spate of kidnappings was enough cause for concern. The political violence that preceded the elections of May 1993 pitted the rival factions against each other, but did not affect foreigners.

Kamaralzaman Tambu, a Malaysian editor of the weekly tabloid *Cambodia Times,* compared the situation with the communist insurgency in Malaya in the 1950s. Even during the insurgency, residents of Singapore visited their relatives on peninsular Malaysia, he said. The same Singaporeans were now the largest trading partners of Cambodia. The sound of cash registers ringing in Phnom Penh was louder than the crackle of distant gunfire.

Deep disorders gnawed at the core of the Hun Sen administration and its huge force of 150,000 civil servants in the nineteen provinces (*khet*) and two municipalities. The *khets* had considerable financial autonomy in raising revenue and collecting taxes, and they seldom reported their financial accounts to the capital. It was nothing new, and had happened in both China and India where the central governments faced resistance from the states. In Cambodia, the provincial governors lorded over their domain, raising and spending their revenue as they chose with little interference from their political bosses in Phnom Penh. It was believed that the provincial governors demanded such autonomy in return for loyalty to the State of Cambodia government. A large part of the problem was that it was difficult for provincial governors to communicate regularly with the central government, as phone connections were almost absent, and faxes unheard of in the remote areas. Provincial revenues remained non-transparent till the elections in May 1993. The new government passed a law on finances making it essential for provincial income to go straight into the national treasury in Phnom Penh. But by mid-1995, First Prime Minister Ranariddh seemed to back off from this law.

In an interview with the authors he justified the old position where the states had greater financial autonomy. The volte-face suggested that Ranariddh had failed to break the stranglehold of vested interests in the provinces.

The national treasury was empty in 1991. The government's revenue could finance only half the budget for the year. In the régime's early days there was no formal tax system, and state firms simply turned their income over to the national treasury. With the birth of a private sector, which owed much to businessmen like Leang Eng Chhin coming back home from France, a tax system was created. But it was abused. Companies haggled with tax officials, and arbitrarily fixed their tax dues. The setting up of a tax department in 1981, and the passage of a tax law in 1985, signalled the arrival of a new breed of bold Cambodian entrepreneur.

Leang Eng Chhin was thirty when he left Cambodia in 1970, the year when Sihanouk was overthrown. He set up a company in Singapore, made money and headed right back to Phnom Penh in 1991 to invest US$1.1 million on refurbishing the run down old White Hotel on Achar Mean Boulevard. He renamed it the Pailin Hotel after the famous rubies of Pailin in northwestern Cambodia, an area that remained under Khmer Rouge control.

"It was all my money," he said. "But we will wait and see if peace returns to Cambodia."

Chhin was a curious mixture: he was the managing director of a Singapore firm, Tristars; he carried a French passport; was a Cambodian by birth, and did not speak a word of English.

Behind the burgeoning business was the hand of an emerging Cambodian business community that had set up seventy private companies, some twelve years after the Khmer Rouge had wiped them out. There were, in 1990, at least one hundred millionaires in Phnom Penh, and as many Mercedes cars. One of them, Kim Chhean, had lofty plans to build a supermarket and a hotel in the capital, but some of his plans fell through. A France-trained building designer, Chhean bounced back, and was soon in business again. But Soviet diplomat Loukianov was scathing about the Cambodian millionaires.

"I agree there are about a hundred millionaires here, but they won't invest a cent in proper development," he said. "They would rather buy foreign cars, villas and clothes."

The country had come to resemble a wild economy where nothing was illegal. With government-owned firms getting into business, allegations surfaced in the newspapers about corrupt officials leasing land and public buildings to foreign businessmen without the approval of the ministry of finance. This allegation would become another dark motif in 1992-93 when UN officials would talk about it in whispers but could come up with no damning evidence to bring the guilty to book. Still, one good thing that the UN did was to recommend the establishment of a ledger of state properties.

The new money, new cars, and new villas added a grimy glitter to the raddled capital where rotting garbage and open drains were yet another motif. Stig Engstrom, a representative of an Australian telecommunications firm, said that he was amazed at the pace of change.

"In 1988, there were only eighty foreigners in Phnom Penh, today there are about 500," he said in 1990.

By August 1991, the government had hurriedly given approval to a dozen foreign companies to build hotels at a combined cost of about US$40 million. Critics called it *ad hoc*, wild, and unplanned. Nonetheless, the reconstruction had started, and the peace accord was only a gleam in Hun Sen's eye.

establishment of a large new car import tax.

Foreign money, new cars, and new villas added a tiny glitter to the would-be capital, where rotting garbage and open drains were yet another motif. She..., a representative of a ... Austrian telecommunications firm, said that he was amazed at the pace of change.

"In 1988, there were only eighty foreigners in Phnom Penh; now there are about 500," he said in 1992.

By August 1991, the government had formally given approval to a dozen foreign companies to build hotels at a combined cost of about US$90 million. Critics called it wishful thinking, and implausible. Nonetheless, the reconstruction had started, and the peace accords gave only a stealth in this September.

1. *Battlefield enemies come face to face: first one-on-one meeting between Prince Norodom Sihanouk (right) and the young Prime Minister Hun Sen in Fère-en-Tardenois, France, on December 2, 1987. Here the ex-guerrilla meets his one-time royal hero.*

2. *Talking across the table, and fighting on the ground: first peace talks between Prince Sihanouk and Hun Sen in France in December 1987. Sitting from left: Son Sann, Sihanouk, and Hun Sen. Standing from left: Sieng LaPresse, Oum Manorine, Khek Sisoda, Norodom Ranariddh, Hor Nam Hong, Dith Munty, and Cham Prasidh.*

3. From ideologue to academic: Hun Sen receiving his doctorate Honoris Causa degree from Iowa Wesleyan College, USA, in October 1996.

4. All the Huns: a family photograph taken in late-1997. From left: Hun Manet, Hun Manit, Hun Many, Hun Sen, Bun Rany, Hun Maly, and Hun Mana.

5. Hun Sen's fortress-like country home: the sprawling three-storeyed mansion in Takhmau, outside Phnom Penh, was built in 1997. It features faux Corinthian pillars, landscaped lawns, a lake, and mini-golf, and was ringed by guards in watchtowers manning machineguns, and artillery. *

6. An elder sibling: Hun Neng, the governor of Kompong Cham in a 1993 photo taken at his provincial residence. He is a brother of Hun Sen. *

7. Passing the hat around: Hun Sen shares a joke with a village woman in Prey Veng who offers him a hat on a sunny day. **

8. Steering through troubled waters: Hun Sen punts across a waterway in 1995 in Koh Tmey commune, Saang district, Kandal province.

9. Preparing himself for golf diplomacy: Hun Sen takes his first swing at a golf course in Kompong Speu province in 1998.

10. Portrait of a powerful couple: Hun Sen and Bun Rany in Puork district, Siem Reap in 1996.

11. *Bringing water to parched ricefields: Hun Sen opens an irrigation pipeline in Stoeung district, Kandal province.*

12. *Two strongmen: Myanmar leader General Than Shwe is greeted by Hun Sen and Bun Rany during his official visit to Phnom Penh in 1996.*

13. Making friends: Hun Sen meets former Thai Prime Minister Chatichai Choonhavan in Bangkok in 1997.

14. Wooing the guerrillas: Hun Sen meets Khmer Rouge people in Pailin in 1996 shortly after their reintegration into society.

15. Hun Sen's bête noire: Prince Ranariddh is welcomed by village folk in Khum Veal, Kompong Speu province in October 1994. *

16. The rebellious Norodom: Prince Norodom Chakrapong (Sihanouk's son and Ranariddh's half-brother) joined Hun Sen's government in January 1992. **

17. The long interview: author Harish Mehta engages Hun Sen in conversation at a Siem Reap hotel in 1997. **

18. An emotionally-charged meeting: author Julie Mehta with Bun Rany in her reception room upstairs at their Takhmau country home.

* picture by Harish Mehta.   ** picture by Julie Mehta.   All other pictures were provided by Hun Sen.

SEVEN

THE PEASANT
AND THE PRINCES

A MERCURIAL MIND

Hun Sen thought no more of the abuse and humiliation that Sihanouk had heaped on him. He buried the hatchet in October 1991 when the peace accord was signed in Paris. It did hurt, though, that Sihanouk had called him a "lackey of Vietnam", and "his bad son". He no longer nursed those grievances, and ordered his government to leave no stone unturned in cleaning up the capital ahead of Sihanouk's return in November. It was to be a grand homecoming.

The changes were visible the moment the worn out tyres of the life-threatening propeller-driven aircraft, operated by Vietnam Airlines, touched down at Pochentong airport. Gone was the run down air control tower that looked like a relic out of the Vietnam war, and in its place a freshly whitewashed structure gleamed in the sun. Like some fruit-topped pastry it was festooned with ribbons and crested by Sihanouk's portrait. The equipment inside the air control tower, however, remained the same.

More surprises were in store. The interior of the terminal had seen the painter's brush and sparkled white. Visitors no longer sweated as they waited in long visa lines. Ceiling fans swished overhead. Travellers' passports were stamped within minutes, and the anticipated inquisition from the customs officers never happened. The entire bureaucratic machinery appeared to be on a public relations exercise. Much had changed since Sihanouk's return.

The streets were swept so clean they looked unreal, and even the cyclos seemed to have been broomed off the main Kampuchea-Vietnam avenue. Apparently the police had ordered them off the main roads, and they could only ride along the side streets. That was one change many residents did not approve of as it robbed the city of its local colour.

The unpainted and dilapidated villas and houses that lent an old grace to the main avenues were given a new coat of paint, and little gardens had been created in roadside niches. Phnom Penh had overnight been transformed into its former self when Sihanouk had been the chief of state until 1970. It was then a city of bistros and dancing halls, all of which gave it the feel of a small provincial town in France rather than a Southeast Asian capital that slumbered oblivious to the million tragedies that lay in store.

Even though the prince was invisible and inaccessible to most Cambodians his presence could be felt. There was little he could do, for he was utterly powerless. The walls of the Royal Palace, once again, wore a new coat of yellow paint, and the royal flag flew above the walls. The prince often emerged from seclusion to deliver public lectures, to open a new school here, a medical dispensary there. He was a changed man. Sources close to him revealed that gone were the days when he would throw lavish parties and play the saxophone for his guests. Now the parties were fewer, and more sober, though he regularly granted audiences to diplomats and foreign politicians, and gave them a sense of his vision. The reason for the prince's sobriety was that he was now an elder statesman, and the head of an uneasy coalition of four parties, the Supreme National Council (SNC).

But he had lost none of his raconteur's wit and sharp tongue. On meeting the American ambassador to Cambodia, Charles Twining, the prince warned America not to meddle in the affairs of Cambodia as it had done in the past. He had not forgiven the Americans for supporting the *coup* against him. Here was a changed prince in yet another way: gone was the man who took sides, and openly criticised some Cambodian politicians while praising others. As the chairman of the SNC Sihanouk was non-partisan and impartial, though covertly he made his likes and dislikes quite evident. In the interest of political stability, he refrained from rocking the SNC's boat too much, though he could never resist an occasional jibe. As he resumed playing a central role in national politics, his words and actions had a deep impact on Hun Sen and his policies.

Appalled by the poverty and the neglect, Sihanouk could not restrain himself from lashing out. Wherever he went, he heard complaints from state employees who had not been paid for several months. On returning from the devastated countryside to the capital, he was incensed at the lifestyles of government ministers who lived in garish villas in an oasis of appurtenances: cars, refrigerators, washing machines, and that ultimate symbol of the rich, the TV antenna. In early 1992, he publicly accused the Hun Sen government of corruption. The story was picked up by newspapers all over the world, and his objective had been served. He had not lost his touch as a manipulator of the media. He still had many close friends in the Western and Asian press to whom he regularly gave interviews. Beholden to him for granting an audience, the press wrote flattering stories. Hun Sen observed Sihanouk's tendency to lambast his government, but he did not react fearing that a direct confrontation with the prince would be seen by the people as an insult to royalty.

Sihanouk fully exploited his status as an elder statesman. So, when he realised that the Khmer Rouge were refusing to demobilise their troops—as the peace accord had called for—he issued a series of statements condemning the guerrillas.

The first time that he revealed his real feelings toward the Khmer Rouge was in reply to a question posed by us. It was his most explicit statement on the

Khmer Rouge. Asked if it would be advisable for Untac to hold three-party elections among Hun Sen's CPP, Son Sann's Khmer People's National Liberation Front (KPNLF), and Norodom Ranariddh's Funcinpec party, he replied: "That would be the best solution because the Khmer Rouge leave Untac no other choice."

It was an extreme position for a neutral head of state to take, but he felt that the larger good of the country ought not to be sacrificed because of the non-cooperation of the guerrillas. Sihanouk became the neutral head of state for what, at the time, seemed sound political reasons. Even before the Paris peace agreement was signed in 1991, he realised that the post that would best serve his future political ambition was not as the head of the Funcinpec party, which he had created after he was ousted from power, but as the head of state. He could, in a sense, kill two birds with one stone. By vacating the leadership of the political party for his son Ranariddh—who was a spitting image of his father—he gambled that his son would lead the party to victory in the elections, and pave the way for him to retake power. By being appointed uncontested as the head of state, he laid the foundation stone to realise his deepest desire—to be elected the president of the country, even as early as 1993. It was vintage Sihanouk strategy aimed at keeping political power within the family.

There was more to Sihanouk's widely trumpeted neutrality than was apparent. Was he staying neutral because the Paris peace accord had limited his powers to that of a non-partisan head of state? Was he refraining from attacking his political enemies because he did not want to be seen as being hungry for power? There was much at stake, and the last thing he wanted was to rock the political boat. He therefore did not align himself with his son's party. Even so, his support for his son did not diminish.

In August 1992 we visited the Royal Palace and met Keo Puth Reasmey, a member of Sihanouk's cabinet secretariat who would, in 1994, become a diplomat. We asked him why Sihanouk had kept a low profile since his return to Phnom Penh ten months before. The quarter of the Royal Palace we caught a glimpse of was not in the best shape—paint was peeling off the walls. A gardener tended the first flowers to bloom since peace officially descended on the unfortunate land. Reasmey, a softspoken man who had served Sihanouk loyally, agreed to deliver a letter from us to the prince. We returned the next day with a letter, and a few written questions, requesting Sihanouk to answer them.

"He is very prompt in answering letters," Reasmey promised.

As a matter of routine Sihanouk personally answered his mail, making little jottings in chaste French. Reasmey told us to return in two days. Sure enough, Sihanouk had answered the questions. All his French comments were there on our letter, written along the margins, and squeezed between the lines. What remained was for Reasmey to translate the replies into English. In less than a week we received a formal letter signed by Sihanouk on royal letterhead. Sihanouk had also taken the trouble of enclosing a document containing his thoughts on the economic reconstruction of his country.

What did his outspokenness concerning the Khmer Rouge signify? That he was fed up with them? That he knew he did not have much time left as his political clock was ticking? The prince turned seventy on October 31, 1992. He was no longer the young rabble-rouser, and the Khmer Rouge still remained the chief spoiler to his ambition of once again coming to power as an elected president. Sihanouk knew that leaving the Khmer Rouge out of the election would worsen the security situation by pushing the faction, still led by a Maoist cabal, deeper into isolation and militancy. But he had little elbowroom at that late stage. A cloud of uncertainty swirled around the capital over whether the elections would be held in May 1993 because of the refusal of the Khmer Rouge to place its troops in cantonments for their eventual demobilisation. The prince, in his reply, dispelled the rumours.

"The elections will probably be held on schedule. And, they will be held only in the non-Khmer Rouge zones," he said.

His instincts were prophetic. He wrote those words in August 1992, and till November the same year nothing had changed to make the peace process any smoother. The Khmer Rouge were still holding out. The statement by the prince also confirmed the widely-held view that the elections were not likely to be held nationwide because the Khmer Rouge had not allowed UN peacekeepers to enter their areas, and prepare for polls. There was also the larger threat of the country being partitioned if the elections were held without the Khmer Rouge. An ominous hint as to how things would turn out was provided by Sihanouk's reply. He guessed that the Khmer Rouge might not participate in the polls. And for their part, the Khmer Rouge accused the UN peacekeepers of various lapses, such as being in league with the Hun Sen government, failing to verify the presence of Vietnamese troops disguised as civilians, and refusing to dismantle the administrative structures of the Hun Sen government. The Untac routinely, and monotonously, parried these accusations with its standard disclaimers that it was not in league with any one faction, that there was no hard evidence of the presence of Vietnamese troops in the country, and that the peace accord did not call for the dismantling of the Hun Sen government.

Sihanouk's sights were set beyond the shenanigans of the Khmer Rouge, beyond the elections. Once again, he wanted to see himself ensconced as a ruler. Besides, there was a rising chorus of demands from various politicians for him to become an elected president in 1993. He was certain to get elected president because there were no credible opponents in sight on the entire slate of possible candidates. If the CPP's leaders such as Heng Samrin and Chea Sim dared run against him, they would have met humiliating defeat at the hands of a prince whose very name had the power of sweeping every vote in the country in the 1960s. The charisma still held.

But Sihanouk set a tough condition. He would run for president only if the presidential poll was held before the general election in May 1993. He refused to run if the presidential election was held at the same time as, or after, the general election.

What were Sihanouk's motives? Was he attempting to consolidate his personal grip on power before the general election? Sihanouk was beset by two worries. One, a fear that if the presidential poll were held at the same time as the general election there was a risk that the Khmer Rouge could scuttle the entire election, and dash his hopes of becoming the president. Secondly, he was genuinely concerned about political stability. Fears that the country was heading down a slippery slope to anarchy had imbued a sense of urgency to a plan to hold an early presidential poll.

On returning to Phnom Penh, Sihanouk quickly restored the capital to its golden era, at least in one sense. The Royal Palace hummed with parties to which he invited diplomats and senior politicians. Although he had just returned from Beijing where he had undergone treatment for an inflamed salivary gland, he was a tireless performer at his palace soirées, singing in his trademark falsetto for as many as four hours in eight languages. The government declared his seventieth birthday a public holiday, and the local papers ran literally hundreds of his photos. The streets were given a dash of colour: scores of giant portraits of a youthful Sihanouk with thick black hair, at odds with the old man with thinning grey hair, appeared everywhere. Sihanouk was young again.

His potential challenger Hun Sen was, till then, not quite his match. But the young prime minister had carefully studied Sihanouk's style, and gave him the respect he demanded. Diplomats in the capital seemed to have reached a consensus at least on one issue—that it would be impossible to rebuild the country without Sihanouk because he was the only leader who could ensure an *entente cordiale* between the factions.

Not many were happy with this reality, for it meant having to endure his mercurial ways and royal whims. Although he was a cultured person with deep affection for his people, Sihanouk was not trusted. For instance, a week before his birthday celebrations, he changed his mind and said that he would no longer run for president, dealing a *coup-de-grâce* to an international initiative to make him president in the sensitive period following the elections of May 1993. The reason why he backed out, he said, was because he had been left out of an initiative by Japan and Thailand to bring the Khmer Rouge back into the peace process.

The world would have to put up with more of his capricious ways. When the French and Indonesian foreign ministers said that they wished to confer with Sihanouk in early November to remove the hurdles confronting the peace process, he agreed on the condition that the meeting take place in Beijing where a birthday party had been arranged for him by his Chinese friends.

True to his word, Sihanouk kept himself out of politics when electioneering began in April 1993. But his name was dragged into the election by Ranariddh who announced on April 6 the formation of a Sihanoukist Front consisting of like-minded parties.

"All the parties in the Front share the same ideals," Ranariddh said, but he would not name the parties that were expected to coordinate their electoral strategy.

Ranariddh's bid to form the Front signalled that the royalist party had lost confidence in winning the election in its own right, and had been forced to rely on Sihanouk's name.

Ranariddh dismissed the charge. "I strongly believe that we will win," he said amid loud cheers from his partymen and women clad in Funcinpec caps and T-shirts bearing Sihanouk's face.

A few days later, Dr. Long Bora, who headed the minuscule Cambodia Free Independence Democracy party, told us that Ranariddh had written to him a week before asking him to contest the elections under a Sihanoukist Front. Ranariddh's secret was out. But it was unlikely that Dr. Bora's participation would tilt the balance in favour of the Sihanoukists, whose main opponent was Hun Sen's CPP.

Sihanouk continued shuttling from the Royal Palace to the "on-now, off-again" meetings of the SNC and, whenever an occasion presented itself, he flew to Beijing or Paris. Without any real power, and shackled by the chains of neutrality that the Paris accord had imposed on him, Sihanouk remained in limbo, and amused himself cutting ribbons and kissing babies, leaving him a great deal of time to pursue his passion to make music and movies.

Back in 1967, Sihanouk commented: "As the first citizen of Cambodia, and chosen by my people to maintain the edification of the country, I have all kinds of professions. Thus, I became a journalist and publisher of newspapers and reviews. I also took an interest in the development of our cinematography, of which I am the leader."

He then added: "Not only was my father, the king, a very good musician, but also my mother, the queen, continued to safeguard the royal ballet's choreography."

The Khmer Rouge put paid to the royal-sponsored arts during its reign of terror, systematically rounding up artistes, and putting them to death. Pen Yet, the vice-minister of culture, said that all but a dozen Khmer classical dancers were killed. Sihanouk did not make films just for the sake of cinema, or to release the artiste in him that struggled to get out. It was a calculated bid to counter anti-

Cambodian propaganda which, he felt, the Western imperialist powers were conducting. In *Apsara,* his first film completed in 1966, he depicted Cambodia with a beautiful capital city, an excellent system of roads, a small but disciplined army, and an air force that was enough to protect national independence. Another film he directed, *The Enchanted Forest,* was the centrepiece of attention at the Fifth International Film Festival in Moscow in 1967.

"I was trying to present a series of tableaux showing different poetic aspects of my Cambodia. The main idea behind this film is to make our arts, traditions, customs, and religious rites better known to foreign countries," Sihanouk said.

Ever since he started making films in 1957, he had directed, produced, composed the music, and often played the lead role. *Four Smiles But One Soul,* and *The Little Prince,* won two awards at the Marseilles Film Festival. His son Norodom Sihamoni played the lead role in *The Little Prince,* shot in the Angkor temples. Sihanouk cast himself as a romantic hero in some of his twenty films that, curiously, imitated his life. The films, shot with a view to project himself as a sensitive and caring politician, were regularly screened for his distinguished guests consisting of diplomats and Untac officials. Upon his return from Beijing in mid-May 1993, just before the elections, the diplomatic grapevine started buzzing with the expectation that he would soon invite people to see his films and, thereafter, to cocktails and dinner at the beautifully lit palace, whose twinkling yellow lights belied the ticking of a political timebomb.

French Brigadier-General Robert Rideau, the deputy force commander of Untac, was often among the list of invitees to Sihanouk's palace to view his films. Rideau told us that guests were, at times, treated to two films: one on a Cambodian ballet, the other on life in Kim Il Sung's North Korea, a leader upon whose largesse Sihanouk depended for material help to maintain his lifestyle.

"I quite enjoyed the Cambodian ballet film, especially since Sihanouk was personally explaining the film," Rideau said. "But I did not like the propaganda film on North Korea."

Sihanouk and Ranariddh had a patron in Kim Il Sung. Ranariddh's election-eve radio campaign blared the "good news" that North Korea would recognise his future government if his party came to power. A diplomat described the closeness of the Norodom family with North Korea as "an alliance of old communists". They maintained that Sihanouk, once an ally of communist Vietnam and the Maoist Khmer Rouge, had the heart of a communist. After Kim passed away in 1994, Ranariddh named a street in the capital after the Korean leader.

Constrained by the Paris peace accord that required him to stay politically neutral, Sihanouk elevated himself above politicking, and again resorted to making films to shape opinions. A feature film, *Revoir Angkor, et Mourir* (See Angkor and Die) shot partly in Siem Reap and Angkor Wat in 1994, was semi-autobiographical, and dealt with many of Sihanouk's own experiences. It starred two Cambodian ambassadors—Roland Eng and Truong Mealy. Other roles were played by Sihanouk's aide, Sina Than, and actors Mam Kanika, San Chariya, and Me Meun. A group of Cambodians produced a stage version of the same film. Eng commented that as an actor it was very difficult to understand what Sihanouk, as a director, had in mind. It appeared that Sihanouk sometimes left his actors guessing what sort of performances he wanted from them. Entertainment in the capital did not cease even though economic development was still not within grasp.

A saxophone player, Prince Sihanouk had played duets with King Bhumibol Adulyadej of Thailand. But now Sihanouk was playing a different tune. Sihanouk wanted power, and it seemed that many influential people wanted him to have it. Hun Sen wanted him to run in a presidential election, and so did Untac chief Yasushi Akashi.

After a closed door meeting with Sihanouk on May 22, 1993, Akashi said: "There's no doubt that he will play a very, very important role."

Ranariddh said much more. After casting his ballot on May 23 in Phnom Penh, he said: "My father will be given full state powers. He will not merely be a figurehead. He will really run the country."

Over the coming days, Ranariddh would derail Sihanouk's bid to take power. Rivalry in the house of Norodom was taking its toll on Sihanouk.

True to form, Sihanouk continued writing letters around the world, and issuing daily statements to the press from the three capitals on his permanent itinerary—Beijing, Pyongyang, and Phnom Penh. A statement he issued from Beijing on February 8, 1993 revealed a fresh lust for power. He would run for president only if the post carried the same powers as that of the American president, he said.

"Due to the grave situation in my country, it is important that the president of Cambodia has the same powers as the president of the USA," Sihanouk said.

On the eve of his arrival in Phnom Penh on February 9, he made clear that he was unwilling to share power with a prime minister.

To allay fears that he would turn into a dark dictator, he added: "Of course, alongside the president there will be a parliament, or a national assembly."

There was panic in the ranks of Hun Sen's CPP and Ranariddh's Funcinpec, both of whom feared that Sihanouk would relegate them to the backbenches. There was no doubting that if Sihanouk ran for president he would win hands down.

Soon enough, he changed his mind again—he did not wish to be an all-powerful American-style president, and preferred remaining a father figure with some executive powers like the French president. Like some retiring grandee Sihanouk occasionally took pot-shots at the four main political parties. He chastised them for their errors and, in the process, continued strengthening his position as he prepared to become the president.

Sihanouk was criticised for spending most of his time abroad, in Beijing and Pyongyang, where he had been given residences by those governments. Beijing also put him on a fat annual stipend, and Pyongyang allowed him the use of a jetliner, and a squad of North Korean bodyguards whom Sihanouk came to trust more than his Cambodian compatriots.

Sihanouk's half-brother, Prince Norodom Sirivudh, was candid when we asked him why Sihanouk spent so much time in China, and North Korea.

"The prince has a special relationship with China," he said. "He has been welcomed by China since the 1970s. They do not take money from him; they extend hospitality. The USA had refused to accept him after he was ousted in a coup in 1970. France had asked him to come, but told him to refrain from engaging in political activities in their country. But China welcomed him. Prince Sihanouk was also welcomed by North Korea because we supported North Korea when the Korean peninsula was partitioned."

Sihanouk was, unfortunately, the only Cambodian with the stature to forge unity among the warring factions, and yet his job as the head of the SNC was a doomed mission. In mid-May 1993 when the political parties began campaigning, Sihanouk was again away in Beijing from where he watched the events at home, and would later play a clumsy political game. Part of the reason why Sihanouk changed his mind so often was because he was surrounded by enemies and, in order to survive, kept them guessing what his real intentions were.

Out of the peace accord came the elections. In party offices across Phnom Penh, strategists were working out their own power combinations. With Funcinpec leading the vote-count, one cabinet line-up was: Prime Minister Ranariddh, and Vice-Prime Minister Hun Sen. Given Funcinpec's lead in the vote-count, this scenario seemed most probable.

Another possible scenario: Emperor Sihanouk, President Ranariddh, and Prime Minister Hun Sen. This formula had just about everything to please everybody. There was a third scenario: President and Prime Minister Sihanouk, and Senior Deputy-Prime Ministers Ranariddh and Hun Sen. Sihanouk would probably have revelled both as the head of state and the head of government, but Ranariddh and Hun Sen were not likely to accept such a patently unfair arrangement.

Even before the election results were finalised in early June Sihanouk launched his plan to take power. Though he was still in Beijing he conducted the operation by remote control. The move to make Sihanouk prime minister started when Chea Sim, the CPP supremo, proposed that Ranariddh and Hun Sen should serve as his deputy premiers. Within days, the victory of Funcinpec was announced. The royalist party, created by Sihanouk to fight the Vietnamese army, narrowly defeated Hun Sen's party. It was still a victory, and a great day for Sihanouk—a party that had fought the elections on the Sihanoukist platform had triumphed. It was clear that Funcinpec had won primarily because of the popular appeal of Sihanouk, whose name Ranariddh used unabashedly during the campaign. Sihanouk's half-brother Prince Norodom Sirivudh had told us before the elections: "We will win. We are the royalist party."

On June 3, 1993, a series of bizarre events unravelled. Even before all the votes were counted Sihanouk launched a palace *coup*. He issued a statement saying that he was forming an interim government with himself as the prime minister. A few hours later Hun Sen's party came out in support of Sihanouk. In effect, Sihanouk had engineered a *coup* against Ranariddh, denying him the first opportunity to form a government as the head of the winning party.

A new chapter in Cambodian history was scripted that evening. Sihanouk appointed himself the prime minister and the supreme commander of the armed forces, and named Ranariddh and Hun Sen his deputy prime ministers. The appointments took immediate effect. The trouble was, Ranariddh had not been consulted. Stinging allegations swirled around the capital that Sihanouk had staged a "constitutional *coup*" with the help of the CPP who wanted to undercut Ranariddh by any means. In Sihanouk, the CPP chiefs found the only man who was able, and willing, to clip Ranariddh's wings. Two hurriedly issued statements by Sihanouk and the CPP in the evening declared that the interim government— named the National Government of Cambodia (NGC)—would remain in power for three months until the national assembly adopted a new Constitution, and a new government was formed. Palace officials said that Sihanouk was confident of Ranariddh's support. A declaration by the CPP said: "The CPP wishes to appeal to all compatriots, public servants, and all categories of the armed forces to remain calm, to be pleased with, and optimistic of, the NGC under the High Leadership of our Samdech Preah Norodom Sihanouk."

With effect from that evening Hun Sen stepped down as prime minister of a country he had led without a break since his appointment in 1985, and his SOC government, installed in 1979 with the help of the Vietnamese, was dissolved. Sok An, the chief of cabinet of the CPP, said in quavering tones: "Yes, it is dissolved."

Hun Sen accepted Sihanouk's decision and stepped down as the prime minister. But several questions remained unanswered. What was the inside story of the attempt by Sihanouk to grab power? Was Hun Sen disappointed at having to step down?

Hun Sen said: "Chea Sim and I had an audience with Sihanouk to beg his royal highness to set up a provisional government immediately to save the situation. I had no reason to be disappointed [to step down] because I had made the proposal. I sent the announcement of the formation of the new government to the radio and television stations to be broadcast."

That evening we asked the SOC's spokesman, Khieu Kanharith, a former editor of the state-run journal *Kampuchea*, whether Hun Sen had been disappointed at having to step down as prime minister.

He said: "Hun Sen is happy that there were no clashes after the election results were announced."

Kanharith wisely left the question unanswered.

The interim NGC was formed after three days of secret talks between Sihanouk and Chea Sim were wrapped up on June 3 at the Royal Palace. Sok An said that the negotiations had gone "smoothly and without disagreement". Curiously, Ranariddh, who was touring Banteay Meanchey province, was not informed of the meetings. It was obvious that a deal had been struck behind his back. That night Sam Rainsy, a rising star in the Funcinpec party, told us that he had been "taken totally by surprise" by the formation of the government.

On June 3 Sihanouk spoke to Ranariddh on the phone and tried to persuade him to join the government but the latter was not convinced. Sihanouk agonised through a sleepless night after he heard that Ranariddh would not join his government as a deputy prime minister. But Sihanouk was convinced that Ranariddh would eventually agree. He felt that his son would have no objections to him becoming the prime minister of an interim government because, after all, the royalist party had won the elections on the strength of Sihanouk's name. His reading of his son, and the top Funcinpec leaders such as Rainsy, was completely wrong.

By giving Hun Sen an equal position in the government with his rival, Ranariddh, Sihanouk had accepted the political reality that since the army and the civilian administration were controlled by the CPP, it would have to be given a major role in government. Sihanouk believed that the formation of the NGC had defused a potentially explosive situation which could have resulted in Hun Sen refusing to hand over power and launching a *coup* against a Funcinpec government. For Sihanouk it was the first executive post he had held since his removal in the *coup* of 1970. It was a very short tenure.

It was widely believed that the CPP had threatened to wage war if it did not get to share power equally with Funcinpec. Was it true that Hun Sen, or the other CPP leaders, had delivered such dire warnings?

"This was not true," Hun Sen said. "It was a total distortion. In fact, Funcinpec had only fifty-eight seats in a 120-member national assembly, whereas a minimum two-thirds majority, or eighty seats, were required to approve the new Constitution. So what could they do at the time if the CPP had refused to establish the provisional government and approve the Constitution? It was complicated enough to say that it was a failure of Untac, which meant that the UN would have to prolong Untac's presence. This would have meant that the UN would have to spend more money, and the State of Cambodia government [headed by Hun Sen] would have continued in power. In this respect, they should have seen the good intentions of the CPP."

On June 4 Sihanouk's hurriedly-formed interim government collapsed after holding power for less than a day. It was shot to pieces by Ranariddh, and a hawkish core within Funcinpec.

An aide to Sihanouk bitterly lamented: "Sam Rainsy is behind the collapse of the government. He is the Funcinpec leader who wants to keep power for himself."

It was unacceptable for Ranariddh to be placed on the same level as Hun Sen, and he demanded a higher post. From being a novice during the peace talks between Sihanouk and Hun Sen in the late-1980s, Ranariddh had won the people's mandate to rule. He now considered himself one notch above Hun Sen.

Ranariddh was advised by his aides that it was politically suicidal for Funcinpec to cede power so tamely to Sihanouk because the party had garnered six per cent more votes than Hun Sen's party. Uch Kiman, a vice-minister in the SOC, said that Ranariddh seemed to be backtracking on his promise to hand over power to his father. He hinted, more diabolically, that Ranariddh had been coached by the Khmer Rouge not to accept the Sihanouk government.

"But this is Cambodia," said Khieu Kanharith, the SOC's spokesman with the rank of a deputy minister, adding: "Anything can happen here." Even though Funcinpec had won more votes its margin of victory was slender and, as a result, the CPP and Funcinpec had no option but to share power, he said. Ranariddh, for his part, refused to accept the treacherous reality that winning an election was not a guarantee of forming a government.

When his own Funcinpec party betrayed him Sihanouk discovered new support among the members of Hun Sen's party who, to a man, backed his bid to become the prime minister, and a future executive president. In return, Sihanouk played the consummate conciliator by urging the Khmer Rouge not to attack Hun Sen's armed forces because they were now under his direct command, and that any attack on them would be construed as an attack on Sihanouk.

Did Sihanouk betray his son's right to form the government as the victor?

"The king's initiative was completely correct," Hun Sen said. "Ranariddh should have been grateful to the king. How could Ranariddh have run the country with less than fifty per cent majority?"

In the coming weeks as the rift in the house of Norodom grew wider, it was Hun Sen's party that gained most.

Next, Sihanouk dropped all niceties, and openly turned against Ranariddh. Appearing on state TV he told the people that Ranariddh had broken his promise to transfer power to him within twenty-four hours of winning the election. He lamented his son's infidelity.

The episode revealed the deep-rooted mistrust that Sihanouk had for his son. Under the influence of his wife, Monique, Sihanouk favoured her own children, and not the sons from his other wives. Ranariddh was not Monique's son; he was the child of a royal ballerina. Rarely did Sihanouk display fatherly love towards Ranariddh, and kept a regal distance between them. It was not surprising that he grabbed the first opportunity to deny his son his legitimate right to form a new government. In the end, Sihanouk backed down, and Ranariddh became the first prime minister in a coalition with Hun Sen as the second prime minister.

Ranariddh was in the ricefields of Banteay Meanchey when he heard the news about the formation of the government. From there he faxed a letter to his father, asking him to explain the legal basis of the creation of the interim government, as well as the legislative structures under which the new régime would function. Ranariddh also demanded that his half-brother, Chakrapong, be kept out of a future government as they did not see eye to eye. Sihanouk failed to come up with a reasonable response to Ranariddh's query about the legal basis of the régime. But he confirmed that Chakrapong would not be included in the NGC.

Sihanouk seemed to have jumped the gun, for there were no legislative structures in place under which the NGC could function. What, indeed, were his motives? It appeared that he intended the interim government to serve as a forum to reconcile the factions under his leadership. It was also a move to pre-empt a refusal by Hun Sen to hand over power. Sihanouk's reply to Ranariddh broke the news of the collapse of the interim government.

He wrote: "Given that some Cambodians, and some UN people, say that the NGC was born out of a constitutional *coup*, I renounce forming and presiding over the NGC. The only goal that I had in accepting the proposal was to avoid a bloody conflict that Hun Sen made me understand would happen. In renouncing the NGC I leave the Cambodian People's Party and Funcinpec to take responsibility for all that will happen."

Indeed, Chea Sim had warned Sihanouk that unless they struck a deal to share power, powerful leaders within the CPP would not agree to hand over power to the new government. There could even be bloodshed.

That day palace officials were spreading the word that Sihanouk had abandoned the formation of the NGC because "some countries in the UN permanent five opposed it". It was believed that the USA was one of them. For what it was worth, Untac chief Akashi lent his support to the NGC during a meeting with Sihanouk on June 3. Palace officials hoped that the NGC could be revived at a future meeting of the SNC. But a meeting of the SNC, scheduled for June 5, was cancelled because Sihanouk said he was "unwell", and would not chair it. In the end, by destroying his father's government Ranariddh not only embarrassed Sihanouk but also lost face as he returned to the capital and resumed talks with the CPP to share power. Later, the members of the national assembly wrote a new Constitution that required a two-thirds majority for any party to form a government. It was thus written in stone that under no circumstances could Ranariddh form a government on his own. He needed the CPP as much as the CPP needed him.

Once again, Hun Sen's canny calculations proved correct. With the collapse of the Sihanouk government, Hun Sen remained the prime minister until a new government could be installed.

That morning, Sihanouk, who probably set a world record for serving the shortest term as prime minister, was accused by diplomats of having carried out a "palace *coup*". A senior Untac official had shot his mouth off to a foreign reporter, labelling the formation of his government a constitutional *coup*. Untac issued a disclaimer saying that such statements were not authorised, and that no lobby within Untac was working against the formation of the interim government, though in fact the opposite was true. It was an open secret that Untac officials from a dozen countries pursued their own national agendas in disregard for what was in the best interests of Cambodia.

Behaving just as unpredictably as his father, Ranariddh performed a volte-face on June 7, saying he was dropping all objections to Sihanouk's idea of forming a coalition government. Ranariddh told Radio France Internationale: "We accept and support the idea of forming this Cambodian national government under my father's presidency." Ranariddh was now saying that his objections covered only minor points. "I only proposed some details to improve this government, and I said that the formation of a government must take into account the will of the sovereign people." Although Funcinpec was ahead of Hun Sen's party with a lead of six per cent of the votes, Ranariddh was candid in accepting the political realities. "One must admit that the situation in Cambodia makes it necessary to form a government of broad national union under the high presidency of my father," he said.

Ranariddh's statement defused tensions between father and son, and patched up an enervating rift in the Norodom family. Prince Norodom Buddhapong, a son of Chakrapong, told us over dinner that week: "It is a good development. We can move on. This is the beginning of everything after so many misses."

Sihanouk's aide, Sina Than, said: "We have been expecting this news. Over the past few days there have been indications that Prince Ranariddh might reconsider his position."

Late at night on June 7 when we phoned Sam Rainsy in Bangkok, he said that he had just heard the news over the Voice of America. Rainsy did not sound happy with Ranariddh's new position.

This time round it was Sihanouk's turn to throw a royal tantrum. Giving vent to his anger he accused Untac officials, the USA, and malicious newspapermen of thwarting his bid to form an interim government. On June 9 he issued a statement, crafted as usual in elegant French, and capping his gauche takeover attempt.

"I absolutely refuse to undertake a similar experience in the present, and in the future," Sihanouk said. "I have learnt my lesson. I must, at all costs, respect the letter of the Paris accords, and avoid constitutional *coups*." Forever a man of *élan*, Sihanouk added pungently: "It is now the duty of others— Untac, the UN, the USA, and others—to attempt a constitutional *coup* in Cambodia, if that makes them happy."

A palace official told us that evening that Sihanouk was annoyed by a malicious newspaper report that claimed that Sihanouk, his wife Princess Monique, and his son Chakrapong were planning to "steal power from Ranariddh".

Meanwhile, a power struggle was intensifying in Phnom Penh, with Hun Sen's party dictating terms in a bid to control the lion's share of the ministries in a coalition government. It became apparent that the CPP's demands would be met because it commanded the army and police, its mailed fists. At the same time, the CPP choreographed another drama. It sent senior army and police officers to pay their respects to Sihanouk, shower him with blandishments, and assure him of their loyalty. In doing so, the CPP took advantage of the rift between Sihanouk and Ranariddh, and succeeded in winning the much-needed support from the former.

Despite their political spat, father and son had not drifted too far apart. But Ranariddh had staked out his turf. Soon after the election results were announced and Funcinpec was declared the winner—in name, not in deed, for the CPP still held the most powerful ministerial portfolios—a newly elected 120-member national assembly met for the first time, and voted to give Sihanouk "full state powers" as the head of state for just ninety days, during which time the assembly would frame, and adopt, a new Constitution. Before entering the assembly house the assemblymen decided to meet every day under the statue of the Buddha— "to make sure they did not tell lies", a UN official quipped.

In a sideshow Sihanouk conferred the highest military rank in the country— five star general—on Heng Samrin, Chea Sim, Hun Sen, and Ranariddh, more as an indication of political seniority than military power. In a decree Sihanouk said that all the appointments were to the Royal Cambodian Armed Forces, the name by which the armed forces were known during Sihanouk's rule. On June 29, Sihanouk changed the name of the country from State of Cambodia to Cambodia, and replaced the national flag in an attempt to reassert his rule and end the dominance of the Hun Sen government.

"The State of Cambodia is now simply called Cambodge in French, and Kampuchea," Sihanouk said in a royal order.

The national anthem, discarded since 1970, was re-adopted. But Sihanouk altered a part of the song that eulogised the king because he no longer wished Cambodia to be a traditional kingdom ruled by an absolute monarch.

Ieng Mouly, a newly-elected MP from the Buddhist Liberal Democratic Party (BLDP), told us at his residence: "The prince has made these changes because he wants to give a fresh start to a new government which will be represented by an older royalist flag and national song, and Sihanouk will become a legitimate head of Cambodia."

By the time the new Constitution was ready Cambodia was again a kingdom, with the king reduced to mere ceremonial status, and real executive powers vested in the co-prime ministers, Ranariddh and Hun Sen. Khieu Kanharith's words rang in our ears: "This is Cambodia. Anything can happen here."

By this time, Sihanouk had flown out to his residence in Pyongyang. His absence imposed tremendous inconveniences on the government. After a twelve-member constituent assembly drafted two versions of the future Constitution, it sought Sihanouk's views on the provisions regarding the monarchy. But Sihanouk was away in North Korea. Ranariddh and Hun Sen were forced to fly to Pyongyang to visit him in September 1993, carrying with them the two drafts. One version set up a constitutional monarchy, whereas the other draft did not.

Ranariddh supported the restoration of the monarchy, whereas Sihanouk, still hankering for power, wanted a greater executive role. After talking to the two co-premiers, Sihanouk agreed to be the king, and gave his nod to the national assembly to adopt the draft of the Constitution creating a constitutional monarchy. The problem seemed to have been solved in Pyongyang.

But was it? Hours after the co-premiers returned to Phnom Penh on September 3, Sihanouk sent them a fax saying he would not be the king. He said he wanted to avoid creating a controversy, and added: "If we discuss the problem of the monarchy, and the nation, we will be responsible for [creating] a new division in our nation."

Just two days later, on September 5, Sihanouk sent a message to the national assembly rejecting the decision to appoint him the king. It would be better, he said, to follow a constitutional path that was neither a monarchy nor a republic. He was then undergoing a medical check-up in Beijing from where he sent a letter to Untac chief Akashi saying he had decided to break off ties with Untac because "inside Untac, some people are anti-Sihanoukist".

Ranariddh was not just perplexed by his vacillating parent, he was annoyed. But palace officials argued that Sihanouk had never wanted to become the king again, and that the co-premiers were trying to foist the monarchy on him.

The most confused group of people in Phnom Penh were the foreign correspondents who would write a report, and discover the next day that whatever they had written had not happened. Here was Sihanouk doing what he knew best—keeping people guessing about his next move. As a result, some reporters covering the country said that they would not send any more despatches to their newspapers until the posturing stopped.

It would prove to be a wise decision. For, on the night of September 24, 1993, Sihanouk surprised his countrymen by taking the oath as king in an elaborate ceremony at the yellow-spired Royal Palace. Earlier that morning he had approved and signed the Constitution that returned him to the throne but restored only a few of the powers that had been snatched from him in a *coup* twenty-three years before. Dressed in regal Khmer finery—a white tunic with gold-buttons set off by purple knee-length silken pants—a dapper seventy-one-year-old Sihanouk and his consort, Monique, were named king and queen after their election by a council of senior politicians and monks. The man who lusted for absolute power had settled for a lesser role as a constitutional king that brought with it supreme power over the armed forces, and the authority to appoint and dismiss cabinet ministers. These, ironically, were powers he would never be allowed to exercise.

It was best that he stayed out of politics. The country was being run by two prime ministers, and interference by a third force, a king, would have made matters worse as there would have been too many conflicting power centres. That afternoon as he greeted the thousands of people who gathered outside the palace gates to catch a glimpse of their beloved king, he seemed such a vulnerable and diminutive figure standing alone on a palace balcony, shielded from the searing sun by a royal parasol carried by an official bearer.

Just two weeks after his return to the throne Sihanouk was back in Beijing where he was operated upon by Chinese doctors on October 7, and a malignant tumour was removed from near his prostate. Sihanouk kept the news of the operation from the people for a few days. Cambodians were dealt a shock on October 12 when he said in a statement issued from Beijing that the tumour, extracted a week before, was cancerous, but had not spread. Identifying the cancer as a type of lymphoma, he said: "If the tumour had not been discovered within two or three months it would have spread to other parts of my body."

A protracted treatment delayed his return to Phnom Penh, setting off fears that his death could shake the country's stability because he was seen as being the only leader capable of keeping the political factions within the coalition from breaking ranks. As the Constitution did not specify a line of succession to the throne, his death or serious illness, was expected to spark off a controversial battle for succession. It was expected that Ranariddh and Chakrapong would make a bid to become king, a position his other sons would eye as well. Th.

mechanism to appoint a future king was through an election in which votes were cast by a royal council consisting of a few senior Cambodian statesmen and monks.

A few days before his seventy-first birthday Sihanouk's life was in grave danger as he underwent chemotherapy and radiotherapy to cure the cancer. At the time, he wrote to the government saying his death was near. He was plagued by worries about the wellbeing of his wife after his death.

"After my death; which is not unforeseen, the royal government, and the national assembly of Cambodia, will please allow my widow, Queen Monique Sihanouk, to live the rest of her life in the Royal Palace, in the house currently occupied by my secretariat, and where my venerable deceased mother, Queen Sisowath Kosomak, lived before being unjustly chased out of the Royal Palace by the leaders of the Lon Nol *coup* in 1970."

If the house was not available, he said, then she should be allowed to live in what was now the residence of the members of his secretariat.

"It was a house I was so familiar with since 1989 when I had first visited the palace," he said, referring to his return.

On his birthday Sihanouk received Chinese foreign minister Qian Qichen at the Beijing hospital. But he said that he would not return home till May or June 1994 because the cancer had turned out to be worse than previously thought, and the fact that his treatment consisted of traditional Chinese techniques.

When he did eventually return to Phnom Penh he received a warning that his life was in danger—not from cancer, but this time from the Khmer Rouge. Curiously, the warning came from Khieu Samphan who told Sihanouk to leave the country for his own safety because the group planned "big trouble in Phnom Penh and throughout Cambodia." Sihanouk said that he had received a "secret letter" from Samphan on April 20, 1994 in which the guerrilla leader asked him to flee. Samphan told him not to wait for a private plane, but to take a commercial flight to Bangkok.

"He advised me to take a commercial flight to Bangkok because he does not want me to be in danger," Sihanouk said. "He said that if I want to remain alive, [I must] run quickly."

The king said that he would stay, and that he would never leave his people in times of trouble. Although Samphan told Sihanouk not to divulge the contents of the letter, Sihanouk could not keep silent.

"I have to tell Khieu Samphan, through television and radio, that I will not run. Ever since I was young I never ran from danger," he said.

Meanwhile, under direct orders from Second Prime Minister Hun Sen, the government drafted a law to outlaw the Khmer Rouge.

Soon, however, King Sihanouk put himself on a collision course with the very people who had supported his ascent to the monarchy—Ranariddh and Hun Sen. On May 7, 1994, Sihanouk called for new elections in Cambodia with the participation of all parties, including the Khmer Rouge. Or, he said, the guerrillas should give up the areas they controlled in exchange for a role in the government. In recent weeks, fighting between the Khmer Rouge and government forces had escalated after the guerrillas recaptured their ruby-rich town of Pailin from the government. But the government, fighting the guerrillas with its back to the wall, dismissed the king's idea out of hand.

The government neither had the money to organise another election, nor could it provide security for an election campaign, and ensure all the factions—Khmer Rouge included—were disarmed. The UN representative in Cambodia, Benny Widyono, said that the UN had spent US$2 billion on the election a year ago, and that the UN, with many competing demands on its money, was already in the red. But certain government leaders such as Norodom Sirivudh and Sam Rainsy, who had come to be close to the king, were not happy to see him being marginalised. In the same month, some supporters of Sihanouk belonging to the parties of Ranariddh and Hun Sen, hatched a plan to give full powers to Sihanouk by amending the less than one-year-old Constitution. The backers of these moves soon had egg all over their faces when their plan was stillborn.

Next, Sihanouk himself began to work the ground in another attempt at grabbing power. In an interview, the king said that he was ready to retake power for "one to two years" to save his country from chaos. Hun Sen was shocked, and he shot off a letter to the king asking him to clarify his statement.

"What I want now is clear information whether your highness wants to be the prime minister?" Hun Sen asked.

Hun Sen was outraged by the king's allegation that he was an obstacle to peace because he did not wish to give a role in the government to the Khmer Rouge. Hun Sen said that he was so upset at being considered an obstacle that he considered resigning.

In a letter to the king, a copy of which took up a full page in several Cambodian newspapers, Hun Sen said: "I was shocked at the point where Sihanouk said that he would not retake power without the support of Hun Sen, or the CPP, because the king does not want blood shed to fight a secession led by Hun Sen. This sentence weighs very heavily on me."

Sihanouk was not alone in lashing out at Hun Sen; Sam Rainsy, too, opposed moves to outlaw the Khmer Rouge. However, he went down fighting, and the bill outlawing the Khmer Rouge was passed by a majority in the national assembly. What many Cambodians found objectionable was Sihanouk's offer to make Khieu Samphan a vice-president at a time when the guerrillas were battling the government's forces in Pailin, and had shown their true colours by taking three Westerners hostage.

The king wrote to Hun Sen on June 18, saying: "I would like to clarify to your excellency I have no intention to act as prime minister in Cambodia. I am an old man and suffer serious illness."

A few days earlier Sihanouk had advocated a reorganisation of the cabinet. He recommended the creation of a cabinet with about sixteen ministers, patterned on his government of the 1960s. It became apparent in September that the king had built a strong lobby of support to advance his causes. One of his staunch supporters was Sirivudh, his half-brother, who served as the foreign minister. On October 25 we phoned Sirivudh at his residence in Phnom Penh, and he asked us to come and see him right away. As we walked up the steps to his first floor library we found him sitting at a table, typing a letter of resignation to his boss, Ranariddh. A TV monitor at one corner of the room helped Sirivudh keep an eye on his front gate.

Why, we asked, did he wish to resign after just fifteen months in office?

Erasing a word that he had typed wrongly, he said: "I am leaving because I don't agree with a lot of things. An idea of His Majesty Norodom Sihanouk to set up a national reconciliation council between the government and the Khmer Rouge was not accepted. Moreover, the king had proposed some solutions to resolve the problems between the government and a Thai firm, but the king's ideas were not accepted."

Hammering the keys of his old manual typewriter, Sirivudh added: "To be honest I did have problems with Mr. Hun Sen, in particular. I did not have problems with Prince Ranariddh who is my boss and the president of the Funcinpec party. But I cannot work with Mr. Hun Sen. He insulted King Sihanouk by writing him a six-page letter. I could do nothing about this, and I was frustrated."

Was he more loyal to the king than to the government he worked for?

"The government is loyal to the king," he said. "We are a kingdom here. But we have found that the suggestions of King Sihanouk are not taken into consideration at all."

Was Sihanouk still in pursuit of becoming an executive head of state with full powers?

"He has already declared that he does not want to take power," Sirivudh said.

As we parted, he said that his resignation was not a mark of protest for the sacking of his close friend, Sam Rainsy, who had been removed as the finance minister.

Sihanouk came to the rescue of Rainsy who was ousted by a majority vote in the national assembly on October 20, 1994. Rainsy had lobbied against his bosses, the two prime ministers, and they had put his future to a vote—ninety MPs voted in support of his removal, and thirteen opposed it. Just before the vote was taken, Rainsy walked up to the microphone and without seeking the permission of the chairman of the assembly, began reading a statement sent to him by Sihanouk.

But Rainsy was prevented from speaking by the interior minister, You Hockry, who belonged to the Funcinpec party. Hockry said that Rainsy breached protocol when he read the statement.

"Rainsy tried to influence the vote," an MP complained.

Outside, in the compound of the assembly, Rainsy distributed copies of Sihanouk's letter.

"In the position of minister of finance, you have given great service to our people, and the motherland," Sihanouk wrote in his letter of October 17 to Rainsy. "If you quit your actual ministerial post, in order to lead other departments, our finance and our national economy will suffer risks, and will confront difficulties that will be hard to surmount. I have no right to interfere in the affairs of the government, but I wish you would remain in the government because our country, and our people need your services, and highly patriotic and highly competent assistance. With profound affection. Norodom Sihanouk."

A member of the government who worked closely with Ranariddh, but preferred to remain anonymous, told us: "Ranariddh was so annoyed with his father. Here he is trying to clean up the cabinet, and make it more efficient, and Sihanouk is actually lobbying against the government."

From Beijing, Sihanouk continued his battle of letters. A few days after writing to Rainsy, he issued a statement locking horns with a brewer. Sihanouk took umbrage at a claim made by a Singapore firm that its proposed brewery in Phnom Penh was the first international brewery in the country.

"This pretension is absolutely unacceptable because in Cambodia in the Sangkum Reastr Niyum (SRN) government there was, in Sihanoukville between 1968-69, a big brewery using French equipment and high technology to make beer of the Alsace type, and of international standard," an outraged Sihanouk said. "Foreigners who come to Cambodia to provide assistance, pretend that my SRN régime (1955-67) did not provide the equipment, infrastructure, and the modernisation of Cambodia. And they make believe that they were the pioneers, and that they came to teach the Cambodians how to build their own country, and to understand what is a modern country."

"There are photographs, and films," Sihanouk wrote, "that can demonstrate, at any time, the people that made this happen, as well as other realities concerning Cambodia. Without mentioning the period of Angkor, Cambodia was modernised in the SRN régime. We are not a savage country."

The Singapore brewery had announced on October 17 that it would build a US$50 million brewery in Kandal province, fifteen kilometres from the capital, and not far from Hun Sen's country home. It said: "With the signing of the joint-venture agreement today, the brewery will be the first international brewery in Cambodia."

Under Sihanouk, some development did take place in the 1960s, but his economic reforms were patchy. On the plus side, his "Buddhist socialism" policies ensured that twenty per cent of the budget was spent on education. His other decisions were less enlightened. He broke the backs of the ethnic Chinese trading community by nationalising trade—an aberration that remained in force for over two decades until it was reversed by the government in late-1993. Sihanouk's repressive measures had forced the traders to smuggle the rice harvest to neighbouring countries where it fetched a better price—a tactic that the traders had followed since that time.

Forever a *provocateur* Sihanouk persisted in taking a confrontational stand against his government. When, in October 1994, Ranariddh was taking roadshows to world capitals to drum up foreign investments, Sihanouk was warning foreigners to stay away from Cambodia. It riled Ranariddh who was working overtime to convince investors and tourists that the streets of Phnom Penh were less dangerous than New York or Belfast. But following the execution in November 1994, by the Khmer Rouge, of three Western hostages—Briton Mark Slater, twenty-eight; Frenchman Jean-Michel Braquet, twenty-seven; and Australian David Wilson, twenty-nine—Sihanouk warned foreigners that his country was in a state of war, and was "clearly insecure".

Wisened by his ham-fisted foray into active politics, Sihanouk said that he would soon resume an old passion, film-making.

"The only plan which I have seriously in my head is not that of my return, which is not desired or desirable, to power, but that of a new 35 mm film entitled,

An Apostle of Non-Violence, for which I am going to write the scenes and dialogue," he said.

The film, he said, had been inspired by the actions of Cambodia's Nobel Peace Prize nominee, Samdech Preah Ghosananda, a Buddhist high-priest. In some respects Cambodia was not a savage place.

Piqued at being sidelined and neglected by the government Sihanouk was eager, in 1995, to see his nominee become the future king. To that end, Sihanouk started a process of grooming his son, Sihamoni, to succeed him, and took him on foreign visits to Indonesia and Malaysia to expose him to foreign leaders, and identify him closely with the palace. Sihamoni, a son from Queen Monique, had unfortunately no flair for politics, nor was he attracted to it, and spent his time in the pursuit of culture and the arts. But Sihanouk did not wish to delay the process of grooming a successor because of his failing health, and his lingering fears for the wellbeing of his wife after his death. He feared that she would be turned out of the palace, just as his mother had been turned out by the Lon Nol régime. To allay such fears, Sihanouk chose Sihamoni in the hope he would take care of his mother. The Cambodian monarchy was not hereditary, and although a future king would be elected by a royal council of two senior monks and senior members of political parties, Sihanouk was leaving nothing to chance.

But the future of the monarchy itself was under threat. More than one-third of Cambodians said in a 1995 poll that they did not think anyone should be the king after Sihanouk. The poll among 700 people, conducted by the Khmer Journalists Association, showed that twenty-four per cent wanted Ranariddh as a future king, six per cent voted for his half-brother, Chakrapong, and thirty-six per cent favoured nobody. Sihamoni's name did not figure in the poll, indicating his remoteness from politics, and the stealth with which he was being groomed.

Having recovered from cancer in a Beijing hospital, Sihanouk did what came naturally. By mid-1995 he had put the finishing touches to his latest film, *An Ambition Reduced to Ashes.* The message of the film according to Sihanouk: "It does not serve any purpose to fight against Fate. An unbounded ambition does not hoist you up to the helm, but rather takes you down to a tragic end. Love is often stronger than political calculation." The film seemed to mirror shades of his own bitter experiences.

As he turned seventy-three in October, Sihanouk seemed to have lost touch with politics, but he still had an eye for the camera.

The political marginalisation of Sihanouk was also the outcome of the rise of Hun Sen. As Hun Sen's influence grew among his own people, and abroad, Sihanouk's star began to sink.

PRINCE VERSUS PRINCE

Hun Sen's·power pulsated out of the capital into the provinces. His party was in complete control of the government and the administration. Yet, in 1991, he was somewhat insecure.

The news that Sihanouk and his son, Ranariddh, were coming back home gave hope to many Cambodians. Isolated, deprived, and poor, they now wanted to entrust their country to the royal family in whom they had blind faith. Hun Sen, and his party, knew that something had to be done quickly to counter the groundswell of support for the royal family.

They saw a chink in Sihanouk's armour. Opportunity came knocking in the shape of Prince Norodom Chakrapong, a son of Sihanouk who broke away from the Funcinpec party his father h· d founded. Chakrapong was displeased with the way Funcinpec was being run, and he sought a meeting with Hun Sen and other Cambodian People's Party (CPP) leaders, for exploratory talks about his political future. The talks went off well, and he joined the State of Cambodia (SOC) government in January 1992. His defection, a year ahead of the general election, worsened relations between him and his half-brother, Ranariddh.

When it came to the pedigree of royal lineage Chakrapong was the purer of the two. Chakrapong's mother, Princess Sisowath Pongsanmoni, was not only a member of the royal family, she was also Sihanouk's aunt. Ranariddh's mother, Neak Moneang Phat Kanthol, was a commoner.

Sihanouk took four other wives besides Pongsanmoni and Kanthol. They were Princess Sisowath Monikessan, who bore him Prince Naradipo; Kanita Norodom Norleak, a member of the royal family who had no children; a Laotian woman named Mam Manivan, who bore him Princess Sucheatvateya and Princess Arunrasmey; and the Eurasian beauty Monique Izzi, who gave him two sons, Princes Sihamoni and Narindarapong. Chakrapong had five siblings, some of whom were killed by the Khmer Rouge, but Ranariddh's only sister, Princess Bopha Devi, survived.

Ek Sereywath, a French-educated Funcinpec official, put it graphically: "Ranariddh is an intellectual with a doctorate while Chakrapong is just an airforce pilot. The two brothers do not get on."

They were slugging it out back in 1992. Chakrapong, forty-seven, and Ranariddh, forty-eight, emerged as political heavyweights in exile. Having built up a formidable international reputation for his role in the Cambodian peace talks, Ranariddh took over Funcinpec's leadership from his father. It was a post that Chakrapong had been eyeing, and when he did not get it, he rebelled and joined Hun Sen's government.

Chakrapong quickly became a household name after Hun Sen appointed him a vice-prime minister. The newest and fastest-rising star in Hun Sen's cabinet, Chakrapong was also given a high rank in the CPP's communist-style politburo, the inner coterie that ran Cambodia. By all accounts, the party intended to cash in on Chakrapong as a vote-puller in the elections of May 1993 in an attempt to counter the appeal of his royal rival, Ranariddh. Chakrapong was the only member of the royal family that the CPP had acquired with the intention of using his appeal to win the hearts and minds of the voters who revered the Norodoms.

The two half-brothers were longstanding rivals with serious differences. Chakrapong and Ranariddh did not see eye to eye on how the Funcinpec party ought to deal with the guerrillas. The only similarity was the striking facial resemblance they had with their father, and the distinctive falsetto all three spoke in. The differences between the half-brothers adversely affected an agreement signed in November 1991 by Funcinpec and the CPP to support Sihanouk's policies.

To gain an insight into the royal feud which raged bright as a Cambodian forest fire we phoned Chakrapong's office in mid-August 1992. His son, the young Prince Norodom Buddhapong who doubled as his assistant, readily arranged a meeting with his father the next morning at his office in the council of ministers' building.

Chakrapong, a swarthy man in a dark suit, walked into the room and greeted us effusively as if we were old friends. Ranariddh was much shorter and leaner than his sibling, who had both girth and height. As soon as he sat down, Chakrapong began explaining why he had broken away from his father's royalist party.

"I joined the royalist party because my father was the president of the party, and I wanted to eject the Vietnamese troops from Cambodia," Chakrapong said in a high-pitched, sing-song voice. "My goal, as a citizen of Cambodia, was achieved the day the Paris peace agreement was signed in October 1991, which ended the factional fighting. My father became the head of state, and my duty was over."

Before joining Hun Sen's government, Chakrapong served as the deputy chief of staff and commander of an élite brigade of Sihanouk's National Army of Independent Kampuchea during the years when Sihanouk headed the Funcinpec party. After the peace agreement was signed, Sihanouk was appointed the head of state and president of the neutral, and powerless, Supreme National Council (SNC). A senior member of Hun Sen's government told us that soon after Chakrapong left his father's party, he tried to join the Khmer Rouge, but could not reach an agreement with them to accommodate him. He entered the CPP as a second choice.

"I was the number two man in Funcinpec," Chakrapong said during our hour-long conversation. It went without saying that his father was the number one.

As one of five vice-prime ministers in the SOC, Chakrapong's responsibilities covered six ministries—civil aviation, tourism, industry, culture, education, and social welfare. The load was too much for the prince who played a figurehead role in most ministries, aside from civil aviation where he performed well. He immersed himself in an ambitious plan to expand the national airline. Part of the reason for his interest in aviation was that he had served as a fighter pilot in the Royal Cambodian Air Force when his father was the chief of state. Sihanouk had, at the time, planned to request the Soviet Union to provide MiG-21 fighter aircraft, but he was ousted in a *coup*. Chakrapong, for his part, said that he would upgrade the Cambodian national airline by leasing a Boeing passenger jet, as well as adding more air connections.

Had he become a leftist by joining the communist-style CPP?

"As the blood of the royal family I would not have joined a party that was communist," Chakrapong said indignantly.

Clearly, the CPP was shedding its communist caul, and Chakrapong's line of thinking sounded logical.

Time and again Chakrapong dropped his father's name to buttress the point that he had won paternal approval for most of his actions.

"Our head of state, my father, has assured us that after the elections, our government's economic policies will not be discarded," he said.

Why would a new government adopt the policies of the Hun Sen régime?

Chakrapong turned red as a beetroot, and his lower lip trembled. We knew that we had stepped on a political corn.

"What do you mean by régime?" he asked, his voice rising. "Are you saying that we are a régime? What is a régime? It is something less than a government? Are we anything less than a government?"

We decided to drop the issue, and changed the subject. But Chakrapong had not quite finished.

"We are the government of Cambodia," he thundered. "The government that may come after us cannot do as much as us because we have already put in place a new foreign investment law, and have taken the best economic systems from foreign countries. We think we can win the election. And if we win the election, there will be a continuity in economic policies. I am optimistic about winning because we are the biggest political party in the country."

Chakrapong began throwing his ample weight around soon after he took office. When Ranariddh wanted to fly into Pochentong Airport on a private airplane, Chakrapong used his clout as the minister of civil aviation to deny permission. Repeated requests by Ranariddh were rejected. It was an episode that Ranariddh would not forget, and he would take revenge at the first opportunity.

While Chakrapong seemed to have sewn himself into a remote corner, another Cambodian prince emerged from the elaborate tapestry of Cambodian politics: Prince Norodom Sirivudh who was Sihanouk's half-brother, and Ranariddh's and Chakrapong's uncle.

In January 1993 tensions were rising as the elections approached. All of a sudden princes of all stripes were entering politics. With his name-tag pinned onto his shirt pocket Sirivudh looked more like a company executive than an aspiring politician. Here was yet another prince who, uncannily, sported many of the mannerisms of his half-brother, Sihanouk—Sirivudh, too, spoke in a high-pitched voice, and had a penchant to stir up controversies.

Sirivudh's story in a nutshell: he had "opposed American imperialism in Indochina" in the 1970s, he said. He took refuge in France where he worked, and wanted to return to Cambodia in 1976, but was "unaware of the genocide being committed by the Khmer Rouge at the time". He waited three years, and joined Sihanouk's movement in 1979. That year the Khmer Rouge was ousted from power. Sirivudh then spent much of his time in the jungles fighting shoulder to shoulder with his nephews, Ranariddh and Chakrapong, who were then united.

Sirivudh made it a point to inform us that he was the first among the Norodoms to return to Phnom Penh from the jungles of Cambodia in November 1991, just a month after the signing of the Paris peace agreement. Sirivudh bristled as he spoke about Cambodia's million mutinies. He said that Untac had failed in its mission to protect his people: at least twenty of his partymen had been gunned down by political opponents.

We asked Sirivudh how the royal family viewed Chakrapong's defection from the royalist party.

"We were disappointed with Prince Chakrapong when he left us, and joined the government of Prime Minister Hun Sen," Sirivudh said. "But Prince Chakrapong was also disappointed with Funcinpec."

He then revealed Hun Sen's strategy to lure young princes away from the royalist party.

"When I returned to Phnom Penh in November 1991 Hun Sen offered to arrange to get my house back, and he offered me a car. I refused because I wanted to win the elections and then take my property."

Sirivudh implied that Chakrapong gladly took the perquisites of high office that were offered by Hun Sen.

Like the Norodoms, several Funcinpec leaders held passports of foreign countries, mainly France, the USA and Australia. This gave rise to the criticism that they were not really committed to Cambodia, and that they craved for the good life abroad. Officials of Hun Sen's government took the moral high ground, claiming that they did not possess foreign passports, and that they had no intention of running away from Cambodia if the Khmer Rouge recaptured power.

Stung by this comment, Sirivudh reacted: "The issue of foreign passports is a cheap and small-scale argument. Who says that Hun Sen's people don't have Vietnamese passports?"

Sirivudh then lashed out at the SOC's links with Vietnam.

"The SOC signed three frontier treaties with Vietnam, and gave some land to them," he said. "But we have not given any land to the Thais. We are committed to the country. The SOC had insulted Prince Sihanouk for ten years, but now national reconciliation is most important. In the 1970s, we played the United States' game, which was a disaster. In 1975, we played the China game, which was also a disaster. In 1979, we played the Soviet game, which was again a disaster. Let us now play the Cambodia game and rebuild Cambodia."

Sirivudh accused the ruling SOC government of intimidation.

"All the killings were organised by the local authorities. They always harass our workers," he said. "Our observers in the provinces say the SOC people tell them verbally: 'You are bad guys, you come to disturb us. We did not see you for a few years, but now you've come to put up your election displays. You are troublemakers. Next time we will shoot you'. Untac, it seems, is not in a position to protect us. Untac has not reacted to the harassment. Untac is not able to investigate. Prince Sihanouk also said that both Untac and the SOC are not in a position to create a neutral political environment."

That allegation would become a motif of Untac's failure. While the political parties and international human rights groups such as Asia Watch criticised Untac for its failure to stop the killings, the much-maligned Untac remained the best hope for the people. For without Untac's intervention there would be no elections.

Not much had changed by November 1992 when Chakrapong and his family arrived in Singapore on a personal visit. When we met him at a local hotel his father's political future was, once again, uppermost in his mind.

"We are backing Prince Sihanouk, and we were the first to propose his name for the presidency," he said.

Over in the rival camp, Ranariddh, too, was openly cashing in on Sihanouk's name as a surefire vote puller. He was telling people that his was a royalist party. Chakrapong, on the other hand, could not claim that his party was royalist in character, as it was made up of former Khmer Rouge defectors, but he tried to link the CPP as closely to Sihanouk as possible. There was tremendous political mileage to be earned in doing so. Chakrapong, Ranariddh, and Hun Sen would have committed political hara-kiri had they set themselves up as Sihanouk's political opponents. One bad word from Sihanouk on national television would have hurt their prospects. All of them, as a result, massaged the ego of the ageing Sihanouk.

How did Sihanouk react to the fact that two of his sons were not just rivals, but political enemies?

"My father has all the Cambodian people in mind," Chakrapong said without flinching. "First, his two sons are Cambodian citizens. Secondly, he is a liberal-democrat. We were shaped by Western-style democracy, and we've had liberty since we were eighteen years old. Now I am forty-seven, and my brother is forty-eight, and we are still liberal-democrats. Besides, in many countries the children of one family are free to join different parties."

He explained why the Norodom family had split.

"If my father was still the president of the party, and all of us were not in the same party as my father, you could then say that we were split," he said. "But please remember that when my father was the president of the party all of us were in the same party."

On returning to Phnom Penh soon afterwards we visited Chakrapong at his villa, given to him as an official perquisite. A couple of guards stood outside a forbidding spiked iron gate. They let us enter without a single question. The only thing that was asked of us was that we remove our shoes before entering the house. We were led into a drawing room whose walls were covered with a combination of rare Cambodian artworks and replicas that looked as good as the originals. After ten minutes Chakrapong appeared wearing his trademark safari suit. He greeted us with a smile and a gregarious burst of laughter. He pressed us to have some tea. The tea arrived, and we got talking.

By this time Sihanouk had turned against the SOC government because it had been harassing members of Ranariddh's party. Sihanouk said that he would no longer cooperate with the SOC.

"That is only half of what he said," Chakrapong cut in. "The other half is that he continues to have a relationship with the SOC like before. True, I am his son, but on behalf of the SOC government I am the vice-prime minister. My brother Ranariddh went to see my father when he was ill in Beijing, and gave him all the wrong reports about the SOC harassing Funcinpec people. Prince Ranariddh is the person who instigated my father, and my father made the statement that he would not cooperate with the SOC and Untac. You know, my father is a humanist, and is very emotional, and he was upset."

As if on cue Chakrapong launched into a long tirade against Ranariddh.

"Prince Ranariddh has said that he does not want to live in Phnom Penh. From the very beginning he has never lived in Phnom Penh. Although he is a member of the SNC, which is based in Phnom Penh, Ranariddh lives in Bangkok, and teaches in France! He does not live in Phnom Penh because he says it is not safe. But what does Ranariddh want? I think this is his tactic to separate my father from Cambodia, and make him stay more and more outside the country because if he stays here he can see the real situation. Earlier he [Ranariddh] thought that he could win the election, but now he cannot win."

His face took on a gaunt expression as he spoke about the mistreatment of Vietnamese settlers and, even here, found an opportunity to attack Ranariddh.

189

"There is another problem—that of the Vietnamese immigrants, which is a human problem," he said. "One cannot ignore history. During my father's rule there were 500,000 Vietnamese who were born in Cambodia. They have been a minority in Cambodia for a long time. Take Prince Ranariddh. He is a French citizen, and a professor at a French university. The majority of the leaders of the other parties are also citizens of Australia, America, or France. These parties claim that they are the champions of liberal-democracy and human rights, but what kind of liberal-democracy is it that does not even grant basic rights to the Vietnamese immigrants?"

He threw a challenge to Ranariddh and his partymen to surrender their foreign passports and assimilate with the Cambodian people.

"In many countries people holding foreign passports are not allowed to run for elections," he said. "Some of these Cambodian politicians have double, even triple, nationalities. Even so, we do not mind if they run in our elections. But why do these people deny the same rights to the Vietnamese immigrants? There will be serious problems if these gentlemen with triple nationalities become ministers. They claim to defend the interests of Cambodia, but they have other allegiances. If these people come to power Cambodia would lose its sovereignty because it would then be governed by foreigners. If these opportunists are really committed to Cambodia why don't they surrender one nationality? If they cannot even sacrifice a piece of paper, how can they make sacrifices for their people? I know why they want to keep their foreign passports. If they win the elections they will come and govern the country. But if they lose and if the Khmer Rouge captures power these foreign gentlemen will just go abroad. The only party that does not have foreign passports is the SOC."

Chakrapong's voice rose several octaves as he rebutted the allegations that Vietnamese troops were present in Cambodia to support the Hun Sen government.

"If the Vietnamese troops were present in Cambodia, my father would not have returned to Phnom Penh!" he said. "My father has a philosophy and strategy against colonialism and imperialism. He stood up for independent governance, and for the people. He was the chief of the resistance forces because the presence of the Vietnamese troops in Cambodia went against his principles. Till 1989 he did not want to come to Cambodia because the Vietnamese were here. Don't forget I was also in the jungles fighting against the Vietnamese, and I had a very hard life. But I am here unlike my brother Prince Ranariddh, and Son Sann, who are registered for the elections but live in Bangkok. Do you think that after fighting for twelve years I would come back and live in a country that had a presence of Vietnamese troops?"

As the minister of civil aviation, Chakrapong had been flying to Southeast Asian capitals on business. He was instrumental in launching the national carrier, Kampuchea Airlines, funded by a Malaysian businessman. But soon, Chakrapong's rising star began to fade. His sudden decline and fall was his own doing. On June 10, 1993, within days of the announcement of the results of the elections, Chakrapong and a cabal of CPP leaders such as the minister of interior, Sin Song, and the governors of seven eastern provinces, refused to accept the verdict of the poll that was narrowly won by the royalists led by Chakrapong's archrival, Ranariddh. Rebels led by Chakrapong formed a self-styled Samdech Euv Autonomous Zone (SEAZ), as a sort of a breakaway state.

Samdech Euv, a term of respect that meant "Papa King", was often used to describe Sihanouk. It was odd that the rebels chose to name their outfit after Samdech Euv because their moves, on the surface, did not have the blessings of Sihanouk. Chakrapong used his father's name in the hope of legitimising the SEAZ. But the people saw through the ploy. They knew that the rebels were simply trying to subvert the results of the elections for which they had turned out to vote in overwhelming numbers. For a few troubled days in June it appeared that the country would be partitioned when province after province broke away. The rebel provinces were Kompong Cham, Kratie, Prey Veng, Svay Rieng, Mondulkiri, Ratanakiri, and Stung Treng—the rural heartland from where the CPP drew its power.

The secession embarrassed Hun Sen. It appeared that the rebels had acted with his approval because one of the rebel leaders was his brother Hun Neng, the governor of Kompong Cham. To quash the rumours and defuse the crisis Hun Sen drove to Kompong Cham accompanied by his aide, Uch Kiman, to persuade his brother to abandon the move to break up the country. Earlier, Hun Neng expelled Untac forces and Funcinpec officials from the province, but he backed off later. Hun Sen succeeded in his mission, and Kompong Cham abandoned the autonomous zone.

After a week of uncertainty this was the first sign that the autonomous zone was collapsing. With Kompong Cham back in the fold it was likely that Prey Veng and Svay Rieng would abandon the secession. Predictably, those two provinces gave up the struggle a couple of days later. The remaining rural provinces followed suit and, within days, the movement was dead. Chakrapong's ham-fistedness lay exposed. Hun Sen suffered a considerable loss of face as the rebels were from his party. He admitted that they were a gang of "misled people".

A few hours after the formation of the autonomous zone on June 10 a senior army officer who served as an Untac peacekeeper told us that he had received intelligence information that Chakrapong was planning to escape to Vietnam in order to avoid being arrested. On June 15 Chakrapong did flee to Vietnam. For its part, Vietnam said that it was unable to prevent Chakrapong from entering the country. The foreign ministry in Hanoi said that it had no information as to his whereabouts in Vietnam. Meanwhile, Chakrapong and Sin Song resigned their seats in the national assembly. With the autonomous zone in its death throes, the stage was set for a bargaining game.

It was widely expected that the CPP would hand over power, albeit reluctantly, and would attach conditions and demand control over ministries such as defence and finance. The CPP was also expected to demand an equal status with Ranariddh for its prime ministerial candidate, Hun Sen. But Ranariddh was striking aggressive postures, saying that he would, at best, offer Hun Sen a ministerial post. The reality was vastly different; Ranariddh was hardly in a position to dictate terms to the CPP which effectively controlled the administration. In the end, the two main parties struck a deal to live and let live, and to share power equally.

The oddest occurences became commonplace. Barely a week after his botched attempt to split the country, Chakrapong was promoted to a four-star general by Sihanouk, but not quite rehabilitated. Phnom Penh politics was as unpredictable as King Sihanouk. At the same time, Hun Sen, Ranariddh, Chea Sim, and Heng

Samrin were made five-star generals. Chakrapong's bid to partition Cambodia was forgotten.

The rebellion was just too seductive a theme for Sihanouk to pass up. In 1995, he shot a twenty-five-minute film, *Heir of a Defeated Secessionist,* that was clearly inspired by Chakrapong's actions. Sihanouk said: "A tiny group of Cambodian figures attempted to achieve the secession of a handful of provinces from Cambodia. I succeeded in putting a halt to their action by promising amnesty to the guilty parties if they accepted to immediately rally to the central government. These amateur secessionists did so and everything fell back into place without any bloodshed." The film was also an allusion to an attempted secession that took place in Cambodia several centuries before, he said. "The Cambodian government of those times had to ruthlessly quash all attempts at secession," he added.

The inside story of Chakrapong's rebellion emerged in early July 1993 when we met him at his residence. Dressed in a safari suit, Chakrapong spoke to us for two hours, tears misting his eyes. He spoke bitterly about the treatment he had received at the hands of the CPP.

"I was betrayed and sacrificed by my party," Chakrapong said in a voice choking with emotion.

The attempt by Chakrapong to form an autonomous zone raised many questions. Did the CPP ask him to stage a rebellion in order to strengthen its bargaining position during negotiations for the control of key ministries? Was Sihanouk informed about the formation of the breakaway zone? It did seem plausible that Chakrapong had ended up as the fall guy.

Still a member of the CPP's politburo, Chakrapong was lying low.

Chakrapong stifled a sob, and said: "Maybe I will leave the party. I was very loyal to the party, but I was very sad that my party is not united. I was very sad that I was sacrificed by my party. I served them with all my heart, but I don't like to be betrayed. I would like to see the CPP defend their members because all of us are responsible. Why only sacrifice Chakrapong and Sin Song for the sake of the so-called national reconciliation? Why sacrifice us to please Funcinpec? I don't know whether I will remain in the party. But I was very disappointed that my party changed its position quickly. They don't have a firm stand."

The betrayal hurt him deeply.

"I was very surprised that the CPP was not standing by me," he said. "When I joined the CPP I thought they were reasonable and united, and would help each other. But now I have begun to understand what some people in the CPP are all about. One day when I come back into active politics I will tell you the entire story."

Chakrapong was already thinking of returning to politics.

"The people of Cambodia know that I love my country, and they have given me justice. The majority say that I am very patriotic, and they understand what I am doing for the country."

What did Chakrapong hope to achieve by forming the autonomous zone?

"The results of the election were full of irregularities," he said indignantly.

What irked him was the refusal of his brother, Ranariddh, to share power.

"My father proposed setting up an interim government with himself as president, supported by two vice-premiers, Hun Sen and Ranariddh," he said. "But Ranariddh's party said that they alone should take power because they had won the elections. My father reminded Ranariddh of his election strategy that 'voting for Funcinpec was like voting for Sihanouk'. But everybody stuck to their stand. Akashi [Untac's Japanese chief] said that the election was free and fair, and he dismissed the irregularities as minor. If something similar happened in Japan, it would not be a small thing."

Chakrapong said that the people in the villages were unhappy with the results of the elections.

"People in many provinces were angry about the irregularities," he said. "Everybody thought what I was doing was impossible. All the leaders had lost control. The only man who could solve the problem was Prince Sihanouk."

Jabbing the air in front of him with his finger, he said: "I want to set the record straight. When I said that I was setting up an autonomous zone, people thought it was a separate country. I called it an autonomous zone in the name of my father. So how could they accuse me, and General Sin Song, of separating from the country? It was not true."

Not only had Chakrapong been ditched by his own party for going too far, but Ranariddh lobbied Sihanouk not to include Chakrapong in a future government, and Sihanouk agreed. Suddenly, all the doors were slammed shut on him.

"How could my brother say that at a time when we were trying to forge national reconciliation?" Chakrapong said. "What kind of national reconciliation is that? Before Prince Ranariddh made his demand I had already told my father that I did not want to participate in the government. But Ranariddh also demanded that Hun Sen should not participate. But now Hun Sen is in the government."

How did Chakrapong manage to win the support of the governors of the seven eastern provinces, and convince them to break away?

"I love the people, and they knew me well, and had confidence in me," he said. "Had I continued my campaign for one more day a lot more provinces would have joined me."

Why did he abandon the idea of forming an autonomous zone?

"I had to stop because I had no access to the mass media," he said. "My mistake was that I did not have a radio or TV station through which I could explain what I was doing. I stopped when I saw that everybody had apparently agreed to solve the problem in Phnom Penh through Prince Sihanouk."

Had he received Sihanouk's blessings to form the autonomous zone?

"My father did not know anything about the autonomous zone," he said. "I was alone with Sin Song. My father said over the radio that autonomous zones were nothing new. Even the Khmer Rouge had its autonomous zones where Untac was not allowed to enter. The only thing that he asked of me was not to indulge in violence. What I did was very peaceful. My movement did not involve the army or the police. It was supported just by the people. I did not kill any Untac personnel. But the Khmer Rouge, in their autonomous zone, had killed more than twenty Untac people. My approach was non-violent, like Mahatma Gandhi. I followed the people, and they were the ones who demonstrated."

Why did he go to Ho Chi Minh City in Vietnam after the autonomous zone collapsed? His sudden departure was interpreted as an escape, and damaged his image.

"Being an army man, I made deceptive moves," he said. "I took my ninety-year-old grandmother to Ho Chi Minh City, that's all. She was with me in Svay Rieng province, and Prey Veng province, during the days of the autonomous zone. I had to take her to Vietnam. I only stayed for a couple of hours in Vietnam, that's all. And everybody was saying that I had fled to Vietnam; but they saw me on TV with my father. I want to laugh at such comments. I never 'escaped' to Vietnam, as the press reported it. What was the need for me to go to Vietnam? Cambodia is a big country, and I had lived in the jungles for more than ten years, and I knew how to live."

After coming back from Vietnam Chakrapong stayed in Prey Veng city for a day to meet Hun Sen who had rushed to him with a message from Sihanouk.

"And then I came back. I would not have come back without his message," Chakrapong said.

What was Sihanouk's message?

"To come back for the sake of national reconciliation," Chakrapong added.

If Hun Sen had not pursued the rebels all the way to the eastern provinces to persuade them to abandon their reckless agenda, the continuing rebellion would have jeopardised the formation of the coalition government. From being an asset to the CPP Chakrapong became a liability.

Hun Sen told us: "Prince Chakrapong and General Sin Song did it themselves. Both of them arrested me on June 2, 1993, and tried to force me to resign as the prime minister so that they could hold power, and oppose the results of the election. Afterwards they led, and formed, the autonomous zone. It was I who solved these problems, and prevented fighting and bloodshed."

Was the idea of forming an autonomous zone a plot hatched by the CPP leaders, who may have wanted Chakrapong to do so in order to manoeuvre themselves into a stronger position to bargain for a bigger role in the government?

Laughing, Chakrapong said, "I have heard about this. I cannot talk about it now. But maybe, one day, I will talk. One day, I will tell you what happened. I am responsible for what I did."

When the controversy had blown over, Chakrapong went to see his father in the capital on June 18.

"My father was very happy to see me and Sin Song," he said. "He then offered me the post of four-star general."

He would return to politics, Chakrapong said, and form his own aid consortium to rebuild the country.

One year later the rebellious prince got into trouble, again. The trio of Chakrapong, former interior minister Sin Song, and General Sin Sen—all CPP members—were accused of trying to engineer a *coup* against co-premiers Ranariddh and Hun Sen in early July 1994. A truckload of rebels was seen moving into Phnom Penh, but they were quickly disarmed before they could put their plan into action. Within minutes it was all over. The attempted *coup* was amateurishly conceived, and clumsily executed.

Chakrapong launched the *coup* attempt after the CPP stripped him of his status as an elected MP in the national assembly. But there was more to the *coup* than met the eye. Chakrapong had become a pawn in a larger political game. Ranariddh, with no love lost for his half-brother, had been searching for ways to teach him a lesson. At the same time Hun Sen's CPP was trying to muster support to pass a law in the national assembly outlawing the Khmer Rouge. It was believed that Ranariddh and Hun Sen had similar ideas on how to deal with the rebellious Chakrapong. They struck a deal. Hun Sen would support strong action against Chakrapong and, in return, Ranariddh would give Hun Sen's party the necessary support to pass a bill banning the guerrillas. The bill, authored by the CPP, had been hanging fire in the national assembly and could not be passed for several months on account of a lack of support from Funcinpec.

With his botched *coup* attempt Chakrapong played right into Ranariddh's hands. A section of the CPP initially resisted the move to punish Chakrapong too severely. But after internal discussions the highly disciplined and secretive CPP reached a consensus to sacrifice him as he had become a political liability. Winning

Funcinpec's support to ban the Khmer Rouge was of much greater importance to the CPP than the future of Chakrapong. The CPP was worried that Funcinpec, a former battlefield ally of the Khmer Rouge, was reluctant to outlaw the guerrillas, and that many of its MPs were good friends of the Khmer Rouge. The time to strike a deal to ban the Khmer Rouge was ripe when the guerrillas inflicted a humiliating military defeat on the Royal Cambodian Armed Forces, and thwarted their bid to capture Pailin and Anlong Veng.

Soon after the arrest of the *coup* leaders Hun Sen said that the trio had wanted to establish a new government, and appoint a new head of state to replace King Sihanouk.

Hun Sen said: "In his first confession Sin Song said, in a letter, that the *coup* was aimed at destroying the government, which he called an anarchist government, in order to set up a temporary national liberation government."

But Chakrapong disagreed. He said that the *coup* was a fiction, a convenient excuse concocted by the government to get rid of him. "How could just 200–300 soldiers pull off a *coup*, when Phnom Penh was such a heavily defended town?" he asked. Moreover, there was no bloodshed, or exchange of fire, as reported by the co-interior minister, Sar Kheng. To make the *coup* theory even more ludicrous, none of the soldiers involved were prosecuted, he said.

The end of Chakrapong's short and flamboyant political career came when he was deported to Malaysia. Sin Song was kept under house arrest in the Cambodian capital. Suddenly, there was no threat to Ranariddh from any member of the royal family.

Hun Sen said: "The exile of Chakrapong was carried out according to the proposal made by King Sihanouk. It was also of use to Ranariddh because these two princes were not on good terms."

Trouble shadowed Chakrapong all the way to Malaysia. He, and his family, reached the Malaysian capital of Kuala Lumpur where they stayed with a personal friend. The Malaysian government allowed Chakrapong to enter the country based on a request made a year earlier by Sihanouk to let him stay in Malaysia after his attempt to form a breakaway zone. On July 6, Chakrapong urged the Malaysian government for permission to live in the country and, at the same time, denied involvement in the abortive *coup* the previous week. Chakrapong made his appeal in a letter to Malaysian deputy prime minister, Anwar Ibrahim. But Anwar said that Malaysia could not let Chakrapong stay until it had conferred with the Cambodian government. Less than a week later, the Cambodian government expressed its unhappiness over Chakrapong's continued presence in Malaysia. Not unexpectedly, the Malaysian government, which wanted to maintain good relations with Ranariddh and Hun Sen, told Chakrapong to leave the country. He was asked to migrate to a third country, and was given enough time to do so.

While France and a couple of other countries were asked to accept him, Chakrapong was spotted with his wife, son, and two friends eating pizza at a fast-food outlet in a Kuala Lumpur suburb. But their life was hardly normal. The Malaysians hoped that Chakrapong would leave before a visit to Malaysia in August by Ranariddh and Hun Sen.

Chakrapong was a shattered man who spoke bitterly about being "forced out of Phnom Penh" and then, Malaysia. He sought refuge in Thailand, but complained that he was "once again compelled to leave Thailand where my wife and child are Thai nationals". Under pressure from Phnom Penh, even the Thais would not allow him to stay.

"Since leaving Phnom Penh I have resolved to settle down to a quiet life with my family, but the Cambodian authorities had, instead, sought to banish me from everywhere I went, as a fugitive," he said. "I could not even enjoy a simple life of a husband to my wife, and a father to my children."

By the end of July 1994, France opened its doors to Chakrapong, releasing Malaysia and Thailand from an uncomfortable diplomatic situation.

Outraged at being stalked by the media, Chakrapong said that the press had "hounded him like a criminal, or even a terrorist". He added: "I cannot even have a quiet meal by myself. I cannot even take a leisurely stroll down the street without worrying whether my every move is stalked like a predator to his prey, by the press."

The rebellious Chakrapong was believed to have joined a new rebel group headed by a Khmer Rouge leader, Chan Youran. The Khmer Rouge said that the new group included some former members of the parties headed by Sihanouk and Son Sann. Khmer Rouge radio said that the group, formed after a split in the Khmer Rouge, consisted of 2,300 members, and was known as a "liberation army". In anger Chakrapong denied the Khmer Rouge radio report.

"Such clandestine political manoeuvring by the Khmer Rouge, and possibly by the government of Cambodia is indeed characteristic of the lowly political play that is now tearing my country apart," he said.

Chakrapong had left Cambodia, but the reverberations of his abortive *coup* continued to be felt in Phnom Penh. The government closed down a popular Khmer-language newspaper, *Morning News,* in early July for linking interior minister Sar Kheng—a brother-in-law of CPP supremo Chea Sim—with the *coup* plotters. While the editor of *Morning News,* Nguon Nonn, was censured, the government banned ministers from talking to the media about investigations into the attempted *coup*. The leak had to be plugged, and the government's plumbers were hard at work.

Cambodia was a forgiving place. It had embraced former Khmer Rouge guerrillas such as Hun Sen, Chea Sim, and Heng Samrin as its present-day leaders, and there seemed no reason why Chakrapong would not ultimately be rehabilitated in the same spirit of national reconciliation and forgiveness.

Chakrapong remained a pariah till November 1997 when Sihanouk pardoned him. In a reconciliatory mood Hun Sen agreed to the king's proposal to rehabilitate his wayward son.

But Hun Sen remained wary of Chakrapong. The trump card that Hun Sen and his CPP colleagues had spotted in Chakrapong when they inducted him into the party had nearly cost them the game.

EIGHT

THE HUN FAMILY

AN ELDER BROTHER

If Hun Sen controlled Cambodia, his elder brother
Hun Neng was the uncrowned king of Kompong
Cham province, the ricebowl of the country. Hun
Neng, the Governor of Kompong Cham, was an
extremely reclusive man, whose life was shrouded
in mystery and secrecy. While his brother's face had
a high visibility in the local press, Hun Neng's was
a rarity.

To uncover the mystery of Hun Neng we flew
to his province before sunrise on May 25, 1993, on
a United Nations' helicopter. Voters were casting
their ballots when we arrived. The first thing that
we did was to hire a couple of motorcycle taxis,
and rode to the party headquarters of the
Cambodian People's Party (CPP). There we met Lay
Sokha, a deputy governor who assisted Hun Neng.

"We will win the election," Sokha said. "We have two teams—team A, and team B in reserve."

Why two teams? Well, if one team was killed the other would live to contest the election, said Sokha who had been a deputy governor since 1985. The CPP would win because Hun Sen had visited the province four times that year which, he said, was an indicator of the good work his supreme leader had done. We told him that we wanted to meet his boss, Hun Neng.

"Impossible," he said nervously. "He does not meet writers."

The veil of mystery around Hun Neng seemed impenetrable, and we almost gave up hope of coming face to face with him.

Back on the road we decided to search for an Indian army battalion that was based in the province. We stopped to cool off under a tree beside the Mekong. Minutes later a patrol jeep of three Indian army soldiers, their heads covered with UN skyblue bandanas, approached. We flagged them down, and asked for directions. They asked us to follow them. A ten-minute ride through narrow roads choked with dense foliage brought us to a clearing where a dozen prefabricated houses stood exposed to Khmer Rouge attacks on three sides. Kompong Cham was a stronghold of the guerrillas who had bases in fourteen of the fifteen districts.

There, we met the battalion commander, Colonel A.N. Bahuguna, who fortified us with a cup of Indian tea followed by a breakfast of *parathas* and curried potatoes. We told him that the purpose of our visit was to meet Hun Sen's older brother, Hun Neng. As luck would have it the colonel knew him personally. He summoned his Cambodian liaison man, and asked him to dash across to Hun Neng's residence with a request for an appointment for the same afternoon. An hour later the liaison man reappeared, and said that Hun Neng's secretary had turned down our request because the governor was too busy.

Unfazed by the rejection from the overzealous secretary we set off for the governor's house after a hearty vegetarian lunch at the Indian army mess. The colonel apologised for the vegetarian fare as it was a religious day for the Indians who were clearly missing their lamb *korma*.

An army jeep dropped us outside a sprawling red-tiled, hacienda-style mansion with armed guards outside and inside. We walked up the stairs to an ostentatious livingroom lined with black rexine sofas, an outsized television set, and Khmer paintings covering whitewashed walls. We found Hun Neng sitting there, alone.

The brothers bore a striking resemblance. They looked like a pair of twins, except that Hun Neng was slightly taller, and was not wearing spectacles. They were young—Hun Sen was forty-one, Hun Neng forty-four. In a well-tailored grey safari suit Hun Neng did not look like a provincial figure from a small town. As he began talking it became clear that they were not just siblings; they were brothers-in-arms who were digging in for a tough election campaign to keep the CPP in power.

To the Hun brothers the electoral battle for Kompong Cham was not an ordinary contest. It was a do-or-die effort to retain control over the province where they were born. They brought in the heavyweights. Some key battles featuring the biggest political stars were to be fought in the province—Hun Sen, Hun Neng, and Prince Norodom Chakrapong. These CPP stalwarts were being opposed by Funcinpec leader Prince Norodom Sirivudh.

With an expansive sweep of his arm Hun Neng said: "The reason why we will win the election here is that the people have no faith in the Khmer Rouge. Kompong Cham is the province where they committed their most terrible genocidal crimes. The people have not forgotten it."

Hun Neng told us a story to reinforce his claim.

"A car dealer in Phnom Penh has wagered that if our party lost the election he would give away free cars," he said. "So confident he is of our victory. The reason why the people will vote for us is that they are suspicious of the Khmer Rouge, and of parties linked with them."

A few days earlier Ung Huot, a political adviser to Ranariddh, had provided the opposing view. He said that the Funcinpec party would win in Kompong Cham. But this opinion flew in the face of conventional wisdom that the Hun brothers were the favourites as they controlled much more than Kompong Cham.

Their influence also spilled over into neighbouring Prey Veng and Svay Rieng provinces, which together with Kompong Cham sent thirty-four members to the national assembly, and comprised thirty-three per cent of the registered voters in the country. Confident of their roots and connections in the three provinces, the Hun brothers were aiming to take the lion's share of the vote.

"That," said Colonel Bahuguna, "is the political significance of these three states."

Kompong Cham's political importance was its strategic location at the confluence of two mighty rivers, the Mekong and the Tonle Sap, that blessed the land of this major rice-producing province. The Tonle Sap ran through neighbouring Kompong Chhnang province, close to the border of Kompong Cham, and the Mekong flowed through Kompong Cham. Its commercial importance was that the traditional trade route to Vietnam ran through it. At the time it seemed that the only negative factor that could muddy Hun Neng's ambitious economic plan to transform Kompong Cham into a booming producer of agricultural commodities was the presence of the Khmer Rouge. But Colonel Bahuguna discounted their ability to inflict damage after a recent violent encounter with the Indian army had scared the guerrillas, who since then had kept a low profile.

Hun Neng's rise coincided with the meteoric ascent of his younger brother, Hun Sen. Hun Neng experienced harsh treatment at the hands of the Khmer Rouge. He was jailed by them in the mid-1970s, punished, and exiled to the hills of Kompong Thom for nine months. His crime: he was the brother of Hun Sen who had betrayed the Khmer Rouge. According to a family member, Hun Neng was forced to perform hard manual labour at a site in Kompong Thom where the Khmer Rouge was constructing a large dyke.

"They wanted to kill him through hard work. He was given no food, and made to work very hard. He was reduced to skin and bones," the family member said.

Like his brother, Hun Neng was a revolutionary. He helped Hun Sen raise the Cambodian forces that, together with the Vietnamese troops, eventually overthrew the Khmer Rouge in 1979. While Hun Neng played an important role in mobilising the military forces in Kompong Cham, Hun Sen sought refuge and political asylum in south Vietnam.

Hun Neng drifted into the past, and began talking about the liberation of Cambodia from the Khmer Rouge.

"In 1979, Hun Sen's forces and my forces met on the left and right sides of the Mekong river, and then got together to launch an attack on the Khmer Rouge," he said.

Hun Neng defended his brother and his CPP colleagues who were then being smeared by their political rivals.

"Ranariddh accuses Hun Sen, Heng Samrin, and Chea Sim of belonging to the Khmer Rouge in the 1970s, but they were never really a part of the guerrilla movement because all three had been jailed by the Khmer Rouge in the 1970s," he said.

This version of history contradicted the generally accepted view that when Hun Sen grew disillusioned with the brutal ways of the Khmer Rouge, he fled to Vietnam, and that at no time was he, or his colleagues, jailed by the Khmer Rouge. However, this may have been Hun Neng's way of saying that Hun Sen was forced to stay on in the Khmer Rouge against his wishes, and that he had been planning to quit long before he actually mustered the strength and courage to do so.

Later, Hun Neng studied economics in Phnom Penh, and served as an economic adviser to the local government of Kompong Cham. He rose to become the chief of a district, and was then appointed the governor in 1985—the same year that Hun Sen became the prime minister. Owing to his background in economics, Hun Neng took a keen interest in the provincial economy, and was a member of the powerful central committee of the CPP. That afternoon he voiced his concerns over the negative propaganda war being waged by Funcinpec that, if it won the elections, it would cancel ali the business contracts the Hun Sen government had entered into.

"The Voice of America had broadcast this warning," Hun Neng said. "Some people were conducting this propaganda campaign to discourage investors from coming to Cambodia."

We sipped tea inside the cool hacienda, and chatted about the security situation. As we said goodbye Hun Neng asked us to return to his province some day, and write about its booming economy.

HUN Neng's confidence was shaken on Saturday, May 29. Early election results showed the CPP trailing in four provinces where Ranariddh's Funcinpec had taken the lead. As the votes were being counted Ranariddh's party was ahead in the constituencies of Phnom Penh, Pursat, Sihanoukville, and Kratie. But by mid-day on Sunday, Hun Sen's party had clawed back in the see-saw battle, and led Funcinpec in seven constituencies while Funcinpec was ahead in five. When the final results came in the CPP had been defeated by Funcinpec by a slender margin of six per cent of the votes.

A diplomat, insisting on anonymity, said: "It was more a negative vote against the Hun Sen government rather than a positive vote for Ranariddh. It was an indictment of the way the State of Cambodia government had ruled since 1979."

Ranariddh's political manager, Ung Huot, said: "When people come out to vote in such large numbers it usually signals that they want a change."

The feared bloodbath did not happen, and Cambodia's first elections since the 1960s turned out to be less violent than those in Sri Lanka where hundreds died. Nor did Hun Sen impose a Burma-type solution by imprisoning the victors of the poll. Hun Sen, and his party, chose the pragmatic option: to share power with Ranariddh. But it left nobody in doubt about who ran the country. Ranariddh was the public face of the government, while real power resided with Hun Sen, Chea Sim, and Heng Samrin.

As for Kompong Cham, Hun Neng remained its supremo. But many Cambodians viewed him as being too authoritarian, and aloof from the needs of the people. In the end, he was a provincial figure, lacking the national appeal and the vast power of his illustrious brother.

THE HUN HOUSEHOLD

The prime ministership changed Hun Sen's tastes. He now lived in an extravagant palatial home where he held political meetings, hosted foreign government officials, entertained guests, and played golf. But he still made the effort to spend time with the family on simple pleasures such as feeding the pelicans that lived on his private lake, playing volleyball, and watching video movies. His taste in food remained very Spartan, very Khmer. He only relished food cooked by his wife.

"So discerning is his palate that he can tell instantly if Bun Rany had cooked a certain dish," a family member commented.

Her menus were uncomplicated. At breakfast it was always rice with some dried fish and fish sauce washed down with a glass of black coffee. For lunch and dinner he ate a dish of bamboo shoots with pork, or *pra hok* cooked with bananas. His favourite fruit was *longan*. In the evenings he enjoyed a couple of glasses of Hennessy cognac mixed with Coke.

Bun Rany had engaged a few cooks at the prime ministerial residence. The cooks prepared the ingredients, and waited for her to come into the kitchen and cook up a quick dish. The Hun family did not like to mix sugar with salt, unlike the Thais who had a penchant for mixing the two, for instance, dousing chilli-hot noodles with spoonfuls of sugar.

A flashpoint in the family was the issue of Hun Sen's smoking. He had smoked forty cigarettes a day since his guerrilla days, and found no reason to stop. His children tried to get him to quit. He set himself many deadlines, but failed each time.

"He does not take too many puffs. At the most he takes four of five puffs of a stick, and lets it burn out," said his brother-in-law Nim Chandara.

Another addiction was his old friends. His sense of loyalty to the people who supported him in his guerrilla days remained strong. Sometimes it caused an invasion of privacy. During his days in the jungles he was so popular that many mothers adopted him as their son, many young women took him as their brother. When droves of these adopted mothers and sisters began arriving at their home in Takhmau, Hun Sen greeted them warmly, swapped old stories, and shared food and cigarettes. But Bun Rany felt that the stream of visitors was invading their privacy, and left no time for the family. She protested to Hun Sen, but he told her he could not turn his back on the people on whom he had relied during his years as a guerrilla. Sometimes when the house was overflowing with people he would tell Bun Rany to send the children to the home of his sister, Hun Sinath, who took pleasure in fussing over them.

Bun Rany and Hun Sen lived as normal a life as possible with their college-going children coming in and out of the house whenever they were home for the holidays.

Like a clucking hen surveying her brood with pride and achievement, she talked about her children and their powerful father.

"He is very soft with the children," she said. "When they were small they would come into his bed, and he would horse around with them."

The children were constantly worried about the safety of their father.

"They used to fret a lot when he went abroad on his trips," she said. "Especially when they were very young they used to be sick at being separated from him."

The family valued its closeness after years of suffering and separation.

"The children would not stay in a separate room when they were young," she said. "They used to come and sleep with us. Only when they grew up did they have their separate rooms. This was especially true of the last three children who still like to come and jump into our bed."

But Bun Rany was realistic about bringing them up with the right amount of discipline.

"Both of us cracked the whip when we had to," she said. "But we've been fairly lucky with them because they have been obedient kids most of the time."

"They were sent to school pretty early—when they were five years old. They didn't really know how to fool around with other kids because they got a large dose of discipline pretty early on at home," she said.

"I only recall one time when their father hit Manet and Manit when they were travelling together. By and large, we have only had to guide them along, and never had to really reprimand them," she said.

The years of shared suffering with her first surviving child, Hun Manet, had fashioned an unbreakable bond between mother and child.

"Hun Manet had always been at the top of the class, or in the worst case, second or third. As a child he was self-driven," said the proud parent.

"Hun Manet is a really unique kid. He's the only one of my children who's cried when I've given him a new shirt," she said.

The boy burst into tears because he had seen his parents suffer so much. He shared their pain. A determined child, Manet surprised his parents by taking computer training and Thai language lessons in addition to his usual workload.

"Manet never went out partying, or asked us for money at any point," she said. "Before going to New York he sat for an exam in Cambodia and topped the charts in mathematics."

Hun Sen was proud of Manet who won financial aid to study at the Westpoint Military Academy in New York state in the US in the mid-1990s. Manet graduated from the academy in May 1999. A rapturous Hun Sen flew to the US to attend the graduation ceremony.

Justifying her extra special love for Manet, Bun Rany said: "It was a hard life for Manet. When I was pregnant with him we only got to eat fish paste and porridge. We hardly ever had the luxury of vegetables or meat. I feel the most sympathy for him. I love all the children equally, but I feel a special bond with him because of what we shared."

Hun Sen's political career took a toll on the time the family spent together.

"We did not have much time to really hang around with them, but they've turned out pretty good kids," she said.

But she was concerned about her daughter, Maly, who studied in Singapore.

"I do occasionally worry about my daughter because she does not live with me. And I know that she is under strict supervision under her uncle who is more of a disciplinarian than I am."

The woman who came through the Khmer Rouge slaughter, said: "I think we are lucky that despite the separation and enormous stress we have remained a fairly happy and functional family."

Hun Sen's extended family had mixed fortunes. His brother, Hun San, worked as a director of transportation in the ministry of communications from 1979 till the early 1990s when he met with a serious road accident. Hun San was a motorcycle enthusiast who enjoyed long journeys on his machine. He was driving in the city when he was run down by a car. He suffered serious injuries to his head, and was unable to work.

Hun Sen's sister, Sengny, married Meas Sovanndy who worked as a deputy director in the border police department. Sovanndy had worked earlier as a driver to Nhek Huon who was one of the four men who escaped to Vietnam along with Hun Sen in 1977.

Another sister, Sinath, married Nim Chandara who worked as a vice director in the ministry of interior, and was in charge of the department of bodyguards. And the youngest sister, Thoeun, remarried after her former husband died. Her second husband, Keo Sokleng, worked as a bureau chief in the economic police department.

Hun Sen's father, Hun Neang, loved his son intensely, but sometimes had his differences with him. For years, Hun Neang worked hard at building a high school in a rural area, but he was disappointed when Hun Sen suggested to him that the school should be named after King Sihanouk. Hun Neang protested, saying that he had put much effort into the school. Hun Sen did not broach the subject for some weeks. When Hun Sen persisted, Hun Neang relented, and the school was eventually named after Sihanouk. A family member said that Hun Neang was not happy with his son's decision.

A YOUNGER SISTER AND HER HUSBAND

Snuggled into the quilting of the ricefields of Stung Trang district in Kompong Cham province was the tiny village of Peam Koh Sna where Hun Sen was born. It was also the birthplace of his younger sister, Hun Sinath. The plucky young girl took to her studies like a fish to water, but her education was interrupted by the civil war.

She joined the *maquis*, led by the Khmer Rouge, in 1971. She was assigned to work as a nurse in a hospital in the same area where Hun Sen later commanded a guerrilla regiment. Her medical unit followed Hun Sen's fighting forces as they fanned out to engage Lon Nol's troops in battle. Brother and sister stayed in close touch during this troubled period.

The Khmer Rouge Angkar arrested her soon after Hun Sen escaped to Vietnam. She was forced to perform hard manual labour. Her supervisors pointed fingers at her, and broke her spirit by calling her an enemy. They accusingly said her brother was half-Vietnamese.

Over in Vietnam, Hun Sen was worried about his family, and he planned a secret search and rescue mission. In late-1977 he led a special team from Vietnam to the family home in Kompong Cham, but he could not locate the family.

"When he found nobody he burned the house. He thought that nobody was alive," said Nim Chandara who later married Hun Sinath. It appears that he burned down the house so it would not fall into the hands of his enemies.

NOT far from Kompong Cham, a little boy, Nim Chandara, was growing up in a scholarly home. He was born in Takeo province where his father was a school teacher. When he was 11 years old his father moved to Svay Rieng province close to the border with Vietnam. Later, the family decided to leave the province because it lacked schools. They moved to Phnom Penh so that the children could go to high school and university.

Chandara studied at the faculty of medicine in Phnom Penh, and completed the second year of his medical studies in 1975. During the terrible Pol Pot years the family was forced to move back to Takeo province. His father, and his elder brother who was a doctor, were killed by the Khmer Rouge in 1977.

After the liberation Chandara stayed on in Svay Rieng where he had many good friends and happy memories. But his city friends called him back to Phnom Penh. He returned and joined the Sixth Battalion in January 1979.

His life took a sudden twist on February 2, 1979 when Hun Sen visited his unit, and demanded that the educational records of all the soldiers be shown to him. On seeing Chandara's certificates, he realised that he was highly educated, and immediately took him out of the unit. Chandara was given a new job as a driver and special bodyguard of Meas Sovanndy, a government official who married Hun Sen's sister, Sengny.

Hun Sen lived alone at the time in his new home at the Independence Monument in Phnom Penh. His family was still missing. He asked Chandara and a group of soldiers to search for his parents, and his sisters Sinath, Thoeun, and Sengny.

"First, we found his father and Sinath in Stung Trang. The difficulty was that everybody had been separated. Then we found Thoeun and Sengny, and at the end we found his wife, Bun Rany," Chandara said.

Hun Sen's parents lay low, and concealed their identity.

"He was smart and kept his identity secret. Hun Sen's mother was also very smart. She had a lot of Muslim and Chinese friends. She was also in the Stung Trang area, but lived separately," Chandara said.

Hun Sen's older brother, Hun San, was forced by the Khmer Rouge to build homes in Kompong Cham. And, sister Sengny stitched clothes for the Khmer Rouge in the same province.

After liberation Sinath eventually completed her education through the 1980s, and went on to study the Thai language and culture with a passion.

Chandara worked very hard for Hun Sen, who grew to trust him. Unexpectedly, in 1979, Hun Sen asked some foreign ministry officials to arrange Chandara's marriage with his sister, Sinath.

"On April 3, 1979 Hun Sen asked us to get married, and we were married on April 9, just six days later," Chandara said.

"Hun Sen wanted me to become a diplomat, but I didn't like the job," Chandara added.

He sent Chandara to Germany. He took German language courses for a year. Chandara did well in his studies, but he told Hun Sen that he did not want to be a diplomat.

"I told him that I wanted to become a pilot," he said.

After returning from Germany Chandara worked in the foreign ministry for a short while before moving to the department of immigration in the ministry of interior where he helped Hun Sen with his security. Soon after Chakrapong failed to engineer a *coup* in July 1994, Hun Sen shifted Chandara to the bodyguards department, a crack unit that took care of the security of the Cambodian leaders.

A TROUBLED FRIENDSHIP

After Hun Sen became the prime minister of the State of Cambodia he began consolidating his power by appointing loyalists to positions of authority, in the process fashioning a vast network of support. One of them was Ung Phan who was appointed the minister of transport, communications, and posts.

But Ung Phan grew ambitious, and tried to set up his own political party as a challenger to the ruling Kampuchean People's Revolutionary Party (KPRP). He was expelled from the KPRP, and imprisoned for 17 months in Phnom Penh's notorious T-3 jail in May 1990 for setting up an underground organisation while still being a member of the ruling party.

The government made a stunning revelation in a radio broadcast on July 31, 1990: "The party central committee decided to expel Ung Phan from the party central committee and the party, because he betrayed the party and the nation's historic tasks." It added that his actions caused a split in the forces opposing the Khmer Rouge that was fighting the government along the Thai border. The expulsion came at a meeting of the sixty-five-member central committee held from July 23-30. Along with Ung Phan, at least five other government and military officials were arrested for trying to form a separate, pro-democracy party. The radio broadcast added that the state had foiled a *coup* plot, but it did not identify the plotters. The Constitution allowed freedom of association, but said that the communist party was the leading force in the nation.

After Ung Phan's release Hun Sen still considered him a friend, and forgave him. In early-1992 Hun Sen presented a silver Toyota Crown saloon car to Ung Phan.

But Ung Phan refused to remain silent, and mounted yet another challenge to the government. By this time the political environment in the country had changed vastly: the rigid one-party state was gradually being replaced by a multi-party system. The new liberal-democratic system was being created by the United Nations Transitional Authority in Cambodia (Untac) that was mandated to organise elections against the backdrop of an alarming rise in political murders by unknown assassins.

Thinking mistakenly that democracy had finally taken root Ung Phan bravely announced the formation of Cambodia's first independent association to protect human rights. But some powerful people did not like what he was doing, and he was shot in the neck and shoulders three times by unidentified gunmen when he was driving with his infant son in his silver saloon car from Takhmau to Phnom Penh in January 1992.

The bullets narrowly missed the child, and a badly injured Ung Phan was rushed to a local hospital where he gradually recovered. The surgeon who operated on Ung Phan said that his patient had told him that he did not hold the government responsible for the attack. But suspicions lingered that some people in the government, or close to the government, were behind the attack.

After being discharged from hospital Ung Phan was placed under the personal protection of Hun Sen. When Hun Sen brought the badly shaken forty-one-year-old Ung Phan to his Phnom Penh residence out of sympathy, he was criticised by some of his partymen for helping a man who had betrayed the party.

The irrepressible Ung Phan then joined forces with Ranariddh's Funcinpec party, an act that severed his links with Hun Sen and the ruling party. He was appointed a deputy prime minister when an interim coalition government was formed in June 1993, and travelled to Malaysia and Singapore to drum up investments. But Ung Phan's honeymoon with first prime minister Ranariddh ended in April 1997 when he accused Ranariddh of incompetence, and said that he was unfit to lead the Funcinpec party or the nation. Hun Sen's Cambodian People's Party (CPP) quickly pounced on Ranariddh, saying that it supported a call by Ung Phan to sack Ranariddh. This development brought out into the open the festering conflict between the two main coalition partners, Funcinpec and the CPP.

But Ung Phan still admired and respected Hun Sen, and tried to prove his loyalty by providing Hun Sen with vital information about a plot to assassinate Hun Sen that was allegedly hatched by Foreign Minister Prince Norodom Sirivudh in 1995. Finally, Ung Phan broke away from Funcinpec in April 1997.

It was apparent that Ung Phan had again grown close to Hun Sen, and that the CPP was using him as a tool to divide the already fractious Funcinpec leaders.

Ung Phan played a key role in preparing the government's case against Prince Sirivudh who was accused of plotting the assassination of Hun Sen. When the case against Sirivudh was heard in a Phnom Penh court the biggest piece of evidence against the prince was a deposition by Ung Phan in which he claimed that Sirivudh had told him that he would kill Hun Sen.

By this time Ung Phan had fallen out with Ranariddh. He accused Ranariddh of fomenting instability by ordering that Funcinpec achieve military parity with the CPP, and that the creation of a Funcinpec-led National Front alliance, ahead of the general election, was a de facto *coup d'état*.

According to Hun Sen's brother-in-law, Nim Chandara, Ung Phan and Hun Sen remained good friends. In 1995 the duo built a high school in Svay Rieng province simply called "Hun Sen-Ung Phan High School".

"Hun Sen is a very forgiving person. He has a large and soft heart," Nim Chandara said.

NINE

THE SOURCE

CONVERSATIONS ALONG THE TONLE SAP

With a fluid wristy movement Hun Sen jerked a packet of 555s at us. We declined the offer, and Hun Sen, prime minister of the State of Cambodia, smiled knowingly the way smokers smile at non-smokers, and lit up. We were talking to Hun Sen on new year's day, January 1, 1992 at the council of ministers' building in Phnom Penh. Hun Sen's tan, impassive face and soft Khmer tones did not betray a hint of fatigue from the celebration the night before.

The revelry in Phnom Penh was unreal. Cambodia had no cause to celebrate. Old hatreds ran deep in spite of the signing of a peace accord in Paris in October the previous year. Although a tentative peace had returned, the Cambodian people remained abysmally poor. The grand accord had done little to improve their lives; instead the approximately 22,000 peacekeeping forces serving under the United Nations Transitional Authority in Cambodia (Untac) had unleashed inflation which took rice and potatoes out of the reach of the common folk. What a new year's gift!

It had not been easy to meet Hun Sen who had a full agenda starting with a meeting with visiting American congressman, Stephen Solarz. Our guide, Leng Sochea, pressed us to approach Cham Prasidh, a top aide to the prime minister. We told Prasidh that we wanted to meet the premier. Prasidh was polite, and said that he would convey our message to Hun Sen. He told us to wait, and hope for the best.

As Solarz arrived we clicked a picture of him ascending the stairs to the council of ministers' building leading up to Hun Sen's chambers, but the flashgun failed to go off.

"Hey, your flash didn't work," Solarz said as he went in to meet the premier.

About forty minutes later an official came running towards us, and said that Hun Sen had agreed to meet us, but he didn't have much time. How much time would he give us, we asked.

"Oh, about forty-five minutes," he replied.

There were four government officials present in the room, all smokers, but they banished all hopes of lighting up in the presence of their great political leader. It was generally believed that Hun Sen was a creation of Vietnam. There was some truth in that perception. The millions of Cambodians who only knew a life of abject poverty had ambivalent feelings about him. Many viewed him as their only hope, and, at the same time, they cynically believed that they deserved their leaders.

Ever since his return to Cambodia on the crest of the tidal wave of the liberation forces, Hun Sen had struggled to win political legitimacy. It was a fight that would cost him more than an eye. His aides said that his health suffered as well. During the peace talks between the four factions, and the permanent five of the United Nations, he had fainted on more than one occasion. Some observers dismissed his passing out as a diversionary tactic, a ploy to win sympathy. Like most things about him even the fainting episode became suspect. The tragic figure that he cut during the years of the civil war was gradually replaced by a more wholesome personality, a maturing politician, one who had managed to pull off the ultimate survival act in the political jungle that was Cambodia. He stayed alive to thrive in a hostile political climate, both at home and abroad. He made very few friends and a lot of powerful enemies not only in the West, and among the neighbouring non-communist countries who viewed his government as a lapdog of Hanoi, but he also had opponents within his own government. For all these hurdles, his rise was meteoric.

He exhibited profound political sagacity for someone so inexperienced in the affairs of state. In early December 1991, less than two months after the signing of the peace accord he predicted that his Cambodian People's Party (CPP) would form a coalition government with the royalist party after the general election in May 1993. It was a public relations master-stroke, delivered in Kompong Cham during Sihanouk's visit to the province, and aimed at reassuring Sihanouk that his royalist party would play a major role in a future government.

On that occasion Sihanouk told the people of Kompong Cham: "The last time I came to this province was in 1976. The Khmer Rouge brought me, but I didn't have much freedom."

Hun Sen did everything to please Sihanouk. He made sure that the 125 kilometre road from the capital to the province was decked with hundreds of national flags, and that the people had been informed about his visit so that they would line the roads expectantly to catch a glimpse of the prince. But beneath the public relations Sihanouk was aware of the painful reality. A year earlier, he had shot a film, *My Village at Dusk,* depicting the harshness of life in a Khmer village. Sihanouk said: "I wanted to show the realities, happiness and misfortune, of a Khmer village whose surrounding areas, including fields and rice paddies, are riddled with landmines; the courage, abnegation, sacrifices of some, the despair of others; the present difference in the way of life between city and country; [and] Cambodia's uncertain future in which the process of domestic reconciliation is still a precarious one."

The man we were listening to on that new year's day did not seem to carry the lodestone of a traumatic past. We were sitting in Hun Sen's palatial meeting room where he held court. Before us he had met congressman Solarz, though nothing much came of it. The Americans were not about to make any concessions, or lift their trade embargo. We sat on grand chairs, elaborately carved and dressed in gold paint. Hun Sen, in a dark suit and a discreet tie, greeted us in his native Khmer language, through his interpreter, Uch Kiman, who held a vice-ministerial rank. Though his education was interrupted Hun Sen had learnt to speak a little English, as well as French, and Russian.

The years sat easily on him. Shiny black hair neatly parted down the side, and glowing skin made him look younger than his forty years. However, his glass eye, fitted after a sensitive operation, did tend to unnerve as he had a nervous twitch. He smoked constantly, inhaling deeply before speaking, and emitting puffs of smoke with his words.

What, we asked, was the biggest crisis that confronted his country? Had his party dropped the idea of putting the Khmer Rouge leaders on trial? And did he think that the people would, at some stage, demand a court trial for the genocidal crimes committed by them?

"I believe that the idea of bringing the Khmer Rouge to trial will not be abandoned because there are many people who would like to see justice done," he said in earnest tones. "The popular anger against the Khmer Rouge cannot be diluted."

He stopped to drag on his cigarette with an air of great gravity and dignity, and continued: "Although a number of countries had subscribed to the Paris peace agreement, all of them wanted to bring the Khmer Rouge back to trial. I think we should let the next elected government decide on this."

But his patience was running thin with the Khmer Rouge who were breaching the peace agreement by refusing to demobilise their forces, and lay down their Chinese-supplied weapons. He sounded a stern warning on that new year's day, even before the Khmer Rouge pulled out of the peace accord by refusing to let Untac disarm and demobilise its troops.

"This peace agreement must be implemented completely—one hundred per cent, no less," he said, breaking into rapid twitches. "I know there will be difficulties, and we are sure that the Khmer Rouge will hide their weapons and army in the jungles. The Untac will have the responsibility of carrying out this task."

Hun Sen, whose own 55,000 troops had been verified by Untac, with some placed in cantonments for eventual demobilisation, was convinced that the Khmer Rouge would fudge.

He had matured considerably. Not once did he evade a question. Neither did he glance at his wristwatch, nor did his four aides gesture furtively at us to bring the interview to an end. To the contrary, he took the time to smoke three cigarettes as he plunged into a debate on the matters of state. Later that week his government was given a big boost when US president George Bush lifted the trade embargo against Cambodia. But the American gesture was not intended as a signal of support or recognition for the Hun Sen government.

The lifting of the embargo was Washington's way of telling the world that Sihanouk was back in Phnom Penh, and that the country was no longer a pariah. It sent a muddled signal to the business community that it was all right to do business with Cambodia, an economy still firmly controlled by Hun Sen. The Bush administration knew the economic realities perfectly well, and yet it figured that the time had come to lift the embargo because it was wrong to punish Cambodia endlessly. It was no small victory for Hun Sen who was given yet another boost in November 1991: the government of Singapore which severed ties with Cambodia when Vietnamese troops entered Cambodia in 1979, lifted its own embargo on investments.

Puffing happily, Hun Sen said: "It is good news, and a great encouragement to hear about the lifting of the economic embargo by Singapore to encourage foreign investments here. I believe that we can develop our own economy only when we have foreign investments coming in very quickly."

Those were happy days for Hun Sen as Singapore emerged as Cambodia's biggest trading partner, with some Singaporean businessmen investing hard currency in hotels and tourism projects even before the embargo was lifted. These businessmen forged links directly with the Hun Sen government which was issuing investment approvals with a vengeance. By the end of 1991, Hun Sen's government had won about US$350 million in foreign investments from businessmen in twenty-two countries such as Thailand, Singapore, France, Malaysia, and Australia.

Hun Sen looked at us, then around the room, as if seeking approval, and said: "I think we should not wait until after the elections in 1993, but rather we should start right now. After a very long war, Cambodia has become a very interesting marketplace for foreign investments despite the fact that peace is not completely restored because the peace agreement has just been reached. But the conditions for investment have been fully implemented."

His lodestar was not just to win investments, but to gain legitimacy. What Hun Sen left unsaid was that foreign investments could also help legitimise his government, and that foreign businessmen, drawn by visions of gold, served his government faithfully. They served as an important symbol at the toughest time in Hun Sen's political career—the peace talks.

It was tragic to see nine million Cambodians suffer because the outside world was hell-bent on punishing the Hun Sen government. Living in their shanties in appalling poverty were the people the world was actually punishing with its crippling embargoes.

He had sloughed off the threats to isolate his country. He was bailed out by friendly countries such as the Soviet Union which granted trade credits and oil, and Cuba which flooded the country with free Havana sugar. But his government still lacked the funds to finance major developments. He dragged furiously on a cigarette, and complained that the country's reconstruction had not budged an inch.

"I have heard, like you, about these ideas. I am expressing some worries too. So far we have not received any budget commitments for reconstruction. The great operation of Untac will have to face the problem of a lack of money."

Hun Sen was right. It was still early days, the peace plan was barely moving ahead, and only three countries had put their money where their mouths were.

"France has provided assistance in the restoration of our water and electricity supplies in Phnom Penh; Thailand has helped reconstruct the road from the border town of Poipet to Sisophon, and other projects as well; and Japan is in the process of discussing the reconstruction of the bridge across the Tonle Sap which was blown up in the war," he said.

Disillusioned by a lack of enthusiasm from the rich countries, Hun Sen said: "For this reason I believe that maybe the private sector will play a major role in economic reconstruction."

Rolling out his grand economic plan, he said: "According to the initial assessment made by our ministry of planning, we will need US$1.2 billion to reconstruct our infrastructure. But we have three priorities on top of all the other priorities. Our country is an agricultural one, and our farmers represent more than ninety per cent of our population. Therefore, any political party in power cannot overlook the agricultural aspects of the problem."

The second priority, he said, related to the lack of transport and communications, and unless his country could quickly develop its roads, bridges, and communications, its economy would remain stunted. A third priority was to put in place electricity supplies without which industrial output could not be raised.

He was in an unenviable position. At a time when his government faced embargoes from countries such as the USA and Singapore, its biggest ally, the Soviet Union, began self-destructing. In 1991 the Soviet Union reduced its trade credits to Cambodia from an annual level of US$100 million to a mere US$12 million. Cambodia'a other faithful ally, Cuba, could not do much either because it was also severely hit by cuts in Soviet aid. Cambodia, which relied on Soviet credits to buy Soviet oil, turned to Singapore to meet its oil needs, and Singapore oil suppliers readily cashed in on the opportunity. These trends were enough to give Hun Sen a headache. The roof caved in on him when the Soviet Union fell apart.

"In the last year our trade relations with the Soviet Union have not produced anything much," he said. "Our students are being shipped back from Russia, and the Russian teachers have also returned home. A number of agreements are in a difficult period. All these problems were not brought about because of any political problems between the two countries. In fact, the Russian people, and the other independent states, continue having a good consideration towards us."

Nothing hurt his government more than Vietnam's decision to also pare down its assistance, much of which was whittled down when Hanoi withdrew its troops in 1989. But after the Soviets reduced their aid to Vietnam in 1991, Hanoi was also hurt. The Paris peace agreement jeopardised any chance of a revival of the Indochinese spirit between Vietnam and Cambodia because the agreement demanded that Vietnam and China, major players in the Cambodian civil war, should no longer interfere in Cambodia.

Hun Sen pondered this point, and said: "Any agreement, or treaty, with Vietnam that is not in conformity with the Paris agreement will be invalidated, and other agreements that are in conformity with the Paris agreement will be continued, especially technical, scientific, and cultural agreements. We will not only continue our cooperation with Vietnam, but also with other countries."

An important defence treaty with Vietnam was suspended because it was incompatible with the Paris peace accord. Vietnam had withdrawn its army in 1989 and, as a result, Hun Sen's image was gradually whitewashed. To international eyes he seemed more and more independent of Vietnam's clutches.

Just when it seemed that Hun Sen was finally becoming more acceptable, he was once again embroiled in a full-blown controversy. In the months before the signing of the peace accord in November 1991, Phnom Penh was rife with talk that Hun Sen's ministers were corrupt. But it was hearsay, and nobody could substantiate the charges. A cyclo driver, who drove us around Phnom Penh, could not resist commenting on the villas the ministers lived in.

"Their salaries are very low. How could they become so rich?" he said, pointing at neat whitewashed rows of ministerial villas as we rode past.

An official in the Hun Sen government remarked: "In 1979 none of them had any personal wealth, and none had houses and cars. But within ten years they have amassed tremendous wealth, and this makes us wonder how most of us have remained so poor, and these ministers have grown so rich?"

When Sihanouk returned to Phnom Penh in late-1991 one of the first things he noticed was that people's lifestyles were a study in contrast. At one extreme were the ministers and officials living in their French-style villas; at the other end were the large numbers of poor citizens who did not even own a bicycle, and earned a pittance to string body and soul together. It was too much for Sihanouk to bear, and his office made a public statement accusing the Hun Sen government of corruption. One of Sihanouk's personal aides, Julio Jeldres, made sweeping allegations that ranged from grand larceny to petty thievery. He said that the officials were selling everything: from government-owned buildings and land, to factories and office fixtures—light bulbs, tables, and chairs. But the palace could only make harmless allegations; it lacked the power to take action.

We were in Phnom Penh when these charges were first made. But we saw no conclusive proof of wrongdoing. We were aware that the government had failed to run its own factories, and had leased them on monthly rents to foreign companies. An official in the ministry of planning informed us that at least sixty factories were leased to foreign investors, but all the deals were above board, and the rent was collected by the ministries.

Hun Sen's response was that the biggest weapon to fight corruption was development. As our meeting drew to an end, a battery of prime ministerial aides that was studiously jotting down every word he had uttered, looked relieved. Hun Sen's face broke into a broad smile as we parted. Our guide, Leng Sochea, looked visibly pleased that we had been able to meet his leader.

Later, Sochea said: "It was incredible. Hun Sen seldom meets writers." Then, he added: "We have to study the text of the interview carefully because he has said many things that set a new policy direction for Cambodia."

OUR next encounter with Hun Sen took place a year later on January 5, 1993, in Phnom Penh. It was the first Tuesday of the new year, and Hun Sen was talking to a group of social workers at the Khmer-style Chamkarmon Palace, meaning 'silkworm fields', which was used to accommodate visiting foreign dignitaries. The palace crawled with workers from non-governmental organisations, UN officials, and mediamen who closed in on the prime minister. Afterwards, as we approached Hun Sen he recognised us instantly.

"How are you two?" he inquired. We asked if he had the time for an interview and, without hesitation, he said yes.

"Come with me. We will go and talk in private in the other chamber," he said.

His demeanour was that of a man who never needed to consult his aides before making a decision about whom to meet. He walked briskly out of the meeting hall, through a corridor packed with diplomats and media, and entered a large hall, followed by his interpreter, Uch Kiman, and a senior general of his armed forces who wore a gold Rolex watch and sat silently throughout the discussion.

It was an elegant room, but not particularly Cambodian in its décor. The floor was covered with a thick carpet that looked typically Vietnamese, a reminder of Hun Sen's close ties with Hanoi, and large paintings depicting Cambodian village life lined the walls. The gold-Rolex-general was at hand to be consulted, but Hun Sen did not need any prompting. The young village lad had matured beyond his forty-one years.

He had one advantage over his political rivals: his age. On that morning, with the elections just five months away, he said that if the polls could not be held in May it would be impossible to hold them until the year 2000.

"By then, I will be forty-eight years old. But I will probably outlive many older politicians," he said.

It had been a tough morning for him. He had heard the news over the BBC radio that Sihanouk had threatened not to cooperate with his government, or with Untac. Sihanouk's move was an angry reaction to the killing of members of the Funcinpec allegedly by activists of the CPP. Diplomats said that Hun Sen was personally not involved, and that the campaign of violence was being conducted by certain hardliners within the CPP who disliked his reformist spirit. There were many in the party who felt that the peace accord had sold out the party's interest, and that they would have preferred to continue fighting to safeguard their political power which faced the threat of the ballot box.

But Hun Sen, who had weathered many political storms, was not fazed by the news that Sihanouk was rocking the boat. Dressed in a blue safari suit he looked less formal than he did a year ago at his office. Minutes earlier, talking to aid workers, he had demanded the ejection of the Khmer Rouge from the peace accord, and that they be branded as insurgents and outlaws. But the country was no longer being run by Hun Sen's party. It was administered by Untac. As a result, Hun Sen could not outlaw the guerrillas who had walked away from the peace process, and refused to disarm and demobilise their troops. Hun Sen's demand went unheeded by the UN. However, the new government that came to power following the elections in May 1993, did succeed in outlawing the Khmer Rouge. Unlike the Khmer Rouge, Hun Sen's party stuck to the peace accord, and handed over the administration to Untac as required. The gesture earned him a few brownie points.

What were his experiences of working with the Untac's dollar-earning generals, and top officials?

"We consider this an obligation that we have to fulfil within the framework of the Paris agreement," he said primly. "With regard to the financial aspect, we consider Untac's control as technical assistance. We are using Untac's control as a way of learning how to combat inflation, and also how to prevent our officials from committing illegal acts."

He inhaled deeply on a cigarette, visibly enjoying the effect of the smoke on his lungs while he waited for the next question.

The CPP had honoured the peace accord by transferring five of its ministries to Untac's control, but the Khmer Rouge had not submitted itself to Untac. How did this anomaly impact on the peace accord?

Looking suddenly agitated, he said: "We are now insisting that Untac exercise the same kind of control over the other parties that signed the peace accord. We know that the Khmer Rouge will not comply. But if we argue that just because the Khmer Rouge will not comply, so we should also not comply, it will mean that we have fallen into the trap of the Khmer Rouge. Therefore, we insist, and demand, that the Khmer Rouge be excluded from the peace process."

He then turned his ire on the parties of Ranariddh and Son Sann.

"Concerning these two parties, we insist that there be similar control by Untac over them, particularly over their finances because there must be no financial influence over the elections," he said. "Right now, the question is, where do these parties get the money to spend on their political campaigns? They do not have the revenue from, for instance, rubber plantations, industry, agriculture, or taxes. So, do they get assistance from foreigners? If they do, is it in conformity with the

Paris accord? Is it also in conformity with the neutral political environment which the UN wanted to create?"

His biggest worry on that Tuesday morning was that the Khmer Rouge had expanded the areas under its control. Earlier that morning, a general from the CPP's armed forces explained how the guerrillas were able to do this. It was a fear that had begun to grip not just the common people in the countryside, that the Khmer Rouge would actually carry out their threat of cutting off the hands of those who dared cast their ballots. Untac electoral officials, stationed in far flung provinces, lived in fear as well.

Hun Sen cautioned: "If we take appropriate and quick measures not to allow the Khmer Rouge to expand further I believe the elections can be held."

The trouble was, Untac had spent about US$2 billion, and had still failed to create the conditions for voting to take place on election day just five months away. The Cambodian and foreign press were not alone in criticising Untac for its failure to bring the Khmer Rouge into the peace process. Hun Sen, too, was annoyed.

"If Untac has no courage to carry out its mandate, and if Untac continues to withdraw all the time [whenever it is threatened by the Khmer Rouge], and if Untac does not allow us our right of self-defence [if attacked by the Khmer Rouge], then it means that the elections will face a lot of difficulties, even to the point that elections may not be held," he said.

As an afterthought, he added: "It is still not too late. We can still find the right measures."

On that calm morning the threat of the guerrillas seemed much magnified. We asked Hun Sen if he would give a piece of Cambodia to the Khmer Rouge if there was no option but to partition the country.

"We cannnot accept the partitioning of Cambodia," he said softly, and added: "We cannot allow insurgency either. Thailand and Malaysia have both addressed this kind of a problem, and have found a common solution."

When asked whether his government would take up arms against the Khmer Rouge if it tried to recapture power using military means, Hun Sen said: "Right now there is no other force in the country apart from us that can face up to the threat of the Khmer Rouge. If we had not exercised our right of self-defence perhaps Untac would already have run away from Cambodia. The other parties can only make a noise about the Khmer Rouge's actions, but they have no ability whatsoever to face them. As long as the State of Cambodia exists, as long as the Cambodian People's Party exists, and as long as Heng Samrin, Chea Sim, and Hun Sen exist, the Khmer Rouge can never bring back their régime. The people have real confidence in our party, not in the other parties."

With a grin, he added: "The Cambodian people are now beginning to joke that Untac is running away from the Khmer Rouge faster than even the Cambodian people because they have cars and aircraft at their disposal, whereas the Cambodians only have bicycles and bullock carts."

His real grouse emerged when we asked him whether he accepted the criticism levelled by Untac's report, *The Short-Term Impact of Untac on Cambodia's Economy,* in which it claimed that inflation, running at about 150 per cent was not caused by Untac, but by the Hun Sen government. Untac blamed it for fuelling inflation by printing money to finance the budget deficit, but independent economists attacked Untac whose 22,000-strong forces had injected some US$2 billion into the economy, pushing prices of food and housing way beyond the reach of the common man. Hun Sen refuted the charge that the indiscriminate use of the printing press had caused inflation.

"We have a domestic consensus that we must keep our spending within our revenue in order to implement our economic stabilisation policy," he said. "For four months already we have not used the printing press to print money. And we are trying not to print any more money."

"Untac", he said, "has tried to avoid its responsibility in Cambodia, on the economic aspects in general. We do not name Untac as the main source of economic instability and inflation. But Untac should recognise that it has not contributed to economic stability. Its presence here, and the increase in local consumption, has created the problem of rising prices. Our production remains the same yet the number of mouths to feed has increased."

"Another reason for inflation is that Untac's troops and civilians have refused to exchange their US dollars into the local currency before spending," he said.

"This has caused a loss of confidence in our currency. This is very important politically because a loss of confidence in our local currency reflects a loss of confidence in our policy, and has a very big impact."

Would he request the Untac chief, Akashi, to order his 22,000 staff to use Cambodian riels instead of US dollars?

"I have raised this issue twice with Mr. Akashi since August 1992, and he promised he would look into it," Hun Sen said. "Two days ago, I signed a memorandum and sent it to him, requesting that Untac personnel exchange ten per cent of their salaries, or revenue, intended for local consumption. So far, I have not received a reply."

Hun Sen did get a reply from Akashi. To all appearances Untac had absolved itself of the responsibility for hurting Cambodians. Vegetable sellers said that due to massive purchases by Untac the price of potatoes had risen from 200 riels a kilogramme in December 1992 to 450 riels a kilogramme. As traders began speculating, the price of rice increased five times. Akashi still did not respond to the emergency, and it was only in April 1993 that he told the Cambodians that Untac was considering bringing extra rice onto the market.

A bigger crisis was playing on Hun Sen's mind. He revealed that the government would run a thirty per cent deficit, which meant there was no money to finance a third of the development.

"According to the World Bank's pledge, by 1993 Cambodia will get US$75 million in assistance, of which US$35 million will be earmarked for importing commodities for domestic consumption," he said.

Smiling again, he added: "If this kind of assistance is forthcoming, our projected deficit will be reduced."

While the Asian Development Bank wasted no time in approving loans to Cambodia worth over US$70 million to generate electricity, and build irrigation canals, the World Bank had other plans. Even as Hun Sen was expressing the hope that the World Bank would lend money, the loan fell through. A few days later, Michael Ward, a World Bank official who worked as a deputy economic advisor to Untac, said that the US$75 million loan, though approved in principle, was blocked at the last minute.

"If it became known in the capital markets that the World Bank had off-loaded US$75 million in Cambodia, and if the political situation in Cambodia deteriorated it would cause a catastrophe in the markets," he said coldly.

A senior World Bank official who was due to visit Phnom Penh in January 1993 suddenly cancelled his trip because the bank now regarded any loans to the country as being too risky. Another reason why the loan was stuck, Ward added, was because it had become harder for Untac to negotiate with Sihanouk who had moved to Beijing to treat his cancer. Before the loan could be sanctioned, the prince's stamp of approval was needed, but he had declined to give his royal endorsement at that stage. It revealed his indifference to the plight of his people who would be made to suffer a little longer.

· The hour-long conversation drew to an end, and we shook hands and departed, leaving Hun Sen, and the gold-Rolex-general, to ponder over the land they had lost to the guerrillas.

Business confidence dipped to an all-time low on May 3 when Khmer Rouge guerrillas launched a lightning attack on Siem Reap, the gateway city to Angkor Wat. They blitzed through the streets firing rocket launchers, and lobbing hand grenades in a bid to bleed the economy, and disrupt the polls at the end of the month. Untac spokesman Eric Falt said it was the biggest attack in the area in over two years. The Hun Sen government revealed that some 300 guerrillas struck at Siem Reap airport, a power station, and the market, as well as the government's provincial military headquarters. It claimed that fourteen guerrillas were killed, and two taken prisoner. One soldier each from the royalists and the government died in the fighting that ended five hours later. But Falt put the number of deaths at seven—four Khmer Rouge, one government soldier, and two Cambodian civilians.

UN troops from a New Zealand army battalion returned fire, and eventually forced the guerrillas to flee. Siem Reap was later back in the hands of government troops. The impact of the attack was mainly economic as tourists stayed away from the country's biggest tourism earner, the Angkor Wat temple. Even before the attack tourism was in the dumps with hotels reporting occupancy rates of fifty per cent, down from ninety per cent a year earlier.

Early next morning we were woken up in our room at the Cambodiana Hotel by a government official. He tipped us off about a meeting with General Pann Thay who had defected some months earlier from Son Sann's Khmer People's National Liberation Armed Forces (KPNLAF), and joined Hun Sen's military. The general, turned out in a khaki uniform festooned with a row of medals and epaulettes, alleged that soldiers from Ranariddh's army had joined the Khmer Rouge in the attack on Siem Reap. A lieutenant colonel and a soldier from Ranariddh's National Army of Independent Kampuchea (Anki) had been captured, the general said. If proved true it would confirm the charge that the royalists were still allied with the guerrillas. Untac spokesman Falt trotted out his stock reply. "I cannot confirm these allegations." However, an Untac military officer told us that some Khmer Rouge guerrillas who were shot dead earlier in the year in Kompong Cham province had been found carrying membership cards of Ranariddh's Funcinpec party.

General Thay said: "We saw a Funcinpec officer in Siem Reap throwing a hand grenade, and another Funcinpec man driving a motorcycle through the city, and we shot him. Later we saw a lieutenant colonel from Funcinpec driving a Chinese-made military jeep and shooting everywhere, and we captured him."

General Thay, however, did not know his name, nor could he say at what time he had been taken prisoner. He said that he had requested Hun Sen for permission to bring the lieutenant colonel to Phnom Penh for interrogation.

"We will hold him for two or three days," he said.

Vice-minister Uch Kiman, Hun Sen's interpreter, who was also present at the briefing, said: "Even previously, we have caught Funcinpec officials redhanded. We conclude that there was collusion between the Khmer Rouge and Funcinpec."

Funcinpec soldiers, he said, jammed his army's radio communications during the assault on Siem Reap by using walkie-talkies that belonged to the Khmer Rouge.

The fires of political violence burned bright in the jungles and the cities. From within the Cambodiana Hotel we would often hear gunshots just as clearly as they could be heard in the streets where soldiers belonging to Hun Sen's army fired into the air just to let off steam.

The period from March 1 to May 14, 1993 was particularly violent as the elections drew closer. A Pakistan army battalion based in Choam Khsan in Preah Vihear province faced a mortar attack by Khmer Rouge fighters on May 7 that left one Pakistani soldier with splinter wounds in his back. Earlier in a grisly episode the Khmer Rouge struck without provocation, killing one Colombian civilian policeman on duty in Kompong Cham province. He was attacked while transporting a colleague to the provincial capital for medical treatment.

Between July 1992 and mid-May 1993, thirteen Untac peacekeepers and workers were killed, and another fifty-four injured in attacks generally attributed to the Khmer Rouge. However, in a few incidents the guerrillas' hand was not clearly established. The dead were from Bangladesh, Bulgaria, Cambodia, Columbia, Japan, and the Philippines.

Untac peacekeepers, performing a thankless job, were not the only casualties. Across the country, Cambodians were killing Cambodians in an orgy of political murders. On May 10, the body of a worker at the Funcinpec party office in the Tbong Khmum district of Kompong Cham province was discovered in a well after he had been kidnapped and killed by members of Hun Sen's SOC government. An Untac study revealed that eight Funcinpec members were killed by workers of the SOC in a continuing spate of political murders. At the same time, the Khmer Rouge murdered three SOC workers, while there was one incident in which a Funcinpec member shot dead an SOC person though the murder was believed to be the result of a personal feud.

Violence was bleeding business and scaring away investors. The profits of trading firms were down by seventy per cent. Businessman Richard Teoh said that half the fifty-odd Singaporeans doing business in Cambodia had scaled down their operations, and had gone home. Teoh said that he would stay put despite the violence.

"No guts, no glory," he said.

Tourism took a rain of blows. Following a statement by the US government that travel to Cambodia was no longer safe American tourists stopped coming in large numbers. A travel agency owned by Japanese and Cambodian businessmen was forced to close down when Japanese tour groups cancelled their visits. Another

Japanese firm pared down its operations to the bare minimum, and its Japanese station manager returned to Tokyo.

A distressed Tep Henn, the vice-minister for aviation, who was also the managing director of Kampuchea Airlines, said that the carrier had reduced its daily flights from Phnom Penh to Siem Reap from seven to two.

"You can imagine how much money we have lost," he said.

Khann Chandara, an engineer with the American giant, Otis Elevator, said that his firm which sold five elevators after the US embargo was lifted in 1992 had not sold a single elevator the following year.

A Singaporean summed up the war jitters: "Foreign firms have cut down their stock inventories, and they prefer to stay liquid just in case the situation deteriorates, and they have to evacuate".

The big scare even affected the Cambodians who were getting rid of their riels, and buying gold and US dollars as a precautionary measure. But the major Japanese trading houses, many of whom had opened offices in Phnom Penh, were unperturbed by the violence. Tsugio Koburi, general manager of a Japanese firm, said that while the Chinese businessmen were in Cambodia for quick profits most of the seventeen Japanese companies would stay put, and compete for major infrastructure projects funded by the Japanese government.

Not only did the Khmer Rouge create a panic with their actions, their words had a devastating effect as well. Their leader, Khieu Samphan, released a statement in the capital blaming the fall of the currency on the imminent departure of Untac at the end of 1993 as well as the flight of foreign businessmen.

Samphan said: "The downfall of the currency will take place because of the closing down of markets in Phnom Penh, the plundering of stores and shops, and the increasing grenade attacks. Everyone lays the blame on the worthless riels. As one can clearly see that the Phnom Penh puppet regime really sick, it urgently needs an injection of dollars. But a legal obstacle must be overcome before such an operation can be carried out."

Samphan was referring to the blockage of the World Bank loan worth US$75 million.

"No international financial institution can deal directly with that régime until it receives the blessings of the elections," Samphan added.

He blamed Untac for its "relentlessness to raise the issue" of the World Bank loan that reflected "Untac's haste to rescue the Phnom Penh régime which was running the risk of collapsing as a result of a very grave monetary crisis". Samphan said that the World Bank loan was "proving to be an urgent necessity to help that régime to survive".

Worried by the flight of businessmen and a miasma of despair that gripped the capital ahead of the elections, Hun Sen gave an assurance to visiting Thai foreign minister Prasong Soonsiri on May 7 that if his party won the elections it would honour the business contracts between the Thai firms and all the four Cambodian parties, including the contracts between the Khmer Rouge and Thailand. In return for his promise to protect Thai business interests Hun Sen extracted an assurance that Thailand would recognise and support his government if it came to power.

It was a canny arrangement—a guarantee covering business contracts in return for political recognition. Here was Thailand shifting allegiances. After aligning itself closely with Ranariddh's royalist party and the Khmer Rouge, it was now performing a high-wire act by reaching out to Hun Sen. Ranariddh's people viewed the deal with suspicion. Thai business interests, they noted, took precedence over old alliances. Apart from business contracts that ran into hundreds of millions of dollars, Thailand hoped to boost tourism by opening a new air route from Bangkok to Siem Reap. The air deal was seen as a major *coup* for Thailand which had been concerned about the fate of its business projects worth at least US$300 million in hotels, banking, tourism, and manufacturing.

Besides doing business with Hun Sen the Thais were quietly earning mega-dollars in clandestine deals with the Khmer Rouge. It was estimated that the Khmer Rouge would earn US$1 billion if all the contracts for logging and gem mining, entered into with Thai firms, were fulfilled.

Quite apart from its legitimate business deals with the SOC, Thailand was also the biggest violator of the UN ban on the export of logs from Cambodia, imposed on January 1, 1993. There were twenty-one instances when Thai firms breached the ban up to February 5, 1993, by when they had carried off 21,800 cubic metres of logs.

Cambodia had come full circle from being a Maoist genocidal gulag, a communist state and, finally, a liberal democracy. A six-week election campaign was due to start in mid-April, but Hun Sen, Ranariddh, and Son Sann were already fanning out into the provinces, soliciting votes as early as January. The pre-election rhetoric stung the protagonists. Ranariddh accused Hun Sen's government of corruption, and the latter hit back on state television alleging that the royalists were on the payroll of the Khmer Rouge. For their part, the Khmer Rouge had begun intimidating the voters.

Reginald Austin, Untac's chief election officer, said: "We know of only twenty cases where the Khmer Rouge had torn up the voters' registration cards."

The guerrillas' tactic was to rip up the cards, and retain the half bearing the voters' names. They warned the villagers that they would come back and kill them if they cast their ballots. A fear of being identified, and singled out for torture and murder, had frightened the village folk.

It did not seem to matter. During the six-day polls from May 23-28, some 4.2 million voters cast their ballots out of a total of 4.7 million who had registered to vote.

IT was drama, vintage Sihanouk. The prince sat on his throne in the Royal Palace wearing Khmer ceremonial trousers, talking to his captive audience—the new government, and the 120 members of the national assembly elected in the first free elections since the 1960s. For four hours on July 2, 1993, he talked nonstop about his life, his arrested aspirations, and how he gave medals to his ministers, and appointed some of them generals. Sihanouk said that he decided to promote his son, Chakrapong, to a three-star general after he abandoned his plan, a month earlier, to form a breakaway state consisting of three eastern provinces.

"But Chakrapong, who was earlier a two-star general, told me that he wanted four stars because he had not been promoted for many years," Sihanouk said. "So, I made him a four-star general to keep him happy. I only have stars to give away. I have no money to give."

From where we stood in the corridor of the palatial ceremonial hall, we watched the soporific royal proceedings. Many newly elected MPs sitting stiffly in their new suits dozed off. They were glad when it was all over, and Sihanouk, shielded from the sun by a parasol bearer, shepherded them across to an open air pavilion for lunch.

It was there that we approached Hun Sen, and struck up a conversation about life after political defeat. He had not lost political clout even though his party took second place in the elections. People across the country still respected him as a man they could trust, as someone who did not bend with the wind. Equally, he had his critics who watched his growing power with alarm. In an odd partnership with Ranariddh, Hun Sen was just settling down in his new role as a co-president of the Provisional National Government of Cambodia (PNGC) which was to run the country till a new royal government was installed at the end of August 1993.

As we walked to the pavilion, Hun Sen, speaking haltingly in English, said. "Our party, and Funcinpec, have joined hands and are working together. It is a very good relationship now."

A week earlier, Ranariddh had also made a similar comment. Those words uttered by Hun Sen and Ranariddh supposedly signalled an end to a twenty-three-year civil war, and set the pace for the emergence of a coalition government of national unity that would put on a cohesive public front.

Cambodian politics was, of course, a strange brew: the winner of the election, Ranariddh, was unable to stake a claim to form the new government by himself because of a major stumbling block—he lacked a two-thirds majority to form a government alone. Quick to realise the political reality of Cambodia, Ranariddh knew that in his country the winner-takes-all formula would again plunge the country into civil war. He realised that the true meaning of national reconciliation was to share power.

When we asked Hun Sen on the lawns of the palace whether the PNGC would continue with the existing economic laws, he said: "Our existing laws on direct foreign investments and banking will all continue. There will be no changes to the basic laws, but perhaps some of the laws will be refined."

The National Committee for Foreign Investments, a body created by Hun Sen in the heydays of his government, still remained the agency that approved investment applications, but the word was out that Ranariddh would make drastic changes as soon as the new government was formed. For a losing party, the CPP had not done badly. It controlled eleven ministries–Funcinpec settled for ten, Son Sann's party was given three, and the small-sized Molinaka party had one.

Asked why Funcinpec had one less ministry than the CPP, Ranariddh said: "We should be splitting them twelve and twelve between us, but we made the concession to accommodate the Molinaka party. We did this for the sake of peace."

Ranariddh's men were placed in charge of the key finance and industry ministries, with Paris-trained accountant Sam Rainsy running the former, and US-educated Pou Sothirak the latter. Hun Sen's men—Chea Chanto, Va Huot, and Kong Sam Ol—were the ministers of planning, commerce, and agriculture, respectively.

As Hun Sen waved and walked away towards the festive pavilion for the royal luncheon thrown by Sihanouk it became apparent that the hostility, the violence, and the reckless posturing that the political parties indulged in during the elections was behind them. The cake had been divided. Ranariddh, who had lashed out at Hun Sen's economic reforms as being a "crude attempt to liberalise the economy," was now happy to work with him.

The new government's national plan—much of it borrowed from the past policies of the SOC—revealed the continuing influence of Hun Sen. The transitional PNGC said that its key home policy was the formation of a national army that would ensure stability. It promised to make the judiciary independent, while laying the foundations for a non-confrontational policy with its neighbours.

Much of the rhetoric was aimed at reassuring the poor villagers that the state would restore the irrigation system, that it would import fertilisers and pesticides, provide seeds, preserve the forests, enforce the fishery law during the spawning season when fishing was banned, and provide land to the refugees streaming back home from camps along the Thai border. As an afterthought, the drafters of the ambitious programme deemed it prudent to enter a caveat to protect themselves just in case they failed to deliver: "In presenting the above-mentioned programme of action, the PNGC focuses only on the tasks needed to be carried out in the three months ahead."

More than the reforms, the PNGC's chief concern was to prevent the country from plunging into anarchy. It appealed to civil servants, the army, and political party members to protect public property, and avoid speculative acts which, it warned, would not go unpunished. There was a very real fear that people would seize public property, taking advantage of a lack of government during the transitional phase.

WHEN Hun Sen flew to Singapore in December 1993 he had a lot more than diplomacy on his mind. First, he wanted to meet Singapore's leaders, and visit a brewery that had long been keen on opening a factory in Cambodia. Secondly, he needed a medical check-up. It was a routine scan for the stressed politician who used to faint frequently at the peace talks in the 1980s.

He had gone through four official avatars in that one year—prime minister of the SOC till May, deputy prime minister in the ill starred Sihanouk government that lasted less than a day, co-president of the PNGC till August, and since September he had been ensconced as the second prime minister.

His country was awakening to the enormous possibilities the region held. A few months before him in August, Ranariddh, the first prime minister, visited Singapore to tap its economic expertise. At that time, it was not clear in what precise direction Ranariddh was steering his country. And although it was Hun Sen's first official visit to Singapore, several ministers from his party had built bridges with the island-state. Chea Sim, Chakrapong, and former foreign minister Hor Nam Hong had visited Singapore before him.

When we went to meet Hun Sen at his hotel on December 17 he began speaking through an interpreter, not Uch Kiman who had been promoted to the rank of an undersecretary in the foreign ministry, but a newcomer named Bun Sam Bo. However, Uch Kiman sat through the interview, occasionally coming to Hun Sen's rescue to fill him in on the minutiae. Also present in the room was Mam Sophana, a US-trained Cambodian architect who was a permanent resident of Singapore, and headed a cooperation committee formed by the two countries.

To get the story from the source itself we asked Hun Sen which ministerial portfolios he was overseeing, and whether there was any conflict with Ranariddh.

"We do not have such an arrangement," he said with the air of a seasoned diplomat. "By and large the two prime ministers are responsible for the whole country. We work things out through a consensus."

Not satisfied with what seemed a motherhood statement we pressed him on whether the two parties in the coalition government would turn against each other, sooner or later.

"I am the one who is involved in these matters," he said. "I don't think there will be any differences. We have the same ideas, and almost the same thinking. Our domestic policy, foreign policy, and policies on the remaining problems, including the Khmer Rouge, are all the same. So, I don't think there is anything that should cause the two parties to split. It is felt within the country, and outside, that the two parties have to work together—not only for today, but for many more years."

The possibility of the winning party singlehandedly forming the government after the elections in 1998 did not seem realistic as no party could hope to win the two-thirds majority necessary to form a government alone. To further complicate matters the entire civil administration was split along party lines. The dividing line between the party, the government, and the civil service had been erased. Civil servants and ministers were required to be members of parties, and this had politicised the entire government machinery and the administration—a nexus that was impossible to sunder.

At this time the future of the monarchy was uncertain. King Sihanouk—named the monarch on September 24, 1993 when the country again became a kingdom—remained under treatment for cancer in Beijing. The seventy-one-year-old monarch who reigned but did not rule had not named a successor, although he often said that he would have liked to do so. He once asked Ranariddh to succeed him, but Ranariddh, chasing a brighter future as a politician, declined. We asked Hun Sen if this meant that the line of succession was unclear, and could spark off a battle for the throne in a replay of ancient Khmer history.

· "It is our hope that the king will live long for the unity of our country," he said. "We need him not only for one or two years, but for many more years. That is what I wish."

Leaving the question unanswered Hun Sen began talking about the improved investment climate. He had matured enough to realise that his country would not get many free lunches. Back in 1992, he told us that he was not too happy about the slow pace of foreign aid to his country, and was revisiting the same theme.

"The world has too many problems like in Somalia, Yugoslavia, Afghanistan, and Angola," he said. "I am concerned there will be more problems in other parts of the world—and then the aid will go elsewhere. What we would like to see is that the money pledged should come in quickly. Some countries like Japan have already disbursed the funds."

He returned to Phnom Penh carrying with him two prizes—a clean health certificate from his physician, and assistance from Singapore to prepare a masterplan to build a 300 kilometre highway—dubbed the "highway for development corridor"—linking Phnom Penh to Sihanoukville. Even before it was built the Khmer Rouge intensified attacks along the same road. Three Westerners travelling by train on a railtrack close to the road were kidnapped, and later tortured and murdered in cold blood.

THE national assembly was in session on October 20, 1994. On the agenda was a cabinet reshuffle. Finance Minister Sam Rainsy was the main casualty. After the MPs unanimously voted to remove him and a few other ministers from their posts, Hun Sen and Ranariddh could be seen talking to Rainsy in hushed tones. At the end of the session, we walked across the hall to meet Hun Sen who informed us that his wife was in Singapore for a holiday.

"I am very busy these days," Hun Sen said. "Perhaps we will sit down together some time soon."

Several months later we unexpectedly met Hun Sen on a flight from Phnom Penh to Singapore. He broke into a smile, and said that he would undergo an operation at a Singapore hospital to remove a small growth in his back.

"It is nothing serious. I will live long, very long," he said, and then went back to the first class section.

IN 1995 Hun Sen's commitment to democracy was questioned because of his government's handling of the Sirivudh affair. Sirivudh, a half-brother of Sihanouk, resigned as the foreign minister in 1994, and was believed to have serious differences with both Hun Sen and Ranariddh. In a bizarre turn of events, Sirivudh was suddenly placed under house arrest in November 1995 for his alleged involvement in a plot to assassinate Hun Sen. Sirivudh denied the charges, but the interior ministry said that it possessed "convincing evidence" implicating Sirivudh in the plot. The ministry produced an audiotape of a conversation that Sirivudh had with a journalist. The journalist had second thoughts, and said that Sirivudh might have been joking when he had said those things. Human rights' groups and diplomats warned that Cambodia was turning into a repressive state. Cambodian lawyers said that Sirivudh could face a ten-year jail term if he was found guilty.

The last thing that Sihanouk wanted was for Sirivudh to face a trial and, three weeks after his arrest, he offered a solution: to exile Sirivudh to France and save him from the indignity of a trial. The proposal was quickly accepted by Hun Sen and Ranariddh, both of whom saw it as an opportunity to remove a political opponent from the scene almost painlessly. Critics alleged that the government was bringing trumped up charges to fix an opponent. Sirivudh won support for his cause in several European countries, and some American senators said that the arrest could derail Cambodia's efforts to win most-favoured-nation trading status. Hun Sen stood firm, warning the USA not to interfere in Cambodia's affairs. Eventually, by 1996, Cambodia did win the trade benefits, and the Sirivudh affair was all but forgotten.

Soon afterwards, Hun Sen fell out with Ranariddh. Trouble began when Ranariddh demanded an equal share of the official posts in the districts for his partymen. Hun Sen flatly refused, throwing their coalition government in jeopardy. It left nobody in any doubt that the real power in Cambodia was Hun Sen, and that Ranariddh played a supporting role.

IN November 1997 the Hun Sen camp began preparing for the general elections—eight months before they were due. Sitting in his fortress-like home in Takhmau he declared that his country was open for business again. Foreign investors who withdrew in panic after Ranariddh was overthrown in July were returning, with one oil deal alone worth US$36 million. In a signal that businessmen viewed Hun Sen's leadership as a source of stability, five international oil giants agreed to explore for gas and oil in the sea off the coast of Sihanoukville. Beaming, he said that more than US$100 million worth of investments had been approved. At the same time, opposition leader Sam Rainsy was warning investors to avoid Cambodia.

Visibly offended, Hun Sen said: "We were accused by the Americans of not having any respect for human rights. We have a free press and a multi-party democracy. I don't think any country could teach Cambodia about human rights. They can be teachers on economy and technology, but not on politics, human rights, and democracy. I feel that human rights in Cambodia is at its peak. But they come from America to teach us about human rights and democracy, and I don't want to be their student."

The greatest destroyer of Cambodian human rights, Pol Pot, was again hitting the headlines everywhere following his exclusive interview with American journalist Nate Thayer. Hun Sen had toppled Pol Pot in 1979, but he had failed to put an end to him, and his movement. Why had he been unable to capture the guerrilla chief?

"If people want Pol Pot to stay alive he will stay alive," Hun Sen said. "If they want to put an end to him that will be his end. There were people who hated Pol Pot, but they also wanted him to stay alive. Pol Pot should have come to an end in 1979, but how could he stay [politically alive] for so long? It was because those who hated him had supported him. If there was no one to support Pol Pot, if there was no one to take him to the United Nations, if there was no one to help him set up the tripartite coalition government, then that would have been his end."

"We should put an end to Pol Pot, but unless the others join us, we cannot," he said. "It's the same for Ranariddh. He relies on Pol Pot to fight. Pol Pot has attached himself to Ranariddh, and those who protect Ranariddh also protect Pol Pot."

Pol Pot died in obscurity and ignominy on April 15, 1998. The seventy-three-year-old terror suffered a massive heart attack. His dead body was found by his wife who came to his bed at night to arrange his mosquito net. The emaciated architect of the genocide had lain close to death for weeks, isolated, despised, and mistrusted by his own cadres who put him on trial for murdering one of his trusted colleagues. He lay dead with an expression of deep hurt on his wrinkled face that was bloated with cottonwool stuffed up his nose. Death cheated Cambodians of the opportunity to prosecute one of the most reprehensible criminals Southeast Asians had ever known.

WHEN we met Hun Sen in early-June 1998 just a month before the elections he was brimming with confidence while the opposition could hardly conceal its jumpiness. Hun Sen used simple math to show that his party would win, and that the fractured Funcinpec party would lose.

"Now we have 51 seats in the national assembly. Divide it by one. What is the result? Another party [Funcinpec] has 58 seats. Divide it by nine. What is the result?" he said.

Funcinpec had split into as many as nine factions, and its MPs belonged to as many different parties. This equation made Hun Sen confident of winning most of the seats in the July 26 election to the 122-member national assembly.

What would happen if the two parties were to win almost the same number of seats as they did in 1993? Would the CPP agree to form a coalition?

Hun Sen said yes, and added: "If we win a majority, even a two-thirds majority, we will still set up a coalition government."

The most significant change was that the two-prime ministers' system would end after the July poll. After that, a single prime minister would take office, as set out in the Constitution. The new prime minister would be named from the party that won most of the seats, and not from an alliance of parties that together commanded the largest number of MPs. Even here, Hun Sen had no fears. The strongest challenger to the CPP was a four-party National United Front set up by Ranariddh, Sam Rainsy, Son Sann, and a smaller party.

In a gesture of goodwill Hun Sen said: "If we do not have enough seats, we will get [the prime minister] from the other parties."

The election was a lot more complex than the one in 1993. There were many more parties in the fray, and more assembly seats were being contested. Yet it cost much less. Untac spent more than US$2 billion on a two-year exercise to organise the last poll, but the 1998 election, organised by the Cambodians themselves, cost merely US$32 million in funds contributed by the European Union, Japan, China, and South Korea, with the UN chipping in a little. The last election featured twenty parties, versus the thirty-nine parties that registered in the 1998 poll. The number of constituencies had increased from 120 to 122 with the addition of Anlong Veng and Kep, the two areas formerly held by the Khmer Rouge.

Hun Sen could visualise victory even before the first ballot was cast.

TEN

STRONGMAN'S GRIP

VICTORY

He did his calculations over and over. The answer was the same every time: the Cambodian People's Party (CPP) would win the elections in July 1998. Yet, beneath the bravado of the math Hun Sen was beset by the fear that his party could lose. The concerns were very real. Opinion polls showed Funcinpec and CPP running in a blood-spattered photofinish.

Hun Sen left no stone unturned to modernise his obsolete party. The strongman went into cyberspace in late-1997 when his party posted a homepage on the Internet in order to soften its image and broaden its appeal. The site was proposed by the party's central committee following fierce fighting in Phnom Penh earlier that year that led to the overthrow of Ranariddh as the first prime minister. Few people in Cambodia ever saw the website owing to the scarcity of computers, but the party said it was aimed at winning friends among Internet surfers around the world.

Hun Sen's critics alleged that the CPP was intimidating voters and attacking the opposition, and that the opposition was denied access to state-run media. As the campaign limped towards its closing days the CPP was given a sudden scare when Hun Sen was rushed to hospital in Phnom Penh for an emergency appendectomy. The operation to remove his appendix was performed by Cambodian doctors.

The emergency surgery put him out of action in the critical phase of the campaign. But he bounced back within days to cast his own ballot at a polling station. The chess player who had learnt the intricacies of the game at a backstreet barbershop had hung resolutely on to the board. He saw the election as a game with four set-piece battles: the registration of voters, the actual polling, the counting of the votes, and the formation of the government.

It was a bittersweet victory. His party lost in two of his strongholds, in Kompong Cham province where he was born and where his brother Hun Neng was the governor, and in Kandal province where he lived. It was a personal disappointment for Hun Sen that he failed to win the support of the people in his own provinces even after pumping in development funds.

The humiliation in Kompong Cham and Kandal lent credibility to the election, to the fact that it was not rigged. The smoothness of the polling process laid to rest the allegations of widespread intimidation. The European Union, Japan, Australia, and the USA endorsed the conduct of the election as generally free and fair.

The CPP won an impressive 41.4 per cent of the votes, Funcinpec garnered 31.7 per cent, and the Sam Rainsy Party a respectable 14.3 per cent. The outcome sprang a surprise as earlier predictions indicated a tight three-way race. But the voters had shown their preference for Hun Sen, and declining confidence in Ranariddh and Rainsy. This was easy to understand. Since the 1993 election Hun Sen had become a Robin Hood figure, a sort of people's prince who spent millions from his party's funds to build schools, hospitals, and irrigation canals across the country. His style was simple, yet it touched the people who came to regard him as one of their own. He sat down with them in their ricefields, smoked a cigarette or two with them, and discussed their problems. On the other hand, Ranariddh's image was hurt by his attempt to import weapons, and his controversial alliance with the Khmer Rouge, while Rainsy's excessively negative tone had begun to jar on many people, particularly the Khmer business community that was disappointed by his frequent warnings to foreign investors to avoid doing business in Cambodia.

Too long had the country been hurt by false hopes and arrested development. A new reign of peace was always just around the corner. A new era of plenty was always about to emerge. But then, something terrible would always happen to plunge the country back into the depths of despair.

After the July election it appeared that the country had a fresh chance to make a new beginning under a powerful leader. But there were plenty of spoilers. Ranariddh and Rainsy, having the lost the election, discredited the entire polling process that had earlier been endorsed by teams of international observers.

Hun Sen's CPP performed better than expected, but it fell short of the two-thirds majority necessary to form a government that could survive a vote of confidence. The lack of a majority forced Hun Sen into a coalition government. He offered to form a government with Ranariddh, but the prince spurned his offer, claiming the election was rigged. The complaints of the opposition were investigated by the election authorities, and were found to be lacking in merit.

In the end, the protests of Ranariddh and Rainsy were discounted by most diplomats. The 800 international observers and 20,000 local election officials said that while the existing administrative structures favoured the CPP, they could find no evidence of massive rigging. They said they could not detect massive fraud. Even US officials dubbed the election "a successful exercise in national self determination". Out of the 5.4 million registered voters, ninety per cent actually cast their ballots, and a majority showed its preference for Hun Sen. The result was a blow to Ranariddh and Rainsy, who, diplomats said, were unwilling to accept any result other than their own victory.

For Hun Sen the electoral triumph underscored an even greater victory: he had won legitimacy in the eyes of his own people. And membership of Asean was only just around the corner. Expectations were riding high in the CPP camp that the government would soon be able to reoccupy its seat at the UN, vacant since the July 1997 military overthrow of Ranariddh.

The passionate chess player who graduated from roadside chessboards to palatial strategies charted his, and his party's, success. He sacrificed an important chess-piece in the 1993 election when he agreed to form a government as a junior partner under the premiership of Ranariddh. From then on he unleashed a series of rapid moves to consolidate himself while wearing down his opponents. First, government critic Sam Rainsy was fired in 1994, and then Funcinpec general-secretary Sirivudh was accused of plotting to kill Hun Sen, and exiled the next year. Throughout 1997, Hun Sen effectively broke up the Khmer Rouge by an expedient alliance with one of its top leaders, former Khmer Rouge foreign minister Ieng Sary, and then he fractured the royalists by the military takeover in July. About a month later Pol Pot was put on trial in the treacherous forests of Anlong Veng by his own cadres, an event that further scattered his enemies.

The final move? Hun Sen had to ensure that the elections were as free and fair as possible. He needed to show the world that he was more popular than the royalists.

That left only one potential threat, Sihanouk. But this danger was swiftly neutralised. The ailing king openly acknowledged Hun Sen's status as a strongman, and treated him with the respect that strongmen craved. After the overthrow of his son, Ranariddh, Sihanouk no longer supported Ranariddh, but backed Hun Sen's claim to the UN seat. Again, when Ranariddh refused to form a government after the results of the July poll were announced, Hun Sen won the support of Sihanouk. The king urged his son, and Rainsy, to form a coalition government with Hun Sen in the larger interests of the nation.

When the results of the election were announced, Hun Sen was overjoyed. Even the embattled riel gained in value after his victory, and businessmen predicted that an era of plenty had finally arrived. The currency strengthened to 3,000 riels to one US dollar from around 4,200 riels before the elections, largely due to renewed hopes for stability.

As a chorus of protests by Ranariddh, Rainsy, and their supporters grew in volume and hysteria, and as their demands for a recount, even a repoll, were screamed across the quiet boulevards of the capital, the emerging strongman drew comfort and confidence from the support that the international community had given him. The pressure exerted on him by the opposition parties to resign was countered by mounting pressure by the international community on them to accept the result of the election, and form a coalition government led by Hun Sen. The Philippines' Foreign Secretary Domingo Siazon urged Hun Sen and Ranariddh to set up a coalition as a first step towards being accepted as a member of Asean.

"It would be highly immoral, or irresponsible, for the political leaders of Cambodia not to form a government only because of their individual ambitions," Siazon said.

French President Jacques Chirac added: "The international observers assessed the election as free and fair. These elections were at first a success for Cambodia, and the Cambodian people. It is today essential that the country's main political forces work in respect of the will expressed by the Cambodian people."

It soon dawned on Hun Sen that the political logjam could only be broken by the intervention of Sihanouk. In early August, after remaining in the shadows for weeks, Sihanouk attempted to break up the fracas with a suggestion to host talks between the three main parties and the National Election Commission (NEC) that had organised the poll. It had little effect on the hotheads.

When Hun Sen saw that the streets in the capital were filling with thousands of protestors demanding his resignation, he could no longer take it lying down. He said that he would amend the Constitution, if necessary, to allow him to rule alone. His partymen gathered enough signatures from the newly-elected deputies to the assembly to ensure that the two-third majority rule could be dropped.

The NEC officially declared the CPP the winner of the election on September 1, setting the stage for a showdown with the opposition. The highest appeals' body, the constitutional council, rejected the complaints of fraud and irregularities. The results showed the CPP winning more than two million votes, just over forty-one per cent of the 4.9 million ballots cast, which gave the party sixty-four seats in the assembly. Funcinpec finished second with 1.5 million votes, about thirty-two per cent of the total, resulting in forty-three parliamentary seats. The Sam Rainsy Party came third with almost 700,000 votes, about fourteen per cent of the total, or fifteen seats.

Rainsy, in particular, did not relish the result of the election. He went beyond the pale in urging Cambodian soldiers to turn their guns on Hun Sen, and suggesting that the USA should attack Hun Sen's headquarters with missiles and smart bombs. The US embassy in Phnom Penh protested against his comments which many diplomats saw as a ploy to provoke Hun Sen into violence so that the entire election would be discredited.

Victory had a predictable effect on Hun Sen. He began to think, and plan, like a prime minister even before he had been formally installed. He pledged to appoint an "economic government" to stabilise the currency, control inflation, and reduce the budget deficit. In an interview with the *Asian Wall Street Journal,* he made a surprising confession: he accepted the criticism that rampant logging had ravaged his country, and promised no longer to rely on revenue from felling trees. He spoke about halving the size of the armed forces now that the Khmer Rouge was not a threat. His country could no longer shoulder the burden of paying for more than 200,000 security personnel, and at most the armed forces should be capped at 70,000 men, he said.

The former guerrilla had finally been legitimised after winning the election, and now he eyed sweeter cherries. He was confident that Cambodia would become a member of Asean in December 1998.

"I will travel to Hanoi with two options: the first possibility is that, after being officially admitted, we will participate officially in the summit. The second possibility is that we would travel there to be officially admitted," he said.

Sensing a breakthrough was close at hand Hun Sen wrote to Thailand's Prime Minister Chuan Leekpai on August 31, requesting membership of Asean. In his letter, Hun Sen said: "Cambodia has always had a strong commitment for Asean membership to achieve Asean's founding vision of all Asean nations in one Asean family."

Asean consisted of nine countries, and once Cambodia became the tenth member the vision of the Asean Ten would be realised, he said. It was in that spirit, that he asked Chuan to press his case at the meeting of Asean foreign ministers in New York at the end of August.

But the seasoned warhorse was disappointed once again. In late-August Asean rejected Cambodia. Asean foreign ministers said that they had delayed the admission because a legitimate government had not yet been formed.

When the constitutional council, the highest appeals' body, stacked with Hun Sen's sympathisers, rejected opposition demands for a recount of the votes on September 1, some 15,000 supporters of Ranariddh and Rainsy took to the streets. Incited by Rainsy's chauvinistic anti-Vietnamese rhetoric a group of protestors set ablaze a monument marking the Vietnamese liberation in 1979. The government did not intervene to break up the mass sit-ins at Phnom Penh parks, fearing they would be accused of subverting the democratic process. But its hand was forced when an unknown attacker lobbed a grenade into Hun Sen's city residence on September 7. His father was at home, but nobody was injured and little damage was done. Hun Sen grew more concerned about the safety of his family.

Clashes broke out as the police moved in to disperse the protestors who were camping in public places. Several protestors were wounded, and one Buddhist monk was believed to have been killed. Hun Sen remained calm in the face of the protests, knowing that it was mere posturing aimed at strengthening the opposition's bargaining stance at talks to form a new coalition government. Even while the protests were going on, at least four Funcinpec members were eyeing the portfolio of tourism minister.

Hun Sen's reading of the situation was accurate. Sure enough, by mid-September Ranariddh and Rainsy dropped all demands concerning the election except two—an accounting of all used, unused, and reserve ballot papers, and the use of a different formula to determine the allocation of assembly seats. They alleged that the seat allocation formula was illegally changed before the vote to favour the ruling party.

To remind the opposition that he was the winner of the election Hun Sen warned that the CPP had three options—to form a coalition government with Ranariddh's Funcinpec; to amend the Constitution and do away with the two-thirds majority rule and govern alone; or simply extend the life of his existing government.

HUN Sen led a charmed life. He escaped unhurt an attempted assassination on September 24 when he was being driven to Sihanouk's residence in Siem Reap. A B-40 rocket was fired at his car, but it missed the motorcade and hit a house just ten metres from Hun Sen's vehicle, killing a twelve-year-old boy, and injuring three others. Hun Sen later joined the MPs who were sworn-in at the ruins of Angkor Wat.

"This was clearly an attempt to kill me," he said. He hinted that the opposition might be behind the attack, and ruled out the involvement of the remnant Khmer Rouge guerrillas.

"Killing Hun Sen will not put an end to the problem. It will make it worse. I feel that if Hun Sen dies the deaths of the opposition leaders would not be far behind. If the leaders of the opposition have advised their people to conduct this type of act, I think their future will not be good," Hun Sen said.

Police chief Hok Lundy accused the opposition of the attack.

"The leaders of Funcinpec and Sam Rainsy Party always say that the army and police should kill Hun Sen, and then they threw two grenades at Hun Sen's house. They have used various means to kill Hun Sen and we believe that Sam Rainsy was the leader. Yes, we are one hundred per cent sure that the opposition parties were behind it, and they cooperated to kill him," Hok said.

Rainsy and Ranariddh both said they knew nothing of the attack. Later, three rockets were discovered near the scene of the explosion. Police said that the hand-propelled rockets were remote-controlled, and that only one cluster had exploded due to heavy rains the day before. A cryptic note was found in a battery pack: "The King Bee will eliminate all the nation's dictators gradually. Today the nation's main dictator must be finished."

Hun Sen linked the attack to the one that occured earlier that month, and he offered a US$200,000 reward to the attackers if they would name their ringleader.

"If the opposition leaders do not instruct their forces to stop conducting activities which threaten my life they would die after the most severe suffering. For a snake, if we don't hit it on the head it can still move and bite back. So we must hit it on the head, not its tail," Hun Sen said.

He cancelled his attendance at an official reception following the swearing-in of the new MPs, and left by helicopter. The next day both Ranariddh and Rainsy departed in haste to Bangkok, leaving their partymen to voice fears that the government was expected to take tough action against them. Police said they were pursuing two suspects, one of whom was a former Khmer Rouge fighter linked to Sam Rainsy's party.

Earlier, an attempt to assassinate Hun Sen was made in 1996. Two snipers had fired at his car as it passed by a garment factory in Kandal city. A bullet hit the helmet of a motorcycle outrider who was wounded. Hun Sen was unharmed, and continued on his way from his residence in Takhmau to the Chamcarmon Palace in Phnom Penh.

JUST before departing for Thailand Ranariddh said that his royalist party would definitely be a part of a new government. The fear of a rebellion within his party forced him to accept the offer of forming a coalition with Hun Sen. Ranariddh had seen his party splinter into several factions, and was aware that his school masterly tone was disliked by many influential partymen, some of whom held secret talks with the CPP to explore what role they could play in a future government.

Sihanouk, too, came down heavily on Ranariddh. The monarch realised that if his son did not form a coalition government he would further wreck the royalist party. Under Sihanouk's goading, Ranariddh ultimately agreed in principle.

Prak Sokhonn, an advisor to Hun Sen, commented: "One day Ranariddh says he will join the coalition, the next day he says he won't."

The future of the government was in jeopardy because the royalists were refusing to negotiate until their demands were met. On October 7 Hun Sen said that his government would continue in office until a deal could be reached with Ranariddh. He told his ministers and civil servants that they should continue doing their job until replacements were selected. But Sam Rainsy's party complained that several ministers who had failed to win back their parliamentary seats had no right to continue in office.

Sihanouk's intervention paid off. The CPP and Funcinpec broke the deadlock, and hammered out a complex deal on November 14 to form a government. Rainsy was left out of the arrangement. Hun Sen would be the prime minister, and Ranariddh the president of the national assembly. In order to accommodate CPP supremo Chea Sim a new senate was to be created headed by him.

Under the deal, the CPP took the choicest ministries of foreign affairs, finance, commerce, agriculture, and telecommunications, leaving them in charge of international and economic affairs. Funcinpec secured the ministries of justice, information, and civil aviation, and a couple of less important portfolios.

Political realities continued haunting the country. It was apparent that Hun Sen had managed to strike a deal with Ranariddh by giving his partymen plum posts in the government. As a result Funcinpec was no longer a vocal opposition party, and had more or less been co-opted by Hun Sen. But, in order to keep his coalition partners happy Hun Sen had to continually walk on eggshells.

The new top-heavy government imposed a heavy cost on the treasury. To strike a compromise the CPP doubled the number of ministerial and deputy ministerial posts so as to co-opt and accommodate a lot of people. The government was forced to find new ways to cut costs and boost revenue. No longer could civil servants import cars tax-free. Their salaries were to be taxed, and their mobile phones taken away. Hun Sen led by example: he slashed his entourage of advisors from more than a hundred to just ten.

The country paid a price in order to achieve political stability. But was it worth the results? For the first time in thirty years the country was at peace. That surely was worth something?

As expected, Prime Minister Hun Sen and his unwieldy new coalition government won a vote of confidence in the national assembly on November 30.

Within days, the UN awarded Cambodia's UN seat to representatives of Hun Sen.

But Cambodia's hopes for a quick entry into Asean were dashed in early December when the leaders of Singapore, Thailand, and the Philippines blocked its accession. The three countries first wanted to see the creation of a new senate. Vietnam, Malaysia, Indonesia, and Myanmar, on the other hand, strongly backed the immediate entry of Cambodia, throwing Asean's prized consensus-oriented approach into jeopardy.

But Asean left the door open to Hun Sen. He was invited to attend an Asean summit in Hanoi in December 1998 as a guest, and he milked the opportunity for all it was worth. In a shrewdly crafted speech Hun Sen made a strong pitch for his country to join the regional group, painting a favourable picture of his country that, to many ears, sounded incredulous. The Cambodian general election was held on time, he said, with the participation of thirty-nine political parties, and a voter turnout of more than ninety per cent. He trumpeted that fact that the election was hailed as free and fair by more than 700 international observers, and was described by some foreigners as a "miracle on the Mekong." He basked in the afterglow of Funcinpec and the CPP forming a coalition government, and the pact between the two parties in setting up a common political platform to strengthen political stability.

Moving to the state of the nation, he said that the economy grew by two per cent in 1997, in line with global and regional trends. In the same year the economy of Thailand contracted by 1.7 per cent after being hit by the Asian economic crisis. Foreign and domestic investment in Cambodia reached US$800 million in the first nine months of 1998, maintaining the same level as the previous year, he said, underlining a point that confidence in his country had not waned after the bloody takeover of 1997.

Then he used the continuing Asian economic crisis to argue that Asean needed to strengthen its cohesion to battle the challenges that had impoverished Southeast Asians. He pledged Cambodia would push forward with its market reforms, and create a liberal and transparent legal system because joining Asean was a priority.

The Asean heads of government, listening intently, were apparently infected by Hun Sen's rustic sincerity.

Four months later Hun Sen's supreme dream came true in just the way he wanted. Cambodia finally joined Asean on April 30, 1999 in Hanoi, the political heartland of his strongest ally to whom he owed his political rise. After two years of wrangling, Cambodian Foreign Minister Hor Nam Hong and nine other Asean foreign ministers signed a declaration formally inducting Cambodia. For Hun Sen it was the ultimate trophy after a frustratingly long search for political legitimacy. His former enemies in Asean had now embraced him, and he them.

A DARK shadow that blotched Hun Sen's career was the speculation that during his years as a Khmer Rouge commander he carried out the instructions of his seniors to kill innocent Cambodians. During their rule from 1975 to 1979 the Khmer Rouge starved, tortured, and killed about 1.7 million innocent people in the urban and rural areas. The victims of the genocide were Cambodia's Buddhist monks, and ethnic minorities such as the Vietnamese, Chinese, Thai, and Cham Muslims.

"It is better [for those who raise such questions] not to ask me, but to ask the people who live in those areas [where the killings took place]," Hun Sen said in reaction to whether he had blood on his hands. "I don't want to respond to any allegations, but the people know the truth. The people in those areas criticise Sihanouk, but they don't criticise Hun Sen. They support Hun Sen. Is there any reason for the people to love a man who carried out killings? The people will have memories of my stay in those areas. Please go to those areas and see for yourself."

An independent investigation into the genocide funded by the United States' department of state, and conducted by Yale University scholars, had failed to come up with any evidence implicating Hun Sen in the killings. The fact was that Hun Sen's influence in the Khmer Rouge was confined to the military. As an army officer he was not required to develop connections with the ruling political cadres. He never met Pol Pot, Nuon Chea (who served under Pol Pot as deputy secretary of the Communist Party of Kampuchea), or Khieu Samphan (who headed the

State Presidium of Pol Pot's Democratic Kampuchea). But he met Ieng Sary once, in late-1972, when Sary entered the liberated zone. Sary, at that time, worked for Sihanouk as a special overseas envoy.

Through the mid-1990s, Hun Sen developed a new, albeit controversial, strategy to break up the Khmer Rouge by encouraging its top leaders to defect to the government. From a strength of 50,000 fighters at the peak of Pol Pot's régime, the Khmer Rouge's numbers were whittled down to about 4,000 by 1993, and to just about 1,000 in 1997. Hun Sen sparked their fragmentation by granting amnesty to Sary, thereby splintering them into smaller factions that sought similar deals to escape punishment. The amnesty given to Sary was not carved in stone. As Cambodians clamoured to bring the Khmer Rouge leaders to trial, the amnesty seemed only a temporary reprieve, a typically Hun Sen-style feint, to break up the guerrillas.

When Khieu Samphan and Nuon Chea surrendered to the Cambodian government in December 1998, the contentious issue of a court trial went on the boil. The duo added insult to injury when they said "sorry" for their crimes against humanity, and then promptly retreated into the cool comfort of their US$105 a night rooms at the deluxe Le Royale Hotel in Phnom Penh, when they should have been jailed in the city's T-3 prison. Clearly, they were literally trying to get away with mass murder.

Hun Sen stuck to his guns by insisting that they face a court trial. Even the government's severest critic, Sam Rainsy, lent his backing to Hun Sen's proposal. But yet another Khmer Rouge general, Ta Mok, also known as "the Butcher", remained on the loose, and new fears were unleashed that if he was allowed to run free in the jungles, he would be able to rebuild his vanquished forces, and again come to control a swathe of Cambodian land. More ominously, bands of Khmer Rouge people might rally around him, and turn into bandits to terrorise the people.

Some Cambodians were disingenuously saying that it was pointless to exhume the issue, and that the best way to heal the nation was to abandon the idea of holding a trial. But this would set an immoral precedent for an unconscionable crime, and take the country down a dangerous road. If anything, the way to heal the wounded people was to bring the buried past out into the open, to confront it boldly, and set an example by punishing the guilty. Without a precedent, every gangster would get the message that they could use the gun without fear of the law, and it would send a signal to the remnant Khmer Rouge fighters that they could regroup and keep alive their ideology.

Equally, it was of crucial importance that a trial be held in a Cambodian court. The Cambodian tragedy was, to a large extent, a result of the American destruction of Prince Sihanouk's neutral régime. It was US President Richard Nixon's secret bombing of Cambodia that inflamed Khmer anger, and set the stage for fanatics such as Pol Pot and the Khmer Rouge to emerge. Pol Pot despised the West for destroying his country, and in his zeal to wipe out all Western traces from Khmer society he killed his own people. As an active and partisan player in Cambodian politics, the USA's relentless bombardment of a poor country and its dark role in destabilising Sihanouk, stripped Washington of the moral authority to sit in judgment on the travails of modern-day Cambodia.

A trial of the Khmer Rouge leaders was in danger of being scuttled by several countries that played a clandestine role in backing Pol Pot. His former backers were well-known. In their attempt to overthrow the Hun Sen government in the 1980s, China, the West and Asean backed the Khmer Rouge. China, in particular, publicly opposed holding a trial because its dubious role would become known. It would be yet another colossal travesty of justice if the narrow self-interest of a few countries, to keep the lid shut tight on their reprehensible support for the Khmer Rouge, was allowed to derail a trial.

There were many who harped on the fact that Hun Sen should also be brought to trial because he was a part of the Khmer Rouge until he defected to Vietnam in 1977. The fact was that he was not a decision-maker in the Khmer Rouge. He was a military commander who fled when asked to attack innocents. If Hun Sen was brought to trial, then King Sihanouk must also be tried because he served as the head of state for a while during Pol Pot's rule. But the investigators had found nothing to implicate either of them.

THE MIND OF A CHESS PLAYER

He lived by the gun and often came close to death by the gun. The teenaged guerrilla who ducked bullets was no different from the grown man, the prime minister who had rockets and grenades thrown at him. His enemies repeatedly tried to assassinate him. They could do him no harm. The hot war into which Hun Sen was immersed and blooded as a boy continued raging through his middle age. He knew no peace, and reacted to every situation the way a guerrilla would. The tangled web that he wove could have destroyed him. But it also kept him alive.

"They cannot overthrow me by force", he commented. "If they want to get rid of me they would have to play a smarter political game than me."

His insecurities stemmed from being surrounded by enemies in the shape of the Khmer Rouge, the royalists, and opposition leaders who wanted him eliminated. Out of the pool of insecurities grew the stem of his security as he layered himself with carefully picked bodyguards, and beyond them an entire armed force that could be called out to support the government.

Hun Sen's critics tended to compare him to Pol Pot and Stalin, but the rationale underlying those parallels was specious and erroneous, for he was revolted by the massacres and escaped from them. He refused to carry out Pol Pot's orders to attack a small community of Muslims. But he lived in violent times, and ultimately the weight of circumstances turned him into an authoritarian figure. He wanted to be that, and no less. Only an authoritarian could control a violent and deeply divided society riven with civil war.

The West showed him no mercy. It wanted him to be a soft democrat. Hun Sen had a low level of tolerance for preachy Westerners. He knew that it would be a mistake to transplant an American-style system in a highly unstable Asian country on the brink of anarchy, where a civil war still burned on a low flame. It could not be done in China, and it would not work in Cambodia. Hun Sen took the challenge, and collided head-on with the West.

"I want to be a strongman, and do something for my country," he said.

Those words had a totemic ring. But he was not the archetypal strongman. He did not believe that murder and genocide could reorder society, nor would it take his country to prosperity. Instead, he created the framework for an authoritarian democracy, he demanded respect from his people, and talked about performing an economic miracle, but within the borders of democracy.

He wanted power, even lusted after it like any politician. He put his vocal cords through a punishing routine, addressing crowds in dusty provinces till he lost his voice. He campaigned like a democrat. He wooed the voters with promises, and actually delivered on some of them, building schools, roads, and irrigation canals across the country. He did not seek revenge against the people who did not vote for him. Far from it. He went back to them, and gave them the things they needed—the schools, the canals. He chatted with them, shared a cigarette, and they responded.

The man carried the child in him. He listened to the child within, and was shaped by the child. Not many people were aware of his early life, and the difficulties he faced. He would not forget the child's pain, the memories of constant hunger, the separation. He would be tormented by the killings he witnessed as a teenager. Those images were seared into his brain. He would wake up at night to a bad dream, bathed in sweat like a veteran of a horrible war.

Those dreams started early. The boy had to leave the warmth and shelter of his home in Kompong Cham, and was forced to live in a pagoda at the mercy of the monks because his parents had fallen on hard times. There, at a tender age, he learned lessons on how tough life could be. He begged for food to feed the monks and himself, carried heavy loads of water over long distances, and slept on hard floors, bitten to sickness by mosquitoes.

He spent long hours on the familiar and friendly streets which became his second home as he went about performing his daily chores. The gamin child knew that he had a sharp mind for chess. He learnt the game at a local barber's shop. Soon, seasoned players realised he could go for the kill.

Even though hunger hacked at his insides he never took his eyes off his books. He read by the midnight lamp, and in semi-darkness, and did fairly well in class. His teachers watched his progress, but they were concerned that he was the silent type.

The widening civil war turned his life upside down, sending him out of the pagoda, out into the wilderness of the jungles. When Sihanouk was removed in a *coup* he joined the resistance to restore him to power. So tantalising was Sihanouk's appeal to the young people that Hun Sen fell under his spell, and was prepared for die for the young prince whose films he had seen as a child. To him, Sihanouk was not just a political hero, but a matinee idol. In one of life's many ironies Hun Sen would later be pitted against Sihanouk. His childhood hero would turn into an adversary during the peace talks.

Hun Sen would have remained an unknown soldier, one who lived and died without even fifteen minutes of fame. But he had learnt to survive. He studied the art of guerrilla warfare, and managed to cheat death when it came calling on countless occasions.

When he joined the resistance he did not realise that it was controlled by the Khmer Rouge. To him, it did not matter who ran the movement as long as the despised Lon Nol régime was overthrown. Even before the Khmer Rouge came to power Hun Sen had proved himself a tough guerrilla.

He had also glimpsed the intolerance, the nanny-like interference, and the paranoia that the Khmer Rouge was capable of. They erected all kinds of stumbling blocks to prevent him from marrying Bun Rany. In the end, the raging fires of their ardour were too much for the Angkar to snuff out. But the process of breaking off with the Khmer Rouge had begun. The young couple realised that this was not the resistance they had joined. It had degenerated into pettiness, thought control, and barbarism.

Hun Sen and his friends were dismayed by the rivers of blood that the Khmer Rouge had opened up. The turning point came when he was ordered to attack a small Muslim community. He rebelled, and escaped to Vietnam.

Were his own hands bathed in blood? An investigation into the mass killings funded by the US department of state and conducted by Yale University came up with no evidence to implicate Hun Sen in the genocide. Hun Sen even welcomed the investigation, and said that he was open to any inquiry. On balance, it did appear that his hands were clean. Revolted by the killings he found it increasingly difficult to stay on in the Khmer Rouge, and fled just when Pol Pot sent a death squad to execute him.

The boy who fought against one injustice by joining the resistance was now a man, and the man struggled against another injustice by defecting to Vietnam. The escape to Vietnam was his only option. There was no organisation that existed in Cambodia at the time to challenge the Khmer Rouge, much less put a stop to the bloodletting. He had to turn to a friendly foreign power.

It was a desperate step, full of dangers both personal and national. The first risk he ran was of being captured and killed by the Vietnamese; the second risk was of endangering his country's interests by playing into the hands of the powerful neighbour. It was a miracle that he survived, and that the interests of his countrymen were preserved. Those victims of starvation and torture that survived the genocide were eventually liberated by the combined armies of Vietnam and the Cambodian rebels.

His training as a guerrilla and a negotiator in the Khmer Rouge's commando schools saved his skin, and then the lives of millions of Cambodians. He always saw his return journey to Cambodia as a life-saving mission, and he accomplished it. It could easily have gone the other way. His Vietnamese captors could have disbelieved his word, and shot him on the spot.

If Hun Sen had been killed the history of Cambodia would have been different. The holocaust could have been on a much bigger scale. The genocide in which about 1.7 million people were killed might have ended with up to four million deaths through starvation and rampant disease alone. And, if Pol Pot had continued with the killings half the population could have been wiped out. Cambodia could have been a bigger human disaster. This would certainly have been the case because there were no indications from Pol Pot's Angkar that any logical economic development was on the cards, other than his failed agrarian programmes.

Hun Sen lived in assorted Vietnamese jails and, with him, the hopes of millions of his countrymen were kept alive. Thousands inside Cambodia defected to join the liberation forces. They prayed for the day that their campaign to overthrow Pol Pot would bear fruit after years of famine, both personal and political.

It was a tribute to Hun Sen's skills as a negotiator that he could convince the military leaders of Vietnam that it was also in their interests to help liberate his country. For Vietnam, it would be an expensive exercise involving several divisions, a potential loss of lives, and the more serious international reaction against intervention. But Hun Sen was able to argue successfully that, in the end, the liberation was essential in order to free the people from an inhuman régime. Reluctant at first, the Vietnamese were finally forced to retaliate when Pol Pot launched repeated attacks against their border villages.

Although Hun Sen was the pointman, he could not have succeeded in his massive enterprise without help from his comrades, Heng Samrin, Chea Sim, Pen Sovann, and others, who banded together to form the United Front. Heng Samrin and Chea Sim, in particular, mustered the support of thousands of people in the eastern provinces whose anger was only waiting to be sharpened.

The liberation was a cakewalk. Pol Pot's forces capitulated, exposing the hollow core of a régime that was foolish and irresponsible enough to attack Vietnam, but ill-prepared to defend itself. The world saw just how ridiculous his régime was.

After a triumphant Hun Sen and his comrades flew in from Ho Chi Minh City to Phnom Penh on a Vietnamese aircraft, the question uppermost in their minds concerned the duration of the Vietnamese presence in Cambodia. Having overthrown the Khmer Rouge, should they depart, or should they stay?

Hun Sen said that he personally asked the Vietnamese armed forces to extend their stay to ensure that the Khmer Rouge were kept confined to the Thai border area, so that the new Cambodian forces could be raised and armed. An early departure would have been akin to opening the backdoor for Pol Pot to return. So shaky was the new régime that diplomats gave it no more than a few months before the Khmer Rouge would fight its way back into the capital.

When his party, the KPRP, elevated the young and inexperienced man to the post of foreign minister, it recognised his tremendous contribution to national salvation and preservation. It was an unparalleled achievement that was richly rewarded once again when he was appointed prime minister.

But any plans that the young premier might have had to develop his country were put on hold because his country was not recognised by the non-communist world. One of Hun Sen's biggest regrets was that his government was denied the loans to build its physical infrastructure such as roads, bridges, power generation plants, airports, and seaports. So, while he saved his people from certain death he could do little to improve their lives.

These troubling realities coaxed the uncompromising former guerrilla to talk to his enemies. The next step was the peace talks with Sihanouk where he got the upperhand over the tired prince who later praised him for his efforts to find a solution. Sihanouk said that Cambodia needed many more Hun Sens. Ultimately in 1991 the peace accord was signed. By this time, Hun Sen, Heng Samrin, and Chea Sim saw the need to jettison communism, and steer their party towards elections.

Never having faced an election in his life Hun Sen was suddenly galvanised into campaigning, presiding over town meetings, and jostling to stay ahead of the other parties. He learned how to become a democrat, but was unprepared to face the verdict of the people in the 1993 elections.

He lost.

Ranariddh won, and became the first prime minister. Hun Sen was appointed the second prime minister. Their awkward coalition lasted only until Ranariddh teamed up with the Khmer Rouge, and secretly imported weapons. Hun Sen saw Ranariddh as a threat to stability, and overthrew him in 1997 after days of bloody street fighting.

Suddenly, the man who had stayed in Ranariddh's shadow emerged as a strongman. He took hold of power, and kept it on a tight leash. The young man who lived by the gun, had used the gun, wiped the barrel clean, and returned it to his holster.

But Hun Sen's image was somewhat sullied by his alleged connections with the richest man in Cambodia, Theng Bunma. Thailand issued an arrest warrant for Bunma on fraud charges on June 22, 1998 alleging that he obtained a Thai passport under a false name. He was also under investigation in Hong Kong for allegedly using a fake passport to register his company, Thai Boon Roong. But in Phnom Penh, Bunma remained a powerful figure. He owned a major hotel, and was the president of the Cambodian Chamber of Commerce. Bunma was banned from entering the USA, which said it possessed evidence implicating him in drug trafficking, though he denied the charges. But he once admitted that he had given millions of dollars to finance Hun Sen's political campaigns.

Unfazed by the Bunma sideshow, Hun Sen had his hands full with the elections in 1998. His party won convincingly, but fell short of a two-thirds majority to rule.

Once again Hun Sen's aspirations were arrested. He had played the democracy game, the elections were seen as being fair by international observers, yet he could not carry the entire country with him.

Be that as it may, there appeared to be no alternative to Hun Sen. Only he was equipped to govern a country torn apart by civil war, remnant Khmer Rouge guerrillas, bandits, and kidnappers. He and his party chieftains, Chea Sim and Heng Samrin, remained the rulers of Cambodia.

Once before Cambodians had gambled by placing their future in the hands of the man who had delivered them from the Khmer Rouge. Once again the results of the 1998 elections showed that the people were prepared to gamble on him as their future leader. It was precisely the opportunity he had waited for.

Cambodia could only be governed by a certain kind of man, a strongman. Hun Sen responded by becoming just that.

The Cambodian people were asking searching questions—what would be the future of Cambodia under Hun Sen? Could he make a clean break with the mistakes of the past? Could he reform his administration to end the corruption, and the tidal wave of violence?

Political punditry in Phnom Penh went into overdrive in an attempt to answer these vexing questions. The consensus in early-1999 was that Hun Sen might, in his best interests, purge many controversial but powerful persons within his close circle of confidants, and within the CPP, in order to send a clear message to the international community that he was intent on breaking with the past, and to give an indication of his commitment to creating a transparent system. It was believed that it would be difficult for Hun Sen to sever relations with people who had remained staunchly loyal to him.

Still, it had become necessary for Hun Sen to start thinking about cleaning up his inner circle with an eye on the next elections in the year 2003. Cambodian voters would assess his term as prime minister with a critical eye. They would not just monitor his contribution to improving their lives; they would judge him by the quality of the people in his administration. He was aware of the needs of his people, and that his every action would be critically judged by them. He had begun his prime ministerial term with a lot of support and affection from rural Cambodians, but he knew that the very same people did not approve of the actions of his key personnel.

Removing long-time loyalists was easier said than done. So, he figured that it might be easier to reform them instead of sacking them. In mid-1999, he warned his partymen to clean up corruption and crime. At a closed-door party congress of 200 delegates, Hun Sen said: "If there is any official who commits wrongdoing, they must change, or else be expelled."

His overarching strategy hinged on the meshing of three factors—political stability, donor aid, and foreign investments. It was clear that he exercised the authority necessary to provide the political stability that foreign and local businessmen craved. It was also plain that he would not tolerate political dissent if it harmed the fabric of political stability. With Cambodia's major aid donors, the USA, Japan, and Europe, supporting his government, it appeared that his country would win the billions of dollars in aid it needed to build roads, bridges, and airports. With political stability and a physical infrastructure in place, it was only a matter of time before private investments flowed in to create jobs and take Cambodians closer towards their dream of peace and prosperity.

"I want to build our economy like the other Southeast Asian strongmen did," Hun Sen had once told us.

He wanted to turn Cambodia into another Asian Tiger economy. The Cambodian people had given him yet another chance to live up to his words.

BIBLIOGRAPHICAL NOTES

At the core of this biography are ten hours of candid face-to-face interviews with Hun Sen conducted by the authors in three sittings in 1997-98. He talked emotionally and passionately of his troubled life and times, and his wounded country. Earlier, an additional six hours of interviews were conducted by Harish Mehta between 1990-1998 when he spoke about the enervating civil war, the genocide, and the phlegmatic process of reconstruction.

Covering a period of eight years these interviews were the compass charting the life of Hun Sen, and plotting his evolution from a communist leader to a Cambodian-style democrat. Moreover, Hun Sen provided written answers to dozens of questions—his last responses coming over the fax in January 1999. He arranged for the authors to travel with him to the provinces, journeys of discovery that gave deeper insights into the man.

A four-hour interview with Hun Sen's wife, Bun Rany, opened a window into their troubled lives. Bun Rany broke down completely during the emotionally-charged interview conducted by Julie Mehta.

A revealing interview with Hun Sen's brother, Hun Neng, was conducted by Harish Mehta in the thick of the general election in 1993. Hun Neng provided him with searing insights into Hun Sen's life.

An interview with Hun Sen's brother-in-law, Nim Chandara, fleshed out some of the unknown aspects of Hun Sen's family life. A series of interviews with Hun Sen's school teachers, school friends, and pagoda boys who lived with him at the Naga Vann Pagoda in Phnom Penh, brought alive his childhood.

Interviews with Norodom Ranariddh, Norodom Chakrapong, and Norodom Sirivudh revealed how the royal family dealt with Hun Sen, and how he responded to them.

For economic data, the authors relied on World Bank reports, Untac documents, and Cambodian government releases from Sihanouk's era to the present. The authors interviewed dozens of Cambodian government officials and UN workers to put into perspective the conundrum of this long-suffering country.

The Players And Their Relationship With Hun Sen

References: *Los Angeles Times*; Charles P. Wallace, "A Humble Populist Hero Emerges In Cambodia: Chea Sim, The Communist Party's No 2 Official, Is Gaining Wide Popularity", September 18, 1990. *The Globe & Mail*, "Election Contenders", July 25, 1998. *The Asian Wall Street Journal*, Urban C. Lehner, "Cambodia's Gadfly Picks A New Target", February 28, 1995. *Phnom Penh Post*, Christine Chaumeau, "Pen Sovann Out To Settle Old Scores", May 1997. Agence France-Presse, "Cambodia's Prince Sirivudh Vows No Politics Yet On Return From Exile", January 20, 1999.

For further reading on the political personalities, see Marie Alexandrine Martin, *Cambodia: A Shattered Society* (University of California Press, Berkeley and Los Angeles, 1994). *International*

Who's Who.
A Sketch Of Hun Sen's Life
Based on Hun Sen's official biodata, and various media reports: Reuters, Agence France-Presse, and *Asiaweek,* from the 1970s through the 1990s.

PROLOGUE

A Short History Of Cambodia

For further readings on ancient Cambodian history, see:

R.C. Majumdar, *Hindu Colonies In The Far East* (Firma Klm, Calcutta, 1992);

Ian Mabbett and David Chandler, *The Khmers* (Blackwell Publishers, Oxford, 1995);

George Coedès, *The Indianised States Of Southeast Asia,* (University of Hawaii Press, Honolulu, 1968);

Michael Freeman and Roger Warner, *Angkor* (Houghton Mifflin, Boston, 1990);

Malcolm MacDonald, *Angkor And The Khmers* (Oxford University Press, Singapore, 1990);

Chou Ta-Kuan, *The Customs of Cambodia* (The Siam Society, Bangkok, 1992);

David Chandler, *A History of Cambodia* (Westview Press, Colorado, 1992).

For more on the 20th century history of Cambodia, see David Chandler, *The Tragedy of Cambodian History* (Yale University Press, New Haven, 1991).

For more on the suppression of the Cambodian press, see Harish C. Mehta, *Cambodia Silenced: The Press Under Six Regimes* (White Lotus Press, Bangkok, 1997).

For Sihanouk's elegantly-crafted anti-American editorials, see *Kambuja Monthly Illustrated Review,* editions of July 1967, August 1967, and September 1967.

CHAPTER ONE

Child of the Full Moon

The centrepiece of the chapter is an extended interview with Hun Sen conducted by Harish and Julie Mehta in Siem Reap in December 1997. It also draws upon Julie Mehta's interview with Bun Rany in Phnom Penh in December 1997, and the authors' interview with Chhim You Teck, medical assistant, Calmette Hospital, Phnom Penh in June 1998.

Pagoda Boy

Hun Sen spoke about his childhood in an interview with the authors in Siem Reap in December 1997. To fill in the missing pieces in Hun Sen's early years, the authors interviewed school teacher Path Sam and medical assistant Chhim You Teck in Phnom Penh in June 1998. Julie Mehta's interview with Bun Rany in Phnom Penh in June 1997 threw new light on the travails of the suffering people.

The Cambodian riel-US dollar exchange rate is based on the *Statistical Yearbook for Asia and the Far East, 1969.* Also see, Reuter, "Cambodian Riel Devalued", November 1, 1971.

CHAPTER TWO

Guerrilla

The authors' conversations with Hun Sen in Siem Reap in December 1997 brought alive his memories of his days in the *maquis*, and his first taste of combat against a US Army unit inside Cambodia. In her interview with Julie Mehta, Bun Rany talked about how she secretly joined the *maquis* without informing her parents.

Romancing Rebels

Hun Sen and Bun Rany spent several hours talking to the authors in Phnom Penh in December 1997. They spoke tearfully about the death of their first child, soon after birth, at the hands of the Khmer Rouge. Early tragedy brought out the songwriter in him.

See *New York Times*, Seth Mydans, "When He Writes A Song, Cambodia Better Listen", 1998. The article quotes Hun Sen as saying: "I can't sing and I can't play an instrument. But I can write." Mydans reports that sometimes the urge to write a song strikes Hun Sen on an airplane or a helicopter, and he scribbles on scraps of paper. He wrote love songs such as: "The Dark Skinned Woman of Krang Yoen", and lyrics extolling peace and human rights.

For details of the executions of senior Khmer Rouge commanders, Chen Sot and Kun Deth, in the eastern zone in the 1970s, see *Genocide and Democracy in Cambodia,* edited by Ben Kiernan (Yale University Southeast Asia Studies, New Haven, 1993).

For further reading on the language and nuances of the Khmer Rouge see, Mary B. Ebihara, Carol A. Mortland, and Judy Ledgerwood, *Cambodian Culture Since 1975* (Cornell University Press, Ithaca and London, 1994). Specifically see John Marston's essay, *Metaphors Of The Khmer Rouge*.

Breaking Off

Hun Sen told the authors in Phnom Penh in December 1997 about his estrangement with the brutal policies of the Khmer Rouge, and his abortive plans to stage a rebellion against Pol Pot within Cambodia.

CHAPTER THREE

Prisoner

During the interview with the authors in Phnom Penh in December 1997, Hun Sen revealed, for the first time, that he and four other defectors crossed the border into Vietnam, and were arrested by the Vietnamese military authorities, and interrogated for months. Bun Rany recounted those terror-filled days when, upon hearing the news of Hun Sen's defection, the Khmer Rouge forced her to perform hard labour, and referred to her as a "widow". She managed to escape from the terror-stricken village just hours before she was to be executed.

For further reading on the plight of Cambodian women, see:

Ang Choulean, *Sahakum Khmae Neu Srok Barang Neng Preah Buddhasasana,* The Cambodian Community In France And Buddhism (Culture khmere, Paris, April–September, 1981);

Chanthou Boua, *Women In Kampuchea* (UNICEF, Bangkok, 1981);

Judy Ledgerwood, *Analysis Of The Situation Of Women In Cambodia* (UNICEF, Phnom Penh, 1991).

Political Asylum

Hun Sen continued his long interview with the authors, talking about how he was rebuffed repeatedly by the Vietnamese when he asked them for political asylum. They asked him to seek refuge in Thailand, but he refused, and eventually managed to convince the Vietnamese to grant him political asylum.

For details on border clashes between Pol Pot's forces and the Vietnamese Army, the authors consulted news reports by the Vietnam News Agency, and Phnom Penh Radio. Also, United Press International, "Khmers Hit Tay Ninh, Says Hanoi", February 2, 1978.

CHAPTER FOUR

Liberation

Speaking with remarkable clarity throughout the interview with the authors in Phnom Penh in December 1997, Hun Sen revealed a sharp memory for dates, places, and events. When he flew by Vietnamese plane to Phnom Penh in 1979, Hun Sen thought that his wife was dead. Bun Rany told Julie Mehta how she hid herself from the Khmer Rouge, and managed to survive until she was found by a search party sent by Hun Sen.

For further reading, see Carlyle A. Thayer, *The Vietnam People's Army Under Doi Moi* (Institute of Southeast Asian Studies, Singapore, 1994). Dr Thayer provides rare insights into Vietnamese involvement in Cambodia.

Other references: Radio Hanoi announced on December 4, 1978 the formation of a Vietnamese plan to overthrow the Khmer Rouge. *New Straits Times*, "Hanoi Front To Topple Pol Pot", December 4, 1978. Radio of Kampuchean National United Front rebels, "Viets Cross the Mekong", January 3, 1979. Radio Hanoi, "Rebels Take Phnom Penh", January 7, 1979. *New Straits Times*, "13 Vietnam Divisions Leading War", January 8, 1979, (based on a *New York Times* report).

The Vietnamese Role

Hun Sen candidly told the authors during the interview in Phnom Penh in June 1998 that his government would not have survived without the assistance of the Vietnamese.

Other references: *New Straits Times*, "UN Support For Pol Pot", January 12, 1979. Reuter, "Chinese Hold The Key To Total Pullout, Says Co Thach", June 21, 1983. Agence France-Presse, "Hanoi Turning Cambodia Into A Vietnam, Says Paper", June 20, 1983. (This report quoted Vietnamese Defence Minister Van Tien Dung, who helped Hun Sen raise a rebel army, as praising the Cambodian armed forces on the occasion of their Revolutionary Army Day). Agence France-Presse, "Phnom Penh Run By A Vietnamese Committee, Says Paper", May 2, 1986. *New Straits Times*, "Viets May Pullout Before '90, Says Rajiv", December 3, 1995. United Press International, "Vietnam's Exercise In Illusion", May 14, 1983. Agence France-Presse, "350 Newsmen Ask To Cover Viet Pullout", September 17, 1989.

For further information on the Vietnamese Army's operations in Cambodia, see Carlyle A. Thayer, *The Vietnam People's Army Under Doi Moi* (Institute of Southeast Asian Studies, Singapore, 1994).

CHAPTER FIVE

Grooming The Guerrilla

In his interview with the authors in Phnom Penh in June 1998, Hun Sen talked about the early challenges of his new job as foreign minister, the difficulties of understanding complex issues of international affairs, how he studied hard, and was coached and nurtured by his leaders.

Other references: SPK, "Mr Hun Sen, Foreign Minister Of Kampuchea, Arrives In Colombo", June 7, 1979. *New Nation,* "Indian Draft Threatens Asean Move", November 13, 1979. *New Nation,* "Dong's India Mission Fails", April 10, 1980. *New Nation,* "Indira's 'Yes' On Ties With Samrin", July 8, 1980. Agence France-Presse, "Residents of Phnom Penh Eating Roots", March 25, 1979. United Press International, "Khmer's Daily", January 27, 1979. *New Nation,* "Heng Outlines Priorities", February 17, 1979. Agence France-Presse, "Sihanouk Expects To Lead Exile Government", July 15, 1979. Agence France-Presse, "Heng Samrin Régime's 2-Stage Plan", August 27, 1981. *Business Times,* Singapore, "Sihanouk Hopeful", September 4, 1981. Reuter, "Piece Of Theatre, Says Phnom Penh", September 3, 1981.

Peaking At Thirty-Three

During the long interview in Phnom Penh in December 1997, Hun Sen spoke about his rapid ascent to the prime ministership after the death of Chan Si.

Other references: *Straits Times,* "Hun Sen Elected Prime Minister", January 15, 1985. *Straits Times,* "Revolutionary Party In Power", May 1, 1979. *Sunday Times,* Singapore, "Cambodia Party Boss Pen Sovann Sacked", December 6, 1981. *Phnom Penh Post,* "Pen Sovann Out To Settle Old Scores", May 1997.

For further details on the KPRP, see "The Kampuchean People's Revolutionary Party", Joint Publications Research Service, Southeast Asia Region, April 10, 1987.

For more on Hun Sen's rumoured rivalry with Chea Sim, see: *Business Times,* Harish Mehta, "Cambodia's Ruling Party Dismisses Talk Of Power Struggle", May 15, 1992; and *Los Angeles Times,* Charles P. Wallace, "A Humble Populist Hero Emerges in Cambodia: Chea Sim, The Communist Party's No 2 Official, Is Gaining Wide Popularity", September 18, 1990.

References to the peace talks include: Associated Press, "Cambodia Dismisses Sihanouk's Overtures", May 29, 1987. United Press International, "Phnom Penh Offers Top Posts to Sihanouk", October 25, 1987. *Straits Times,* "Sihanouk Opens Paris Talks With Hun Sen", December 3, 1987. Reuter, Agence France-Presse, United Press International, "Cambodia: Kim Wanted As Mediator", December 5, 1987. Agence France-Presse, "Sihanouk Cancels Talks", December 11, 1987. United Press International, "We Must Fight As Well As Negotiate: Hun Sen", December 13, 1987. United Press International, Agence France-Presse, "Hun Sen Takes Back Foreign Minister's Post", December 30, 1987. Reuter, "Sihanouk Picks France For Further Talks", January 3, 1988. *Straits Times,* "Rajiv And Hun Sen Discuss Cambodia", January 15, 1988. Reuter, Agence France-Presse, "Positive End To Paris Talks Despite Discord", January 22, 1988. *Straits Times,* Paul Wedel, (reported by United Press International) "Rise Of A Rural Revolutionary", February 7, 1988. United Press International, "Heng Samrin Gets Squadron Of Mig-21s", June 22, 1989. *Straits Times,* Tan Lian Choo, "Sihanouk Steps Down As Head Of His Political Body", August 28, 1989. Agence France-Presse, "Western Overtures To Phnom Penh Worry Resistance, US", November 22, 1989. Agence France-Presse, "EC Urged To

Recognise Phnom Penh Régime", November 24, 1989.

The Four Escapees

Background information on the four Khmer Rouge defectors who escaped to Vietnam with Hun Sen in 1977 was provided to the authors by Nim Chandara, a brother-in-law of Hun Sen's. Further information about one of the defectors was given to the authors by Hun Sen via fax in January 1999.

Defeat

For further readings, see a 49-page booklet published by the United Nations, "Agreements On A Comprehensive Political Settlement Of The Cambodian Conflict", Paris, October 23, 1991.

Other references are a series of reports in *Business Times* by Harish Mehta: "Road To Democracy Full Of Potholes—And Landmines", February 16, 1993. "Funcinpec Captures Lion's Share Of Seats In Hun Sen's Stronghold, Leads By 6% Overall", June 8, 1993. CPP Demands Re-poll In 4 Areas Or It Will Not Accept Results", June 8, 1993. "Hun Sen's Military Officers, Troops Reject Poll Result", June 9, 1993.

For full text of Hun Sen's objections to the election, refer to his statement delivered to the Supreme National Council at its June 10, 1993 meeting in Phnom Penh.

The Real Power

Information in this chapter is culled from an interview with Hun Sen in Phnom Penh in December 1997, and an earlier interview with Prince Norodom Ranariddh in May 1996.

For further details of Ranariddh's complaints about the CPP's dominance and its reluctance to share power, see "Two-PM System Must Go" by Harish Mehta, *Business Times,* June 4, 1996. For details of Ranariddh's alliance with the Khmer Rouge, see "Prince's Khmer Rouge Deal Laced With Treachery", *Phnom Penh Post,* May 22-June 4, 1998.

Strongman

Hun Sen explained the background to the fighting, and the overthrow of Ranariddh, in an interview with the authors in December 1997.

The events surrounding the military overthrow of Ranariddh are based on official documents issued by the Cambodian government, and on statements made by Ranariddh and opposition leaders who described his removal as a *coup*, and an illegal act.

See "White Paper: Background On The July 1997 Crisis", 27 pages; and, "Crisis In July: Report On The Armed Insurrection—Its Origins, History, And Aftermath", 84 pages. Both papers were issued by the ministry of foreign affairs. Also, see a statement issued by Hun Sen on July 13, 1997 explaining the causes of the fighting, and the need to maintain stability.

For more on the overthrow of Ranariddh, see Harish Mehta's paper on Cambodia published in *Regional Outlook Southeast Asia* (Institute of Southeast Asian Studies, Singapore, 1998-99). Other references: *Straits Times,* "Heavy Fighting Rages Amidst Civil War Fears", July 7, 1997. *Phnom Penh Post,* "Prince's Khmer Rouge Deal Laced With Treachery", May 22-June 4, 1998. *Straits Times,* "US Condemns Hun Sen For Cambodian Violence", July 10, 1997. *Bangkok Post,* "Ranariddh Opts Out Of Civil War", July 19, 1997. *Thailand Times,* "Ranariddh Gives Up Armed Fight", July 19, 1997. *Straits Times,* "Ranariddh Meets Top Asean Team", July 19, 1997. Agence France-Presse, "Evidence Against Ousted PM Found", July 20, 1997. *Bangkok Post,* "Ranariddh Fears Another Civil War", July 20, 1997. *The Nation,* Bangkok, "Support Plunges

For Ranariddh In Party Division", February 2, 1998. *The Nation,* Bangkok, "Cambodia Will Elect New First Premier Today", August 6, 1997. *Straits Times,* "Asean Puts Off Cambodia's Entry", July 11, 1997. *Straits Times,* "US Refuses To Recognise New Cambodian First PM", July 18, 1997. *Bangkok Post,* "Sihanouk Appoints Co-Premiers To UN", September 6, 1997. *Far Eastern Economic Review,* Nate Thayer, "The Resurrected", April 16, 1998.

CHAPTER SIX

Phnom Penh's Communists

In an interview with the authors, Indian Minister for External Affairs Inder Kumar Gujral revealed that Hun Sen had requested India to supply weapons to his government in 1990. The authors met Mr Gujral in Singapore in 1993; at the time, he was a member of parliament representing an opposition party.

Other significant interviews conducted by the authors in Phnom Penh, as they appear in the text, were with Soviet Union embassy counsellor V. Loukianov in May 1990, Cambodian architect Mam Sophana in October 1993, Cambodian Minister of Culture and Information Pen Yet in May 1990, State of Cambodia Prime Minister Hun Sen in January 1992, General-Director of tourism Sam Promonea in May 1990, and Deputy Governor of the National Bank of Cambodia Ti Julong Saumura in 1993. The authors also met Khmer Rouge spokesman Mak Ben at his press conference in May 1993, when he announced his party would not take part in the elections.

For details on the economy and life in Phnom Penh, see a series of reports by Harish Mehta in the *Business Times,* Singapore: "Peace Dividend", *Singapore Business,* April 1992. "State Of The Soviet Economy Causing Problems For Cambodia", October 1991. "Peace At Last For Cambodia", August 29, 1991. "The Killing Fields II?", October 12-13, 1991. "Cambodia Acts To Stop Theft Of Ancient Treasures", September 30, 1991. "Hun Sen Régime Set To Transfer Key Ministries To UN Control", June 30, 1992.

Also, Agence France-Presse, "India Can Help Resolve Cambodia Conflict: Hun Sen", October 9, 1990.

The Embargo

The authors interviewed Michael Ward, a World Bank official attached to UNTAC, in January 1993. The encounter yielded information on how the Cambodian government was printing currency notes in Moscow, and flying the cargo into Cambodia.

Other interviews conducted by the authors in Phnom Penh were with Prince Norodom Chakrapong in August 1992, Lt Gen John Sanderson in May 1993, *Cambodia Times* editor Kamaralzaman Tambu in May 1993, First Prime Minister Prince Ranariddh in May 1996, businessman Leang Eng Chhin in January 1992, and Australian telecommunications firm representative Stig Engstrom in May 1990.

For details on the air-flown riels from Moscow, see *Business Times,* Harish Mehta, "Untac Has Tough Job Keeping Tabs On Cambodian Currency", February 1993. The report, in part, said: *A flight from Moscow carrying a secret cargo of Cambodian currency notes touches down at Phnom Penh's Pochentong Airport, and within hours the cash is injected into the Phnom Penh economy.*

The cargo of 11.2 million riels (US$500,000) is put into circulation by the central bank, the National Bank of Cambodia, and the local market reacts instantly. As soon as the notes find their way into the system, the riel slumps. Last year, notes printed in Moscow were flown to Phnom Penh several times, and the last delivery was made on December 11, 1992. The UNTAC is monitoring the movement of the riel—both in the financial market, and aircraft movements. And it's not an easy job. Michael Ward, deputy economic advisor to UNTAC said that as the State of Cambodia's (SOC) budget deficit rises, it prints more money. The state, however, maintains that it has stopped printing notes to finance its budget deficit. Mr Ward, a principal economist at the World Bank on a year's attachment to UNTAC, said that the SOC's budget for 1993 is 200 billion riels (about US$100 million), and the deficit is as high as 30 per cent. About 80 per cent of the budget is spent on wages for the armed forces and the civil service. UNTAC has moved to exercise tighter control over the state's income and expenditure by taking over its five key ministries. "We are now in a better position to say that the state cannot spend more than it has got", Mr Ward said. But there would seem to be little that UNTAC can do to prevent notes being flown in. The World Bank and the Asian Development Bank have been urging the state not to print money to finance its deficit.

See Law On Foreign Investment In Cambodia (State Council No 58 KR) decreed on July 26, 1989.

Also see various reports by Harish Mehta in the *Business Times:* "Foreign Firms Bid For Cambodian Oil Blocks", February 1, 1992. "No Hang Ups In Phnom Penh, Mate", March 22, 1994. "Missing In Action: Economic News About Cambodia", March 12, 1993.

Also see a series of reports by Julie Chatterjee Mehta: "Angkor At Last", *Straits Times,* October 10, 1992. "The Great Cambodian Hope", *New Paper,* Singapore, May 20, 1993. "Thrilling Fields", *Straits Times,* December 19, 1992. "Cambodia Goes Through Slow, Uncertain Growth", *Straits Times,* March 16, 1994.

For details on the inefficiencies in the telecommunications system, and other public utilities, see *Cambodia: Agenda For Rehabilitation And Reconstruction,* (The World Bank, East Asia and Pacific Region, June 1992).

For further reading on the genocide, see *Report By A Group Of Cambodian Jurists, People's Revolutionary Tribunal Held In Phnom P nh For The Trial Of The Genocide Crimes Of The Pol Pot-Ieng Sary Clique* (Foreign Languages P blishing House, Phnom Penh, 1990).

CHAPTER SEVEN

A Mercurial Mind

This chapter contains correspondence between Prince Norodom Sihanouk and Harish Mehta. Sihanouk, in his letter dated August 16, 1992, answered several questions posed by the author in his letter dated August 14, 1992. Sihanouk replied on his official letterhead, and offered his views on the troubled peace process.

To glean an insight into Sihanouk's political strategy, the authors interviewed several players in the peace process in Phnom Penh: Prince Chakrapong in November 1992, State of Cambodia spokesman Khieu Kanharith in May 1993, deputy UNTAC force commander French Brigadier-General Robert Rideau in May 1993, Prince Norodom Sirivudh in January 1993, Hun Sen in December 1997. They interviewed Sam Rainsy on the telephone in Bangkok in June 1993.

For more on the working relationship between Ranariddh and Hun Sen after the 1993 election, see Harish Mehta, *Cambodia: A Year Of Consolidation, Southeast Asian Affairs* (Institute of Southeast Asian Studies, Singapore, 1996).

For further reading on the pre-election scenario, and the elections, see a series of reports by Harish Mehta in the *Business Times:* "My, What A Facelift For This Lady", January 4, 1992. "Princes And Power Brokers In Cambodia", November 27, 1992. "Ranariddh Forms Front To Fight May Cambodia Polls", April 7, 1993. "Sihanouk Changes His Mind, Will Continue To Lead SNC After Polls", April 8, 1993. "Cambodia Free Independent Democrats To Join Sihanoukist Front If Communists Kept Out", April 1993. "Jockeying For Power In Cambodia", June 3, 1993. "Can Sihanouk Call The Shots If He Becomes President", May 24, 1993. "Sihanouk Government Collapses In Face Of Resistance From Funcinpec Hardliners", June 5, 1993. "Sons And Rivals: Rift In The House Of Norodom", June 7, 1993. "Ranariddh Agrees To Back Sihanouk's National Government", June 8, 1993. "Sihanouk Refuses To Form Interim Government", June 10, 1993. "CPP Demands Control Of Key Ministries", June 10, 1993. "Hun Sen's Military Officers, Troops Reject Poll Result", June 9, 1993. "Will Hun Sen Wage War If He Loses The Elections?", May 28, 1993. "Cambodian Assembly Gives Sihanouk Full Powers As Head Of State", June 15, 1993. "Sihanouk Changes Country's Name, Flag", July 30, 1993. "Cambodia's Foreign Minister Threatens To Quit", October 24, 1994. "The King Is Being Ignored", October 26, 1994. "Cambodian Finance Minister Rainsy Ousted", October 21, 1994. "Sihanouk Rejects APB Boast About First Brewery", October 22, 1994.

Also, a series of reports by Julie Chatterjee Mehta in *Straits Times,* Singapore: "I Survived Pol Pot", March 1, 1994. "Age Old Khmer Dance Revived", March 1, 1994. *The Nation,* Bangkok, "Apsaras In Angkor", January 17, 1999.

Prince versus Prince

The core of this chapter are a series of interviews conducted by the authors in Phnom Penh with Prince Chakrapong in August 1992, Prince Sirivudh in January 1993, and Hun Sen in December 1997. These conversations revealed the depth of the rift in the Norodom clan.

For further reading see Milton Osborne, *Sihanouk: Prince Of Light, Prince Of Darkness* (Allen & Unwin, Australia, 1994).

Also, see a series of reports on the rise and fall of Chakrapong and Sirivudh by Harish Mehta in the *Business Times:* "Princes In Politics", September 3, 1992. "The Rise Of Another Norodom", January 28, 1993. "Princes And Power Brokers In Cambodia", November 27, 1992. "Hun Sen Refuses To Hand Over Power, Six Provinces Breakaway", June 11, 1993. "Kompong Cham Decides Against Seceding After Hun Sen Visits Brother", June 15, 1993. "Cambodian Secession Fails, Chakrapong Flees To Vietnam", June 16, 1993. "The Week When Cambodia Almost Broke Up", June 16, 1993. "Four Stars For Chakrapong", June 22, 1993. "Chakrapong's Bid To Secede—The Inside Story", July 10-11, 1993.

For more on UNTAC and its media, see Julie Chatterjee Mehta's "Crucial Days in Cambodia's History", a review of *Radio UNTAC* by Zhou Mei, published in *Straits Times,* October 15, 1994.

Also, see "To Whom It May Concern", and "The Cambodian '*coup d'etat*': Fact Or Fiction?", a press release posted on the Internet by Chakrapong on August 27, 1994, and "Memorandum of Opinion", posted on the Net by Chakrapong on August 28, 1994. Chakrapong made an impassioned plea of his innocence, and rued his shabby treatment at the hands of the Cambodian government.

CHAPTER EIGHT

An Elder Brother

Harish Mehta conducted a rare interview with Hun Neng, governor of Kompong Cham and older brother of Hun Sen, at his residence in Kompong Cham in May 1993. The interview was a *coup* as Hun Neng never gives interviews. The same day, he also interviewed three other players in the province: Deputy Governor of Kompong Cham Lay Sokha, Indian Army Colonel A.N. Bahuguna at his battalion headquarters, and Funcinpec's political campaign manager Ung Huot.

For further reading on the Hun brothers, see a series of reports by Harish Mehta in the *Business Times:* "Kompong Cham To Be Developed If Hun Sen's Party Wins", May 26, 1993. "Hun Brothers Fighting The Ranariddh Wave", May 31, 1993. "Funcinpec Snatches Slim Lead Over CPP", June 1, 1993.

The Hun Household

This chapter is based on an in-depth interview with Bun Rany conducted by Julie Mehta in Phnom Penh in December 1997, where she talked about her family life, and bringing up her children. Further information about the family was provided to the authors in an interview with Nim Chandara, a brother-in-law of Hun Sen's, in Bangkok in May 1998.

Also, see Reuters, "Cambodia's Hun Sen To Son's West Point Graduation", May 23, 1999.

A Younger Sister And Her Husband

Information about Hun Sen's siblings was provided to the authors by Nim Chandara in an interview in Bangkok in May 1998.

A Troubled Friendship

Information about Ung Phan was provided to the authors by Nim Chandara in an interview in Bangkok in May 1998.

Also see, *Straits Times* for various reports: "Cambodia's Ruling Party Expels 'Traitor' Minister", August 1, 1990. "Former Minister Ung Phan Placed Under Hun Sen's Protection", January 31, 1992. "Cambodian DPM To Visit Singapore", August 6, 1993. "New Spat May Be Last Straw For Cambodia Government", April 17, 1997.

CHAPTER NINE

Conversations Along The Tonle Sap

This chapter is based on a series of interviews with Hun Sen conducted by Harish Mehta in Phnom Penh on January 1, 1992 at the Council of Ministers' Building; on January 5, 1993 at the Chamkarmon Palace; on July 2, 1993 on the lawns of the Royal Palace; on December 17, 1993 in Singapore; on October 20, 1994 in the national assembly; in December 1997 and June 1998 at his Takhmau home.

The authors interviewed World Bank/UNTAC official Michael Ward in Phnom Penh in

February 1993 on the state of the economy. Also, see *Sunday Times*, Singapore, "US May Establish Contacts With Phnom Penh To Ensure Fair Polls", July 22, 1990.

For more on Hun Sen's views on his country, and its international relations, see a series of reports by Harish Mehta in the *Business Times:* "The Political Maturing Of Hun Sen", January 8, 1992. "Cambodia Needs US$1.2 Billion Urgently For Reconstruction", January 3, 1992. "Cambodia Welcomes Lifting Of US Embargo", January 6, 1992. "State Of Soviet Economy Causing Problems For Cambodia", February 1992. "Creating Confidence In Cambodia", January 8, 1993. "Evict Khmer Rouge From Peace Process: Hun Sen", January 6, 1993. "UN Troops In Cambodia Send Prices Soaring", August 12, 1992. "Untac Has Not Curbed Inflation Nor Stabilised Currency: Cambodia", January 5, 1993. "World Bank's US$75 Million Loan To Cambodia Falls Through", February 5, 1993. "Major Khmer Rouge Attack On Siem Reap", May 4, 1993. "Ranariddh's Troops Joined Khmer Rouge Attack: Phnom Penh", May 5, 1993. "Cambodia Violence Is Bleeding Business, Scaring Off Investors", May 6, 1993. "Top Cambodia General Quits Funcinpec To Join Hun Sen", April 5, 1993. "Defecting General Accuses Ranariddh Party Of Sabotage", April 6, 1993. "Two More Generals Leave Ranariddh's Party For Hun Sen's", May 11, 1993. "Khmer Rouge On Reasons For Currency's Fall", April 6, 1993. "Hun Sen Gives Thailand His Word On Business Contracts", May 8, 1993. "Sihanouk Urges Singapore And Hong Kong Firms To Invest In Proposed Duty Free Zone", July 3, 1993. "Beholding An Economic Vision For Cambodia", December 24, 1993. "Cambodian Finance Minister Rainsy Ousted", October 21, 1994. "Cambodia's Open For Business", December 22, 1997. "Hun Sen Is Sure His CPP Will Win", June 29, 1998.

Also, Julie Chatterjee Mehta's reports in *Straits Times,* "Phnom Penh At Peace", October 9, 1993; and, "Rural Cambodians Reeling In Poverty", May 6, 1994.

For more on Cambodia's economy, see "The Short-Term Impact Of UNTAC On Cambodia's Economy" (Report by the Economic Advisor's Office, UNTAC, Phnom Penh, December 21, 1992).

For more information on the spate of violent attacks during the 1993 elections, see UNTAC document, "Incidents Of Political Violence, Harassment, And Intimidation", covering the campaign period from March 1, 1993 to May 14, 1993.

For further details about Sihanouk's films, see website: NorodomSihanouk.org

CHAPTER TEN

Victory

This chapter is based on a comprehensive interview with Hun Sen conducted by the authors in June 1998.

Other references: Agence France-Presse, "Cambodian Strongman Hun Sen Enters Cyberspace", December 2, 1997. *Bangkok Post,* "Conciliatory Hun Sen Launches His Campaign", April 30, 1998. Agence France-Presse, "Hun Sen Officially Declared Winner", September 2, 1998. Agence France-Presse, "International Calls: Accept Polls", August 1998. Agence France-Presse, "Sihanouk Ready To Try And End Turmoil", August 3, 1998. *Business Day,* Bangkok, "Ranariddh Eyes Vote Row Compromise", August 3, 1998. Agence France-Presse, "Hun Sen

Set To Alter Law For Solo Rule", August 28, 1998. *Asian Wall Street Journal,* Barry Wain, "Asean, UN, Will Admit Cambodia, Hun Sen Says", September 1998. *Bangkok Post,* "Hun Sen Asks Thailand To Lend A Hand", September 7, 1998. *The Nation,* Bangkok, "Asean Rejects Cambodia Yet Again", August 25, 1998. *Asian Wall Street Journal,* Barry Wain, "Ranariddh Must Play The Statesman", September 4, 1998. *Bangkok Post,* "Opposition Vows Not To Give Way", September 10, 1998. *The Nation,* Bangkok, "Cambodia Foes Agree To Talk", September 23, 1998. Agence France-Presse, "Hun Sen Escapes Unhurt In Rocket Attack On His Car", September 25, 1998. Associated Press, "Hun Sen Blames Political Rivals For Angkor Wat Rocket Attack", September 25, 1998. *Bangkok Post,* "Hun Sen Presses For Global Endorsement", October 27, 1998. *Bangkok Post,* "Coalition Deal Ends Three-Month Stalemate", November 14, 1998. *Asiaweek,* Dominic Faulder, "The King Comes To The Rescue", November 27, 1998. *Bangkok Post,* "King Praises 'New Unity', Reconciliation", November 15, 1998. Agence France-Presse, "Rivals Share Of Power Uneven", November 23, 1998. *Bangkok Post,* "Hun Sen Wins Stamp Of Approval", December 1, 1998. Reuter, "Annan Hails New Cambodian Coalition", December 2, 1998. Kyodo, "Sihanouk Asks Asean To Admit Cambodia", December 4, 1998. Agence France-Presse, "Committee Credits UN Seat To Hun Sen", December 6, 1998. *The Nation,* Bangkok, "Cambodia's Quick Asean Entry Hopes Dashed", December 15, 1998. *Straits Times,* Lee Kim Chew, "Yes To Cambodia, But Timing Not Fixed", December 16, 1998. *Bangkok Post,* "Cambodia Becomes Part Of Asean", May 1, 1999.

Also, see Hun Sen's 6-page statement delivered at the Asean ministers' meeting in Hanoi on December 15, 1998.

The Mind Of A Chess Player

This chapter draws upon a comprehensive interview with Hun Sen conducted by the authors in June 1998.

Other references: Agence France-Presse, "Clean Up, Hun Sen Tells Party As Local Polls Near". *The Vision,* Cambodia, M.H. Tee, "Hun Sen Might Have To Redesignate Some Key Lieutenants To Placate International Community", October 21, 1998.

Note: Some of the articles by the author, Julie B. Mehta, listed above, were published under the name, Julie Chatterjee Mehta.

INDEX